Speak Out!

A Brixton Black Women's Group Reader

Edited by Milo Miller
Introduction by Jade Bentil

VERSO

London • New York

This work was supported by funding from the Economic
and Social Research Council (grant number 1508787).

First published by Verso 2023
Collection © Verso 2023
Contributions © Contributors 2023

1 3 5 7 9 10 8 6 4 2

Verso
UK: 6 Meard Street, London W1F 0EG
US: 388 Atlantic Avenue, Brooklyn, NY 11217
versobooks.com

Verso is the imprint of New Left Books

ISBN-13: 978-1-80429-197-9
ISBN-13: 978-1-80429-198-6 (UK EBK)
ISBN-13: 978-1-80429-199-3 (US EBK)

British Library Cataloguing in Publication Data
A catalogue record for this book is available from the British Library

Library of Congress Cataloging-in-Publication Data
A catalog record for this book is available from the Library of Congress

Typeset in Sabon by MJ & N Gavan, Truro, Cornwall
Printed and bound by CPI Group (UK) Ltd, Croydon, CR0 4YY

Contents

Contents

Editor's Preface

Milo Miller

The Brixton Black Women's Group (BBWG), which formed in 1973 and lasted until 1989, was a Black socialist feminist organisation based in Brixton, south London. It is thought to be the first autonomous Black women's group of its kind to be established in London, and to be among the first in Britain more broadly (indeed, it was initially known simply as 'the Black Women's Group').[1]

The group was central to radical struggles against racism, fascism, sexism and class oppression in London and beyond. As will become clear over the following pages, the group organised extensively around the policing and criminalisation of Black people, reproductive justice, housing, labour, legislation on immigration and nationality, education and more. The BBWG worked closely with a number of community groups and organisations; it was also actively part of networks of women's groups nationally and internationally (as part of which it provided support for radical political groups, particularly in the Caribbean and in Central America). It was instrumental in establishing the

---

1   See B. Bryan, S. Dadzie, and S. Scafe, *The Heart of the Race: Black Women's Lives in Britain*, 2nd ed. (London: Verso, 2018 [1985]); Tracy Fisher, *What's Left of Blackness: Feminisms, Transracial Solidarities, and the Politics of Belonging in Britain* (New York: Palgrave Macmillan, 2012); and Julia Sudbury, *'Other Kinds of Dreams': Black Women's Organisations and the Politics of Transformation* (London: Routledge, 1998). Readers will see the group referred throughout this book as 'the BBWG' or 'the BWG'.

Organisation of Women of Asian and African Descent (OWAAD), which existed between 1978 and 1983 and was the first national Black women's organisation in the UK.

Crucially, the BBWG organised on the grounds of political Blackness. 'Blackness', in this formulation, was not understood as a *descriptive* category referring, for example, to 'race' or skin colour; rather, it was understood as encompassing all those exploited in Britain through historical and modern forms of colonialism, imperialism and racism. 'Blackness', in this sense, functioned as a site of active and relational re/articulation; as a site of resistance, of solidarity and of coalition.[2] This conceptualisation of Blackness was prevalent (though far from settled or uncontested) in Britain's Black Power movement in the 1970s and 1980s, and the BBWG's members, accordingly, included women from and with ties to the Caribbean, Asia and Africa.[2] This approach was central to – and further developed by the BBWG's critical involvement in – OWAAD, which explicitly marked it by referring to women of Asian *and* African descent in its name.[3]

Along with the Mary Seacole Craft Group, the BBWG established the Mary Seacole House, later renamed the Black Women's Centre, in 1979. For much of its existence, the centre – the first centre of its kind for Black women in Britain – was managed by the BBWG. It became a focal point for the meeting of women's

---

2   For example, as stated in Bryan, Dadzie, and Scafe, *The Heart of the Race*, with regard to the Organisation of Women of Asian and African Descent (OWAAD), 'When we use the term "Black" we use it as a political term. It doesn't describe our skin colour, it defines our situation here in Britain. We're here as a result of British imperialism' (p. 170).

As noted by Nydia A. Swaby in '"Disparate in Voice, Sympathetic in Direction": Gendered Political Blackness and the Politics of Solidarity', *Feminist Review* 108, no. 1 (2014), 11–25, however, 'resistance to deploying black, politically or otherwise, was an issue even in the founding days of the organisation' (pp. 21–2); further, 'from the outset, OWAAD expressed gendered political blackness in a way that could not account for certain kinds of internal differences'. For in-depth analyses of the uses, limits, tensions and contradictions presented by the concept of political Blackness, see also Sudbury, *'Other Kinds of Dreams'*; Fisher, *What's Left of Blackness*; the editorial ('On Black Women Organising') in issue 5 of *Speak Out* on p. 257 of this collection; and 'From the Inside Looking In: A Reappraisal of *Heart of the Race*' on p. 309 of this collection.

groups and political organisations working across London; it was also the postal address for OWAAD. The centre hosted a regular legal and welfare rights information and referral service; a craft workshop; a health group providing, among other services, advice on contraception and pregnancy; a crèche; children's activities during school holidays; and a library and resource centre specialising in women's literature and Black history. In the aftermath of the April 1981 Brixton Uprising, the centre also functioned as the headquarters of the Brixton Defence Campaign's Legal Defence Group.

The BBWG's newsletter, *Speak Out*, detailed all of this. It contained reports on the BBWG and other grassroots groups' work on a variety of fronts, in-depth political position statements, analyses of proposed legislation, explainers on health issues and accounts of liberation struggles across the Global South. Alongside these, there were poems and illustrations by BBWG members, as well as reviews of plays, films and novels – emphasising the group's understanding of culture and political struggle as inseparable, and of art and self-expression as integral to movements for liberation. More broadly, the BBWG was prolific in its writing. Collectively written pieces – on, for example, the issues the group organised around, the coalitions the group was part of, and the group's political positions – appeared in publications such as *Race Today*, *Spare Rib*, *Red Rag* and *Feminist Review*.

Over the years, many individuals and groups have devoted a considerable amount of effort to honouring the BBWG's work – not least the writers of the landmark 1985 book *The Heart of the Race: Black Women's Lives in Britain*. The first sustained account of Black women's history in Britain written by Black women, *The Heart of the Race* was written by BBWG members Beverley Bryan and Suzanne Scafe with OWAAD co-founder Stella Dadzie, and features an extended section on the BBWG. Elsewhere, Dadzie's personal papers, held at the Black Cultural Archives in Brixton, have long included the most comprehensive collection of BBWG documents available. Despite efforts by a great many people, however, the wealth of writing produced by the BBWG has remained scattered and often difficult to access. This book brings together, for the first time, all of the issues of

Speak Out as well as statements, articles and book chapters written by the Brixton Black Women's Group. It also contains other hard-to-access archival material essential to understanding the group's work and trajectory.

This book has assumed many forms over the seven years preceding its publication. The gathering of the material included in this collection began in 2016, as I was writing my PhD thesis. My thesis focused on squatting – living in or otherwise using a building without the consent of the owner – in Brixton from the 1970s to the 2010s; it includes a chapter on the BBWG. From my own experience of squatting in south London, I knew of Olive Morris, a heroic figure in London's squatting histories. It took some time, however, for me to learn that, far from the individualised figure she is often portrayed as, Morris was very much part of a collective in Brixton and that she had spent much of her adult life organising with the BBWG, which she co-founded.[3]

As part of my research, I began compiling as much of the BBWG's writings as I could find, in addition to writing by individual members of the group. I visited archives and typed up issues of *Speak Out*, as well as leaflets produced by the group; I tracked down out-of-print books and journals, typing up chapters and articles written by the group or by individual members. Initially, this was solely so I could easily revisit this writing and quote from it as needed in my thesis; over time, however, this gathering of the BBWG's writing became a project in its own right. The group's visionary work speaks, as you will see over the following pages, urgently to the conditions we face in the present. I began to share the material I was collecting with friends, whose excitement was palpable. Many of them had never heard of the group; some had but had never encountered the group's writings. My own excitement was beginning to be mixed with frustration: Why wasn't this material more widely known and accessible? Why was the Brixton Black Women's Group so absent from accounts of any number of key political issues, campaigns and events in 1970s and 1980s Britain to which they were central? Why wasn't the

---

3   Many thanks to Nazmia Jamal and Sita Balani for key early insights into this.

group's trailblazing work as celebrated as it deserved to be and available as a resource in combatting current, seemingly intractable and ever-intensifying crises?

In 2017, at the mid-point of my PhD, I did an internship at Verso Books' London office. It was during my four months there that I began the process which would culminate in the re-publication of *The Heart of the Race* in 2018. Seeing the excitement around the release of that book – as well as the necessity of having it back in print and reaching new audiences in these troubling times – made it very clear: the collected writings of the Brixton Black Women's Group *had* to be published.

Over the following year, I worked on the collection whenever I could. I continued typing up articles and chapters; I tracked down an elusive *Speak Out* issue; I found photos of the Black Women's Centre; I carefully removed photocopier static from images in issues of *Speak Out*. As the Covid-19 pandemic swept across the world in 2020 (with risks, vulnerabilities and burdens impacting in systemically unequal ways along classed, racialised and gendered lines), I often found it a comfort, during lockdowns, to sit with this writing and to assemble this collection. In November of that year I contacted, with the support of Verso editor Rosie Warren, members of the BBWG and sent them what I had put together, with the offer to take this forward should they be willing. Meticulous discussions then took place between us: What should the scope of the book be? What material was perhaps beyond that scope, and what material had yet to be included? It was at this stage, for example, that the decision was made to include the first issue of *FOWAAD!* (OWAAD's newsletter) in this collection, given the work that the BBWG devoted to OWAAD, to the National Black Women's Conference organised under its aegis in 1979 (the first of its kind in Britain), and to the assembling of *FOWAAD!*'s first issue. Members looked to their personal archives and sent me more material to include, from leaflets and statements to photographs.

The pieces in this collection have been arranged chronologically, with one exception. The first issue of *Speak Out* has been placed at the start as it does a lot of important introductory work for this collection, despite its 1977 publication coming after the

1974 publication of the 'Black Women and Nursing: A Job Like Any Other' report. Obvious typos have been corrected (a much easier task now than when working with typewriters, as the BBWG did) but care has been taken to retain the spelling of the original texts in cases where variations and ambiguities may carry political significance (some texts capitalise 'Black', for example, while other texts don't). Given the sheer range of people, laws, campaigns, organisations and texts mentioned in the group's writing, I have included 'editor's notes' in the footnotes, in order to provide background information and cross-referencing; these notes also provide useful details for those wishing to read the texts the BBWG read and discussed as part of their collective theorising and political development.

The year of this book's publication – 2023 – marks fifty years since the Brixton Black Women's Group was founded. As fascism sees a resurgence around the world, as the struggle against police brutality and racism must continue unabated, as attacks on reproductive rights and bodily autonomy rage on and as border regimes and capitalism continue to exact their deadly toll, the work and legacy of the Brixton Black Women's Group remain as vital and necessary as ever. This book is offered in the hope that it might provide tools to not only understand and confront this current conjuncture but also prefigure and enact practices of mutual aid, solidarity and resistance so urgently needed to overcome it. It is offered in the hope that it might provide tools to imagine a radically different world; a world beyond – as Jade Bentil writes in the introduction to this collection – the brutal entanglement of conquest and empire.

Milo Miller is a Fellow in Gender, Media and Culture in the Department of Gender Studies at the London School of Economics and Political Science.

Acknowledgements

In making this reader available, we want to acknowledge as many as possible of the sisters who contributed to the Brixton Black Women Group (BBWG) through its long history, from 1973 to 1989. The group could continue in its groundbreaking work over this extended period because, at different times, different sisters came forward and took up the baton.

Some of those sisters are featured here in these photographs from 1979, which capture one moment in time. The photos were taken after the first conference organised by the Organisation of Women of Asian and African Descent (OWAAD), a national organisation our group helped to establish. The BBWG went to Bushey (a training centre in Hertfordshire) after the event to reflect on what had been a momentous gathering, our most inspirational up to that point.

Some sisters who were in the group at the time are not included in the photos; others joined the group later: Sindamani Bridglal, Anne Chan, Ramani Chelliah, Donna, Liz Fajemisin, Pat Gordon, Iyamide Hazeley, Delia Jarrett-Macauley, Amina Mama, Angela McNish, Liz Obi, Sona Osman, Suzanne Scafe, Farah Sharif, Rif Sharif, Dorothea Smartt and Neelim Sultan.

Call their names; our sisters for a season: Annette Blair, Marlene Bogle, Monica Dawkins, Sylvia Erike, Clover Graham, Olive Morris and Caroline Redfern. RIP ... in everlasting blue peace.

A special mention of the women who were interviewed for this reader: Beverley Bryan, Stella Dadzie, Liz Fajemisin, Sindamani Bridglal, Takumba Ria Lawal, Gail Lewis, Amina Mama, Monica Morris, Suzanne Scafe and Jocelyn Wolfe.

Love and respect in a special mention to Gerlin Bean, who

could not make the roundtable interview but who we all agreed was the connecting link for us all – a true sister from the very beginning.

Lastly, this acknowledgements page has been an act of collective remembering by just a few members of the BBWG (the Afterword group) as we collaborated through email, WhatsApp and Zoom. But what of the gaps? Memory is contingent: it will elide, alter and re-edit; so there will always be a longer version of this list that could have been made. We acknowledge those absences.

Standing, from left to right: Melba Wilson (partly visible behind Beverley), Beverley Bryan, Joan Morris, Lindiwe Tsele, Clover Graham, Gerlin Bean, Gail Lewis, Claudette Williams, Kamedea Brown, [name unknown], [name unknown], Jocelyn Wolfe, Pat Adams.
Sitting, from left to right: Olive Gallimore, Judith Lockhart, Monica Morris, Sylvia Erike, Vanessa, Glynis Neslen.
Photographer: Takumba Ria Lawal.

Standing, from left to right: Melba Wilson (partly visible behind Beverley), Beverley Bryan, Joan Morris, Sylvia Erike, Clover Graham, Kamedea Brown, Monica Morris, [name unknown], [name unknown], Jocelyn Wolfe, Pat Adams.
Middle, from left to right: Claudette Williams, Gerlin Bean.
Sitting, from left to right: Olive Gallimore, Judith Lockhart, Takumba Ria Lawal, Gail Lewis, Vanessa, Glynis Neslen.
Photographer: Lindiwe Tsele.

Introduction

Jade Bentil

> The bourgeoisie is fearful of the militancy of the Black woman, and for good reason.
>
> –Claudia Jones, *An End to the Neglect of the Problems of the Negro Woman!* (1949)

The project of freedom is often imagined as a linear, forward march towards an undefined future. The official record of history indexes the radical potential for imagining what freedom might be by measuring society in silos of 'progress'. In this narrative, the importance of awarding the colonised and the nominally free with a seat at the table of power becomes a placeholder for liberation. The structures of power that distribute limited life choices, gratuitous violence, economic repression and exposure to premature death to the colonised and the nominally free remain intact. The *vertical hierarchy of life* continues; the future falls out of reach.[1] Revolution is deferred once more.

The prevailing arrangement of social life has attempted to erode the critical labour of transforming our current conditions, eradicate our capacity for love and care, and foreclose the possibility of a world beyond the brutal entanglement of conquest and empire. Yet, even as the forces of anti-Black racism, free markets and state-engineered precarity have sought to wither away the belief that another set of arrangements is possible, 'freedom' is a

---

1   Saidiya Hartman, 'The Belly of the World: A Note on Black Women's Labors', *Souls: A Critical Journal of Black Politics, Culture, and Society* *18*, no. 1 (2016), 166–73.

word that continues to form the nucleus of the Black radical imagination. The long history of Black resistance has been marked by the insurgent longings of those whose lives are rendered surplus and disposable under the regime of racial capitalism. 'Freedom' names that which remains out of reach even as we endeavour to create it in the here and now, and 'freedom' brings together a set of practices that allow us to imagine what *might be*. Living within the 'interminable catastrophe' that structures Black life, political education, mutual aid, general strikes and riot have provided tracts for survival, a discourse of dissent, a love language for a liveable future, and a rehearsal of a radically different world.[2]

At the heart of the revolutionary ideals that emerged under the press of death on the plantation, in the colony and in the metropole is the sustained labour of Black women. In 'The Belly of the World: A Note on Black Women's Labors', Saidiya Hartman notes that the ritual theft and regulation of Black women's sexual and reproductive capacities 'defined black women's historical experiences as labourers and shaped the character of their refusal of and resistance to slavery'.[3] Describing the acts of subterfuge and autonomy that enslaved women engaged in – such as poisoning slaveholders, utilising abortifacients, giving birth, completing suicide, and dreaming of destroying the master and his house – Hartman draws an atlas of a world that continues to be shaped by the dispossession of Black women. Under a deathly calculus that renders our lives expendable, the collective refusal of Black women has been critical to both the formation and the survival of Black life throughout the diaspora.

In the mid- to late twentieth century, Black women in Britain drew upon the traditions of rebellion cultivated by the enslaved and the colonised to fight back against a 'Mother Country' that had only ever been hostile to their presence. Revolutionaries such as Claudia Jones, Althea Jones-Lecointe, Olive Morris, Liz Obi, Gerlin Bean and countless others whose names remain unrecorded were foundational in honing an analysis of the material conditions that made Black people vulnerable to both state and

2   B. Alagraa, 'The Interminable Catastrophe', *Offshoot Journal*, 1 March 2021, offshootjournal.org.
3   Hartman, 'The Belly of the World', 166.

interpersonal violence. Understanding that to be Black in Britain was to be positioned outside the boundaries of the nation and that, in its corporeality, the state was antagonistic to Black life, Black women radicals endeavoured to find ways of being in the world that were not tethered to the ruse of citizenship, the fallacies of the nation-state or the horizon of empire.

As the chant for Black liberation reverberated across the globe, the labour of Black women activists was integral to the burgeoning Black Power movement in Britain. Inside groups such as the Black Panthers, the Black Liberation Front and the Black Unity and Freedom Party, Black women taught at supplementary schools, staged campaigns against police brutality, fought racism within the education system and struggled against the epidemic of substandard living conditions that defined Black life in the late twentieth century. They produced literature and distributed pamphlets that analysed the historical dimensions of their experiences as Black people living on the underside of the capital; they sustained their comrades, cooking and cleaning and typing long after the men had finished lamenting the super-exploitation of the Black worker, put their coats on and turned the lights off. Black women's labours, however, are often positioned as a footnote or entirely written out of grand narratives of Black struggle and feminist revolt. Recalling the liminal space in which Black women were placed in the Black Power movement during the early 1970s, Black feminist activist and author Melba Wilson recalls that 'it was a struggle to get Black women's voices to be heard in that context. A lot of the women who came from the Black Liberation movement were doing the "backroom jobs" – the typing, the cooking … they were on the pickets for sure, but they were expected to follow, not lead!'[4] Having been a member of the Black Unity and Freedom Party (BUFP), Gerlin Bean remembers the reproductive labour that sustained Black liberation organisations: 'We were the women, we had the responsibilities, we were doing childcare, we were doing everything and we should be

---

4 Amrit Wilson, 'Charting South Asian Women's Struggles against Gender-Based Violence', in *Violence against Women in South Asian Communities: Issues for Policy and Practice*, ed. R. K. Thiara, and A. K. Gill (London: Jessica Kingsley, 2010), 55–79.

recognised and should have a voice in the organisations, not just be their secretaries ... because that's where we were relegated.'[5]

Refusing to capitulate to a worldview that overwrote their lives, Black women activists insisted that their voices be heard. Within what had by then become the Black Workers' Movement of the early 1970s, they set up a women's caucus and sought to attend to the nature of Black women's subjection throughout the world. Reflecting on her participation in an early reading group, Marlene Bogle details the circumstances that shaped Black women's practices of convening: '[The] lack of resources in the Black community made it necessary for us to meet in each other's homes,' she recalls, 'as we had no other suitable place to do so.'[6] A space for political education, the women's caucus afforded Black women the breathing room to think with each other, learn with each other and challenge each other outside of the rigid, patriarchal hierarchies that had come to define what had by then become the movement. More than fifty years later, these radical practices of intimacy, comradeship and care continue to defy dominant metrics of visibility precisely because of their incisive critiques of power. Black feminist labour, then, is stitched through the tapestry of Black radicalism even as it falls out of the frame of representation.

It therefore comes as no surprise that when I first learnt of the existence of the Brixton Black Women's Group, it was through a chance encounter that would change the course of my life. It was 2014, and I was in my final year of an English Literature and Spanish degree. Having been taught everything from Civil War literature to the poetry of the Romantic period, I was hungry to read and learn about the narratives of Black people; those who had been omitted and erased from the lectures I attended but whose lives were woven within and beyond the whitewashed narratives that shaped the course. More than anything, I was

---

5   Gerlin Bean, interview, January 2010, ORAL/1/3, Oral Histories of the Black Women's Movement: The Heart of the Race, 2009–2010, Black Cultural Archives, collections.blackculturalarchives.org.

6   Marlene T. Bogle, 'Brixton Black Women's Centre: Organizing on Child Sexual Abuse', *Feminist Review* 28, no. 1 (1998), 132. *Editor's note:* The text quoted here is on p. 315 of this collection.

yearning to find traces of Black women's lives in Britain, longing for anything that documented the voices of women who were never bound to appear in any of my modules but who I knew must have existed. This opportunity would finally arrive on a visit home to my family in south London in November 2014. Walking around Brixton, I bumped into an old school friend who was volunteering at the newly reopened Black Cultural Archives (BCA). As we talked and I regaled him with tales about the narrow landscape that had been my experience in higher education, he invited me to join him in viewing the BCA's inaugural exhibition, 'Re-imagine: Black Women in Britain'. Charting more than four hundred years of Black women's experiences within the imperial core, the exhibition was my first taste of the radical possibilities that resided within Black women's everyday practices of refusal: the echoes of their voices, the textures of their memories and the rhythms of their lives, which not only challenged dominant forms of remembering and forgetting but also cleaved through the current arrangements of the world and imagined it anew.

Making my way through the beautifully curated space, I eventually arrived at a display mapping the history of the Black women's movement in 1970s and 1980s Britain. Watching footage from the First Black Women's Conference held in 1979 by the coalition of groups that made up the Organisation of Women of Asian and African Descent, I found myself yearning to know more about these women: who they'd been, who they were now and the aspirations that had incited them to come together as a critical mass and demand liberation for Black women everywhere.

Inspired by this brief encounter, I returned to Brixton a few months later to view archival papers related to the movement. Painstakingly collected and preserved by sisters of the movement across decades and eventually donated to the BCA, these pamphlets, meeting minutes, yellowing photos and scraps of ephemera provided a window into the thoughts and feelings of the women who were the heartbeat of the Black liberation struggle in Britain. Casting my eyes over the *Speak Out* newsletters fanned across the desk in front of me, I drank in the words of the Brixton Black Women's Group, women who were writing four decades prior to the moment in which I encountered them, women who were expressing so many of the thoughts and feelings that I had yet to find a way to articulate. In the first issue of *Speak Out*, the group argue that attending to the specificity of Black women's subjugation is a prerequisite for the liberation of all Black people: 'In order to change our entire situation, we must strive to fully understand the nature of the oppression we face as black people, and particularly as black women. We have brought to this country a history of exploitation and a tradition of struggle which has never been documented.'[7] Having spent the entire day in the reading room poring over *Speak Out* issues, the light began to dim outside, and soon enough it was time to leave, but the experience had left its mark on me. Reading BBWG's insightful, urgent and prescient analyses of racism, sexism and capitalism, as well as all that exceeded these deathly entanglements – the conversations about art, the meditations on literature, the verses of poetry, the dreams of freedom – struck a chord that would continue to chime nearly a decade later. My growing desire to seek out Black feminist counter-narratives – other ways of knowing, other ways of living – was the same one that animated the group of Black women who came together to form the BBWG (then known simply as the Black Women's Group) in 1973.

When I met with sisters of the group in the autumn of 2022 for a virtual roundtable discussion, they emphasised that when they began organising, they did so with a shared longing to deepen the struggle for Black liberation by forming an analysis of Black women's position within it. As the first autonomous Black women's organisation in Britain, BBWG member Gail Lewis noted, the group was focused on 'the specificity, not just of "woman's condition" but of woman's role in the struggle'. Gathering every Sunday at Sabarr Bookshop at 121 Railton Road, the BBWG extended the traditions that began in the women's caucus of the early 1970s by first coming together as a study group. Seeking to incorporate the various political histories and understandings that shaped each member's trajectory within the

---

7 *Editor's note:* This is a passage from the editorial to *Speak Out*, no. 1 (1977), which is included on p. 19 of this collection.

group, the collective read and analysed Marxist, socialist and anti-colonial literature and endeavoured to formulate an analysis that moved Black women from the margins of these texts to the centre. During our conversation, founding member Beverley Bryan emphasised the significance of exploring and interrogating texts collectively:

> In the Panthers, we read some Black texts like Fanon's *Wretched of the Earth*, and we read some Marxist–Leninist texts.[8] That's where I read Marx and Engels's *The Communist Manifesto* ...[9] We continued that because the women coming into the group were also interested in understanding Marxist analysis, understanding the economic foundations of the society we were living in and what capitalism was doing to us as Black women. I remember we re-read *The Communist Manifesto*, and that was really useful because one thing about being a women's study group, I think we certainly felt freer to discuss, to ask questions. There wasn't so much a teacher giving an opinion of how you should be thinking. We could work it out together.

The group's non-hierarchical, communal process of learning illustrates their commitment to developing a political consciousness that could speak to and, ultimately, transform the social conditions in which the lives of working-class Black women emerged. As more and more sisters joined the organisation in the mid-seventies, the group formed a critical mass that was intent on not only naming the sources of their oppression but also, importantly, crafting a theory that could be mobilised in practice. Arriving at the term 'Black socialist feminism', BBWG sought to illuminate how the intersection of race, gender and class undergirded their position within the social order. When I asked the sisters how

---

8 *Editor's note:* First published in French in 1961, an English translation (by Constance Farrington) of Fanon's *The Wretched of the Earth* was published in 1963. It was republished by Penguin Modern Classics in 2001.

9 *Editor's note:* First published in 1848, an edition of Karl Marx and Friedrich Engels's *The Communist Manifesto* was published by Verso in 2022.

they defined Black socialist feminism, Lewis explained that it was important to the group that alongside an understanding of the ways in which racism and patriarchy functioned, 'class was also central' to their analysis.

> We came from working-class life in one way or another. Even if people had been middle-class in terms of their social location and cultural practices back home, they became working class once they were here. We *had* to understand class. Reading Marx meant you had to understand how a class dynamic was also central ... We weren't just 'socialist feminists', we were *Black* socialist feminists, and we understood that class struggle, gender struggle and anti-racist struggle were all part of the terrain in which we operated.

BBWG's vision of Black socialist feminism sought to redress the overlapping crises of anti-Black racism, economic deprivation, patriarchal violence and the state's organised abandonment of working-class Black women and children. Understanding that the mundane and the ordinary were staging grounds for revolutionary change, the group was foundational in forging links with fellow sisters in the local community and forming a network of initiatives and campaigns that could adequately address their needs. BBWG member Olive Gallimore formed the Mary Seacole Craft Group, which brought together a community of Black single mothers for craft sessions and provided a forum for them to voice the issues that imbued their everyday lives. Bryan, then a primary school teacher in Brixton, was also active in the West Indian Parents Action Group and agitated alongside parents and other local activists to uproot a racist educational system that routinely criminalised and underserved Black children. Reflecting on the expansive network that the group cultivated, Monica Morris described the polyvocal nature of BBWG's organising:

> We had a good model. People would go along to other organisations and then report back and tell us what was going on elsewhere ... We'd discuss it, and we'd form a group view on it, a strategy that we would follow when we went out to meetings. It was a

really good learning experience in terms of how you operate in these spaces with different dynamics.

This was Black socialist feminism in practice, theory in the flesh that was energised by an unyielding dedication to being in solidarity with those who were rendered forgotten, missing and disappeared within both the women's liberation movement and the Black liberation movement.

In a landscape where intersectional analyses of race, gender and class fell outside of mainstream narratives of women's liberation, the organisation's insistence that Black women's freedom had to be central to any notion of a feminist future was a radical undertaking. When white-led women's groups organised for greater abortion rights and campaigned for 'A Woman's Right to Choose', BBWG argued that this framing failed to account for the scale of reproductive injustice waged by the state against Black women. Noting that Black women were systematically coerced into having abortions and sterilised against their will and that many were given the contraceptive injection Depo-Provera without their consent, the organisation campaigned against the insidious practices of reproductive regulation that were illegible under a singular focus on abortion rights. In their demand for reproductive freedom at every level, including the autonomy and resources to raise their children with dignity, the group fundamentally shifted the terrain of feminist struggle.

Within their analysis of Black social life, the sisters of BBWG focused their energies on the granular, the local and the everyday, while never losing sight of who their enemies were or the historical dynamics that informed the political stakes of their organising. The coercive power of the state and the colonial roots of Black women's oppression were always at the forefront of their minds. Recognising that borders and nation-states were sites of imperial enclosure, the group understood that their subjection in Britain was inseparable from the subjection that Black women experienced throughout the world. Sisters of the group hailed from different cultural and organisational backgrounds and brought with them a lens that was rooted in a transnational vision of Black liberation. Prior to joining BBWG, members such as Suzanne Scafe and Sindamani Bridglal had spent years organising in women's labour movements in Jamaica and Guyana, respectively, and Jocelyn Wolfe had organised around politics and education, first in the youth movement and later in the People's National Movement, in Trinidad. Amina Mama grew up in Nigeria where her politics were shaped by relatives who had been involved in the struggle against British colonialism. Claudette Williams, Melba Wilson and Gail Lewis travelled together to form links with women's groups in Nicaragua, and eventually Gerlin Bean and Monica Morris went to work in Africa – in Zimbabwe, Tanzania and the Gambia.

Bringing together different diasporic contexts and perspectives at their weekly study sessions, the group crafted a Black internationalist framework in which they understood that the movement against racism, against patriarchy, against capitalism and against imperialism was a global one. 'Black socialist feminism was about race, sex and class, but it was also about what was happening on the ground; what was happening to us and to other women,' Bryan explained during our conversation.

> We came from migrant families. We could still see what was happening to migrant families, to our families ... So the idea that class was part of Black socialist feminism was totally about our experiences, and we connected those experiences to other women in our community. That's why we had to support women when they went on strike. By doing that, you made the connection that it was also about *our* economic life. That was how the system worked. It might have been Caribbean workers in one iteration, or it might have been African women in another iteration. The system was fed by the impoverishment of our different countries of origin.

Mobilising alongside sisters from across Africa, the Caribbean, Asia and Central America as well as strategising with the growing number of Black women's organisations throughout Britain, the group carved out an anti-colonial movement of Black women that was expansive enough to envisage their collective freedom while holding space for the specificity of their different locations and material conditions.

The spirit of collaboration that lay at the foundations of BBWG's organisational practices found its expressive language within the pages of the group's *Speak Out* newsletter, first published in 1977. Lewis describes the newsletter as 'the "organ" of the group', a vital contribution to the Marxist–Leninist tradition, in which producing literature that could articulate the organisation's political vision and provide a resource for mass mobilisation, an essential part of revolutionary struggle. The group resisted their work being assimilated into an institutional frame, seeking instead to speak to the grassroots – those who they were organising in community with and those who were not yet part of the movement but could become comrades of tomorrow. 'With *Speak Out*, we were very concerned to not just talk to ourselves, so it wasn't going to be something that was primarily intellectual or hard to digest,' Morris notes. 'We were hoping to bring up issues that were relevant to people on the street.'

Speaking to many issues with many voices, the group's newsletter was a groundbreaking endeavour in which the capacity for imagining what freedom could be was centred around Black women's lives. *Speak Out: A Brixton Black Women's Group Reader* is alive with the energy that coursed through the group's organising and brings together the threads of their work that have remained out of view until now. The book documents more than a decade of BBWG's activism, illuminating the colossal scope of the group's political vision, the relationships that they nurtured and the lives that they touched. In their writings and speeches, sisterhood becomes a verb, an action that the group committed themselves to over and over again.

The kinship, relation and struggle that brought BBWG together can be felt everywhere throughout their work. *Speak Out* is written in a collective grammar, and there are rarely any names under the editorial pieces collated throughout the newsletter, signifying the group's desire to eschew individual acclaim and celebrity in favour of a shared vision of liberation. The book also doesn't shy away from the tensions and failures that mark any attempt at revolutionary change; in the editorial to *Speak Out*, no. 5 (1983), 'On Black Women Organising', the group reflect on the marginalisation of lesbian women within the organisation and reaffirm their commitment to fighting racism, sexism, classism and homophobia on all fronts. The piece is an important meditation on how conflict within organising spaces can be handled with accountability and care, and on the vital role that Black queer women have played in Black struggle.[10]

Speak Out acts as an archive to the lesser-known aspects of the group's political work. In coalition with the Mary Seacole Craft Group, the organisation opened the Black Women's Centre (BWC) in Stockwell Green in September 1980. Offering a space for other political groups to gather, as well as a crèche, a library and a place for Black women to come together and produce music, theatre and art, the BWC became a crucial site of resources and service provision for an underserved community. The BBWG was also instrumental in the Black People Against State Harassment (BASH) campaign, where, in coalition with a number of local Black organisations, they fought back against the police's pervasive use of Section 4 of the 1824 Vagrancy Act ('sus' law). The BBWG spearheaded protests against the legislation by disrupting police attempts at making arrests and demonstrating outside police stations and courts. Among their expanding network, the group strove to raise the collective consciousness by holding meetings at the BWC and documenting the discretionary power the law granted the police to prey on Black people. The group's ceaseless organising would prove critical when, in 1981, Black people throughout Britain rose up against the endless cycle of police harassment. Orchestrating the Brixton Defence Campaign in the aftermath of the Brixton uprisings, the BWC became the epicentre of anti-racist organising in the local area, with the BBWG providing care and legal support for Black communities experiencing the brunt of state warfare. An open revolt in the face of state racism and police power, the group provided a critique that helped to lay the groundwork for contemporary demands for the abolition of the police and the carceral state.

As our conversation came to an end, I asked the sisters of the BBWG to reflect on how their political work in the seventies and eighties is in conversation with our present moment. 'I think that

---

10   *Editor's note:* This piece is on pp. 257–68 of this collection.

question needs to be asked to another generation,' Scafe replies. 'It is important that the generation who's experiencing what it means to be a Black woman or experiencing issues around Blackness and gender and sexuality speaks for itself in relation to how they might be in conversation with other generations.' Scafe's response encourages me to return to the young woman I was in 2014, when I first learnt of BBWG, and to all the women I've been in the wake of that first encounter. Nine years later, we continue to live in a state of emergency that produces precarity around Black women's lives. *Speak Out* is a love letter to all those who yearn for another world, a reminder of the foundations that have been laid and a call to action for what remains to be done. In returning to the speeches, poems, articles and archival fragments assembled here, I retrace the steps of the working-class women, daughters of migrants, single mothers and queer people who came together as the Brixton Black Women's Group. In returning to the Black feminist labour that held the organisation together, I am able to hear the soundscape of rebellion that echoes into the present.

Jade Bentil is a writer, critic and historian from South London whose work is situated within Black feminist thought. Her debut book, Rebel Citizen, *explores the everyday rebellion of African and Caribbean women who migrated to Britain in the aftermath of the Second World War and is forthcoming from Allen Lane.*

SPEAK OUT 15p

Issue No. 1

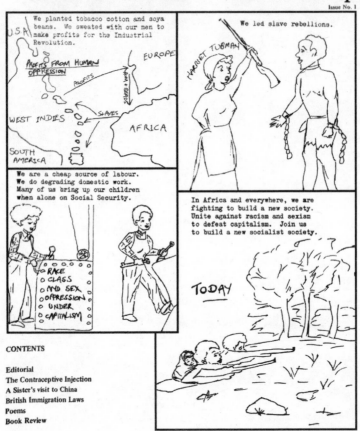

We planted tobacco cotton and soya beans. We sweated with our men to make profits for the Industrial Revolution.

We led slave rebellions.

We are a cheap source of labour. We do degrading domestic work. Many of us bring up our children when alone on Social Security.

In Africa and everywhere, we are fighting to build a new society. Unite against racism and sexism to defeat capitalism. Join us to build a new socialist society.

CONTENTS

BLACK WOMEN'S GROUP BRIXTON

EDITORIAL

Brixton Black Women's Group
First published in Speak Out, *no. 1, 1977, pp. 2–3*

The Black Women's Group began in 1973, mainly with women who were involved in the black movements in the late '60s and early '70s. Since then, many other women have joined the group. Over the years, we have attempted to study and analyse the situation of black women in Britain and the Third World, because such an analysis has been long overdue.

In attempting this analysis, we have met with many obstacles and misunderstandings regarding the need for black women to meet and organise around their specific oppression.

Some argue that we are splitting the black movement. We disagree with this argument because we recognise that our struggle is the struggle of black people, and also that we have an important contribution to make to the overall struggle of the working class in Britain. It is only by coming together and analysing our situation as black women in this society that we can make an effective contribution to this struggle. Out of our experience in the Black Women's Group and the black movement in general, we have come to realise the necessity for a means through which we can express our ideas and political understandings around the issues which affect black women in Britain today.

We are a small group, and consequently our ability to initiate and sustain activities is limited. We meet regularly as a study group and, with the support of the group, individual sisters are involved in various activities in their communities – activities such as West Indian Parents Action Groups; educational, cultural and recreational programmes for young black people. Through the Sabarr Bookshop Collective we are able to keep in contact with schools and other institutions with whom we discuss educational material available in the bookshop for their use.[1] We are also in contact with other black women's groups in London and Manchester, and we hold joint meetings in order to exchange and discuss our ideas. This exchange, we feel, is an important part of our political development and understanding of the capitalist society in which we live.

Capitalism exploits the majority of people for the profit of the few. This is so because working people own nothing but their labour power (i.e. the ability to work and produce wealth). In order to make their profits, capitalists pay the lowest wages for the most work. This exploitative system is maintained through such divisive measures as sexism and racism.

Sexism creates the division between the sexes, while racism sets white workers against black workers, which prevents the working class from organising as a class – both to the benefit of the owners of the means of production, the capitalists. This situation forces black people into the worst paid jobs, poorest living conditions and limited educational opportunities. For black women, the situation is much worse. We are forced to take on the worst paid jobs under the worst conditions in order to help maintain our families.

In the home, our situation is not much better. In keeping with its goal of destroying black people's will to resist its subjugation, capitalism has found it necessary to create a situation where the black man finds it impossible to obtain meaningful or productive employment, thus making it more difficult for him to help maintain the family. The black man, not understanding fully the true nature of the forces working against him, attempts to treat black women as domestic slaves, denying us the opportunity of a creative life and often blaming us for his emasculation. This is coupled with the myth of the powerful black woman central to

---

1   *Editor's note:* For more on the Sabarr Bookshop, see 'Writing Our Own History: Talking Personal, Talking Political' (pp. 321–37 in this collection), as well as footnote 7 in 'Memories of Olive: A Very Strong and Fearless Black Sister' (p. 178 in this collection).

the black family. What the myth does not reveal are the burdens, responsibilities and real powerlessness of that role. Often, we are left to face the difficulties of bringing up a family in a racist society that oppresses and exploits the working class. We and our children have to face the hostile police on the streets, indifferent housing officers in the council, unsympathetic teachers in the schools and prying social security officers in our homes.

In struggling against this overwhelmingly difficult situation, individual black women have made heroic attacks upon the system, resisting oppression in whatever way possible. In trying to solve our bad housing conditions, we have had to occupy empty council houses to find shelter for ourselves and our children. One such example is that of a sister who, with her five children, occupied an empty house in Notting Hill Gate in 1970. This individual action not only gave great encouragement to other homeless black women, but to the whole squatting movement. There are many more examples of individual resistance which have furthered the struggles of black people in this country, but they have also indicated the need for collective organisation: we can only achieve so much on our own. Therefore, organisation is necessary. It is for reasons like these that we have felt it necessary to come together as a group of women.

In order to change our entire situation, we must strive to fully understand the nature of the oppression we face as black people, and particularly as black women. We have brought to this country a history of exploitation and a tradition of struggle which has never been documented. It was as a people, black people, that we fought against our oppressors under slavery and colonialism, and, in this fight, women were able and are still able to make an important contribution to the ongoing struggles of our people.

In Britain, we face institutionalised racism, sexist laws and practices, and male domination in the home. Our sisters in Asia, Africa, the Americas and the Caribbean not only have to face these exploitative conditions but they also have to contend with being used as guinea pigs in 'the field of medical research'. It is clear from this that our oppression is not just confined to this society – it is international. The black women's movement is an important part of the movement throughout the world for change and the destruction of capitalism. In that movement, women are coming forward to take part in the struggle for personal and finally political emancipation. Advances for us can be made only if and when our organised attacks contribute to the erosion of the capitalist system. We are fighting against the system that oppresses us and keeps us subjected to drudgery and exploitation.

Although the women's movement has highlighted many important issues, we do not subscribe to that tendency within it which regards men as the primary source of oppression and which sees women's liberation solely in terms of sexual emancipation. Neither do we support the call for wages for housework. We regard all these tendencies as middle-class deviations from the real issues of women's liberation.

We in the Black Women's Group see whatever activities we participate in as being part of the general struggle of black and working-class people against a worldwide system of exploitation. As women, our task must be to take up those issues that face us at work and in the community, making clear that the struggles in which we participate are linked with the general fight against international capital.

WE FREE OUR MINDS TO FREE OUR BONDS AND OUR SISTERS' BONDS!

THE CONTRACEPTIVE INJECTION

–Some Important Findings

Brixton Black Women's Group
First published in Speak Out, *no. 1, 1977, pp. 2–4*

For most women, it is easy to get pregnant – each month, for over 30 years, our body gets ready, carefully and in detail, for us to get pregnant. A man has 300 million or more sperms on call at any moment. But we are the ones who get pregnant, not he, so we do the worrying.

We need birth control. It must be good, cheap, safe, and easily available. At this moment in time there are some good methods, but we must always remember that they nearly all have side effects, and one sort might be o.k. with me but bad for you.

We must also remember that we live in a profit-motivated society, and profit calls the 'tune', hence any development which seems to make our lives easier ought not to be accepted without any questioning. And especially where women and Black people are concerned, this problem is acute, because we know that this society is also involved in a programme of containment and oppression of Black people, women and all working people. As working-class people, we thus have to double-check all information given to us. This is particularly important for us as women trying to take control of our lives, deciding when and how we will have children, and not leaving it up to the rest of society and our men to decide. As women struggling to separate sex from childbirth, we are confronted with the problem of contraception, how to get it, what is best for us and so on. The information we get from our doctor and others is, most times, inadequate and, anyway, they are informed by the profit-orientated drug companies.

Norethisterone: The new injection

It has come to our notice in the Black Women's Group that a contraceptive injection called Norethisterone is now being used at two London hospitals. We have also spoken to women who have received this injection. The women we spoke to were not very happy with this drug because of various side effects, such as headaches, dizziness, putting on a lot of weight in a short time, increase of size of bust from 36" to 44", and scant and irregular periods or no periods at all. One woman reported the deepening of her voice. But some of these women were reluctant to stop having the injection because it was such a convenient method of birth control.

As a result of talking to these sisters, we felt that it was important for us to gather some information on this drug. In investigating it, we found that there was little written information available to those on this drug or potential takers. We also found that the staff at the family planning clinics where the injection is given could not tell us much about it, either. The women who are being given this drug (a large percentage of whom are Black) are in a sense being 'experimented' on.

What the doctors say

We spoke to a doctor at one of the London hospitals involved in giving this drug. This type of contraception is given in the form of an injection. It is effective as a birth control for 3 months. We were told that it was only given to women who had children already or had had several abortions, those women who have just given birth and those who have difficulty in using any other

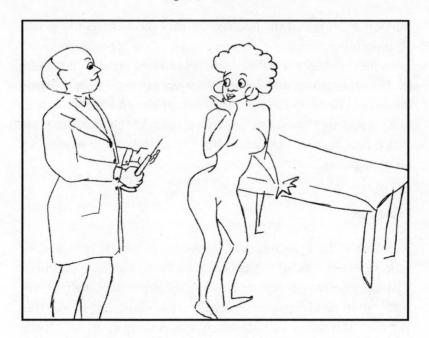

form of contraception, but we found that it was also given to those who tend to be 'forgetful', and women who want to keep their use of contraception secret from their men.

The injection is oil-based and is stored in the muscles, to be released slowly into the blood stream for its effect. It is therefore not possible to change one's mind between jabs, as one might be able to do with oral contraception. Doctors admit that it can affect your reproductive system for at least one year.

This drug has been in use for about a year, and we were told that up till now no woman has become pregnant while taking Norethisterone. We were also told that the women who [...][1] so either because of the absence of bleeding each month or other side effects. The doctor we spoke to dismissed either of these reasons as being valid.

He attributed the lack of bleeding to the absence of oestrogen in the injection, pointing out that it was normal for some women taking birth control to cease having periods. He thus concluded that the women who came off the Norethisterone injection for this reason did so because they 'enjoyed bleeding every month'

---

1 *Editor's note:* Original text illegible.

and felt abnormal if they didn't, i.e. they did not feel like a real WOMAN!

As for the other side effects experienced by a number of women on Norethisterone, this doctor believed that some people blame whatever disorders they already have or would have had on to whatever drug they are taking at the time. He claimed that this was especially true of women, but particularly those women on contraceptives.

How safe?

Research so far indicates that, unlike the pill, there is no risk of blood-clotting related to the use of the Norethisterone injection. The injection may therefore be given to women who suffer from high blood pressure or are prone to thrombosis. Although this is hailed as a major breakthrough, blood samples are still being taken once a month for the purpose of research from [...][2] that there is no concrete proof as yet that the absence of blood-clotting is necessarily a good thing.

We also learnt that many of the Black women on the injection were reluctant to give blood samples each month, because they felt that they would be used as guinea pigs. However, we suspect that their reluctance is due to the fact that doctors do not spend time explaining to these women the nature of their work and that doctors generally operate on the assumption that working class women are not concerned about being well-informed. In fact, we were told that middle class women tended to take more interest in the drug and the research connected with it, hence they were the ones who volunteered to give blood samples.

Depo-Provera: The first injection that failed

The people who produce Norethisterone have been at pains to tell us that it is not the same as Depo-Provera,[3] which has had a

---

2   *Editor's note*: Original text illegible.

3   *Editor's note*: Depo-Provera is also known as depot medroxypro-gesterone acetate.

lot of bad publicity over the last 10 years and more recently in the *Guardian*, 6 July 1977.[4]

Depo-Provera (DP for short) is also an injectable contraceptive, manufactured by Upjohn Co. of the U.S.A., who by 1975 had sold 11 million doses (see *Spare Rib*, no. 42).[5] It started life in 1960, and was used as a drug for the treatment of threatened abortions and for a disease of the womb called 'endometriosis'. It was widely used up until 1974 (in the U.S.A., at any rate) when the American Food and Drugs Administration decided that the drug was no good for either of these problems and could in fact cause damage to the foetus if taken during early pregnancy. It was also found that DP could cause breast cancer in beagles, and so the oral form was banned, but they continued to allow the use of the injectable form.

The drug is still being used in many countries and especially in the underdeveloped countries, in the same way that the pill was first used in 1956 in Puerto Rico for 4 years before it was approved in this country. Some European countries also still use DP, but on nothing like the scale it is used in our countries of origin or of our other sisters of the Third World. In 1974, the largest shipments went to Thailand, Sri Lanka, Uganda, Kenya and Costa Rica.

The *Guardian*, 6 July 1977, carried a very long article on the use of DP in Third World countries despite the ban on its use in most Western countries. It also pointed out that DP has been tested in the 'slums of Glasgow' and at Charing Cross Hospital, and that its short-term use has been approved by the Committee on Safety of Medicine 'for women whose husbands have had a vasectomy (pending final medical clearance) and for women immunised against German measles'.[6]

In other words, clinical trials and experimentation are being

---

4   *Editor's note:* See C. Sweeney, '"Banned" Birth Jab Used in Third World', *Guardian*, 6 July 1977.

5   *Editor's note:* See J. Rakusen, 'Depo-Provera: 3rd World Women Not Told This Contraceptive Is on Trial, *Spare Rib*, no. 42 (January 1976), 22–3.

6   *Editor's note:* Sweeney, '"Banned" Birth Jab Used in Third World', 24.

carried out on thousands of women without their informed consent, because someone else has decided that the benefits outweigh the risks.

Our right to know

It has become apparent to us in the Black Women's Group that there is a great need for independent research on birth control methods, because few drug companies take much notice or are even interested in feedback from doctors or women taking birth control about side effects and complications. Doctors tend to give us reassurance rather than information we need. They assume we don't want to know, or they snigger at our ability to handle the information we seek. These doctors will put women on the pill and other contraceptives without proper examination, put in an IUD (coil) without explaining that it has a failure rate, or will send a woman home with a cap without letting her practice putting it in so that she will know what it feels like when it is properly inserted.

Most important of all, many women are being used as guinea pigs without being told, and this is what we in the Black Women's Group would like to bring to the attention of other sisters. We are being used as a main supply for medical experiments, because of our social and economic position in this society. Some

people believe it only happens in the Third World, but we know it happens here. They have always used working-class people and other poor people the world over to test their drugs on, and if and when the drugs are perfected at our expense, it is then passed on for use by more 'important' people who live off and exploit us in every way possible.

The women's liberation movement in this country and America

has done a lot to encourage and support women (although it has been more beneficial to middle-class women and those in a position to follow or take part in their campaigns) to take a more positive interest in our bodies, and especially where birth control is concerned, since it is one of the spheres in which we are most exploited and kept as second-class citizens.

But, of course, as long as a system of exploitation exists, the oppression of women, Black people and all working-class people will continue. This is one of the reasons why we, as Black women, have found it necessary to come together to support each other and to pool our knowledge and resources to help and inform each other.

A SISTER'S VISIT TO CHINA

Brixton Black Women's Group
First published in Speak Out, *no. 1, 1977, pp. 6–9*

This is a report by a sister from the Black Women's Group who visited China in August/September of this year on a student delegation organised by the Society for Anglo Chinese Understanding (SACU). The Society has made possible many trips by workers and others to enable them to see for themselves how the Chinese people are building socialism. In later issues of this paper, we plan to have more reports on other aspects of this sister's experience in China, including reports on women, education and children.

China and its relation to the rest of the Third World

All African and Asian people are members of the Third World, or developing world, with a common history of colonialism and imperialist exploitation. Many of our countries have kicked out the foreign exploiters and some are still doing so, but in many where independence has been achieved we are still not in full control of our affairs and destiny. There are many reasons for this, one being that the foreign exploiters have been replaced by a privileged section of our own people who are the stooges of imperialism. However, we have examples of ex-colonies which have been able to uproot the old oppressive society and replace it with a people's government. China is a very good example of the achievement by a once-exploited and colonised part of the Third World. Since her liberation in 1949, China has always expressed support for the struggles of the people of Latin America, Africa, Asia and the Caribbean against imperialism and colonialism.

Examples of support

One example of the support China gives to the developing countries is her help in building the Tanzam Railway in Africa, which serves as a vital link between Tanzania and Zambia. This railway has given the people of the two countries greater independence from the racist Rhodesian regime, in that they no longer have to ship their produce through there.

The Chinese have always pointed out that their help and aid to the Third World is never a one-sided affair, because there are many things which the Chinese can and do learn from other developing countries.

In helping these countries to attain independence and revolution, China is advancing herself in building socialism and, finally, communism. It is not possible to build true communism in one country as long as imperialism and capitalism exist in other parts of the world, because socialist countries will have to continuously be on their guard against aggression. This task becomes easier when more countries are encouraged and supported in taking the socialist road. The task of protecting a socialist country or those which may have socialist views is very costly, and a lot of resources which should go towards building and developing socialism have to be channelled into defence.

Right up until 1949, China was described as the 'Sick Man of Asia'. She hardly had any industry to speak of; disease, starvation and poverty were rampant. In the short space of time from 1949 to today, she has got to the stage where she is now able to manufacture everything needed to feed and clothe her people, producing agricultural equipment of all kinds, excelling in the medical field and so on. China is also able to help the rest of the Third World with farming implements and the teaching of farming techniques (as far as the Third World is concerned, China is second to none). In passing on this knowledge, they stress the fact that their aim is to teach people to master techniques so that they can be self-reliant. This idea is central to China's policy in helping Third World countries. The Chinese say that since they have been successful in their socialist revolution, it is their duty to help others without claiming anything in return. Hence no strings are attached to aid, no interest is demanded for loans. Loans are given on a long-term basis (10 to 20 years), and, if the repayment time expires, nine times out of ten the Chinese will treat the loan as a gift.

The role of the people in China's great revolution

China's achievements and successes are due to the people's role in their country's development. They have been and still are 100% involved with this great leap forward, unlike in some other so-called socialist countries, especially the Soviet Union and the Eastern European countries.

There, industrialisation and technological advancement have been achieved in a short time, but at the expense of the working people, with only a few people, the bureaucrats, in control of its development. In the Soviet Union, industry has been developed at the expense of agriculture; this in turn has meant the crushing of the peasants and the almost complete oppression of the working class in general. The Chinese leadership has always put great emphasis on the role of the people.

Many of the new techniques and methods of work have been developed by ordinary Chinese people, peasants and workers, some with only a very basic education. This has been made possible because, since the struggle began over 50 years ago, the leadership has put great emphasis on the ability of the people to build socialism by their own efforts.

We spoke to many peasants, workers and students, who related to us how they are taking part fully in the building of socialism. They told us how their own ideas have been used in whatever field of work they were involved in, to improve their work and make their task easier and more beneficial. This involvement is encouraged by the Communist Party. We were shown examples of how workers had developed new techniques in their factories, and how ordinary people had set up factories on their own initiative to make use of their waste material for the betterment of people and the country as a whole. This at first was very difficult for us to understand, because we are so used to being told that workers can only do the mere minimum, like standing in front of a machine or pulling one lever at a time. We as Black people, of course, are used to being told by racists that we can only learn one thing at a time.

In the factories we visited, all workers we spoke to, no matter what jobs they were doing, knew the whole process of their work and what happens to the end product, because they all took part in the running of the factory. For us, in this society, all inventions and innovations are left to the experts and kept secret from the 'non-experts'. But it is clear that it is the people at the point of production in the factories and on the land all day and every day who will know the most about their needs, about what will make a job easier and so on, rather than some 'expert' who may never have seen an agricultural area or a shop-floor. This type of participation is possible in China because, unlike in capitalist countries, profit does not rule people's lives, deciding when they will sleep, eat, have holidays, even when they are allowed to go to the toilet.

I was very impressed by the great advances in agriculture and the tremendous amount that had been achieved over the years, as we could see from the charts and photographs we were shown, and from the personal experiences that older people related to illustrate how things had been right up until liberation and at ten-year intervals since liberation. The achievements were very, very impressive. I was struck by the way every inch of land is being put to use today for breeding pigs, cows, fish, chickens, sheep and other livestock, and, of course, for agricultural crops, the mainstay of China. The land which could not be used for one of these purposes was used for planting forests or for pleasure gardens.

I found this type of development very relevant to my country, Jamaica, which I revisited in 1974. In Jamaica, I noticed the large quantity of land not in productive use. One of the obvious reasons for this was the lack of irrigation systems produced for poor farmers, and the lack of confidence and self-reliance (which came for the Chinese people through their long and hard struggle for freedom) among the poor people as regards their ability to fulfil their goals. This was reinforced by the lack of encouragement from the government.

In China, I saw the people directly taking part in solving the problems and shortcomings of trying to cultivate what was once seen as barren and useless land but which they have now put to productive use. We met educated youths in these areas and in the countryside. They were passing on their technical knowledge to the peasants and also learning a great deal about the past and present life of the peasants and about their needs and their aspirations. We were told by the people that in order for the educated youths to contribute effectively to the life of the peasants they have to be educated by the peasants. This involvement by students and intellectuals in the practical aspects of life in China is very important for the reducing of class divisions, which is essential to the success of socialism. So, once again, we were able to see learning being conducted as a two-way process. Students are encouraged and expected to spend a certain amount of time in the countryside.

All Third World peoples rely a great deal upon the land for survival, and seizing the land has always played a great role in our independence struggles. So, too, in China, in the early stages of the revolution, great emphasis was put upon poor and landless peasants reclaiming the land from the big tyrannical landlords. This land reform movement was only the beginning of a continuous revolution in the countryside.

The People's Commune and its origin

After the People's Republic was founded in 1949, the peasants were freed from the exploitation of big landlords and a system of collective production began, which over the years has gone through many stages. Today, it takes the form of the 'People's

Commune', which combines all social activities. It organises the running of small factories, schools, medical teams, clinics, cultural activities and, of course, agriculture. The People's Commune has furthered the people's confidence in dealing with the job of planting, protecting and harvesting crops, guaranteeing food for the mass of Chinese people all year round.

The People's Commune developed out of collective production, during the land reform movement which began in 1949. The peasants were guided by the Communist Party of China in the setting up of mutual aid teams which worked on the basis that the land remained under private ownership but members helped one another with manpower, draught animals and so on, on an exchange basis. This type of collective organising to work on the land is practised in other Third World countries today. The mutual aid teams developed into elementary cooperatives which were semi-socialist. Its members were remunerated for the amount of work they did and in addition drew appropriate dividends for their labour. Land, draught animals and bigger farm implements were pooled in the co-ops as shares and placed under a unified management. This system later developed into the advanced co-ops, which were fully socialist. All the income of its members came as reward for their labour. Land and other principal means of production were owned collectively, and no dividends were paid for them.

The Great Leap Forward

By 1956, agricultural co-operatives were the general rule in China's countryside. Then the Great Leap Forward took place in 1958, a movement which aimed to release the full potential of China's new socialist economy by involving the whole people in iron- and steel-making, water conservancy projects, land reclamation and industrial construction. This movement set a mass of peasants to work on large-scale land improvement and water control projects. They also began to reform farm tools and increase production. The movement was very successful, and it gave impetus to the 'People's Commune'.

Although the advanced co-ops were far superior to the mutual aid teams and elementary co-ops which went before them, it was still inadequate as a method to deal with the rapid growth in production which came with the Great Leap Forward. Many important tasks such as building roads, installation of high-voltage power lines and the speeding up of farm mechanisation required the co-ops for their coordination to combine their activities. The new organisation is not only larger than the advanced co-ops, but it is also different in nature. Its name was changed after a discussion among the people to 'People's Commune'.

We visited a commune in Shanghai called Hung Chiow Commune. It has a population of 26,000 and a size of 1,300 hectares. They supply 270 tons of vegetables to Shanghai per day. This provides for 600,000 people. The average income of the people on this commune is 290 yuan per year (3 yuan equals £1). They pay 1 yuan per year for medical treatment, no house rent is paid, and a small plot of land is provided for individual members who want to work it in their spare time. The workers get two days off per month.

The 'People's Commune' is organised on three levels: Production Team, Brigade, and Commune level. The Production Team owns most of the land and big equipment, while the Brigade owns things like walking tractors and the small-scale production equipment. Pipelines, irrigation channels and power stations are the kinds of things owned at the Commune level. The aim of the people is to move from the three levels of ownership to a two-level system of ownership, then to a one-level system and finally to the stage of ownership by the State, which will mean a common ownership by the people. This last stage, we were reminded by the people of Hung Chiow Commune, could only be reached through the attainment of more material wealth.

Structure of the communes

Each commune has a revolutionary committee, which is at its head. Members are elected by the people. The revolutionary committee has representatives from various groups – peasants, women, youth and so on. Each commune has a scientific research worker attached to it who takes an active part in the life of the commune as well as teaching their scientific skills, helping to improve soil and protecting plants from pests. They also do manual work. We found that, on the commune, the scientific graduates did not only play the role of teachers, but a lot of the time they were students of the peasants.

Although these communes are mainly engaged in agricultural production, they are also nearly self-sufficient. They are able to repair their agricultural machines and make spare parts for them.

Communes in China vary in size from 20,000 to about 200,000, but the administrative function of the commune is the same all over China. This gives unity to what are often very different physical and social economic communities. The commune is an organisation which integrates government administration and economic management. The role of the communes is therefore social and economic as well as political.

China is important to the Third World because it serves as an example of a peasant society which has had a successful revolution of something in them taking the only certain road for

development today – socialism. And although the working class was in the forefront of the revolution, its success would not have been possible without the active support of peasants, who were then and still are the majority. This is an encouraging fact for the rest of the Third World, where industrial workers are only a small part of the population. There are some people who still believe that socialist revolution is only possible in a highly technological developed society. This theory rules out socialist development in the Third World altogether.

China has in practice knocked this theory squarely on the head, showing it up for what it is: a western chauvinist myth. China's example is also important in showing an alternative to the countries who follow their former masters after independence has been achieved, or who change one master for another. China has not allowed itself to be colonised by Soviet social imperialism, which has great designs on developing countries.

China backs up this alternative with material help and aid, which does not in the long run bleed the receiving country dry, leaving them still dependent on some other outside power. China does not insist on a country being socialist or promising to become socialist as a condition for aid. Each country, China believes, has its own specific conditions for revolution and therefore the revolution cannot be exported: the people of that country will, in the final analysis, determine their own destiny.

China has had a long history of floods and other natural disasters which have caused great losses in lives, crops and animals, resulting in famine and other ills. Today, the great rivers responsible for the floods have been tamed by the people and put to their use. All the lessons which came from the Chinese experience in this field are today placed at the disposal of the rest of the developing world. The Chinese people make up one quarter of the world's population, and 80% of the people are involved in agricultural work. They are able to feed all the people themselves. In this, China has a lot to teach us, not only in the Third World but to all oppressed peoples, including those in developing countries.

BRITISH
IMMIGRATION LAWS

−An Attack on Black People

Brixton Black Women's Group
First published in Speak Out, *no. 1, 1977, pp. 9–10, p. 12*

We, the Black Women's Group, do not see ourselves as isolated from wider society, and are joined in our efforts with Black men to triumph over racism in every form.

So, our battle is two-fold. Our ideological standpoint will not allow us to concentrate merely on sexual discrimination, though we are bound to recognise it. Indeed, we justify an article on immigration laws taking up so much space in a women's paper in that if we probe deeper into the problem of institutional racism, which is a characteristic of capitalism, we will see that racism, along with class divisions and sexism, are established capitalist tools which have successfully served to keep certain groups subservient (Black people, women and the working class as a whole).

With this mature conception of our place in society, it is our duty to analyse and uncover, as we find it, all the levels of exploitation that come to mind.

It analyses contemporary capitalist and racial exploitation by demonstrating that the 'numbers game' is primarily a tool for exploiting Black people in Britain by using us as a scapegoat for the present crisis of capitalism. Having set the scene in this way, the paper helps to aid any comprehension of sexist exploitation of Black women in Britain, e.g. by explaining why and how Black men have the lowest paid jobs, which obviously has repercussions for Black women, and puts important issues such as police attacks against Black people in perspective.

West Indians have, up to now, felt that the immigration laws have serious implications only for the Asians whose plight has received extensive and racist publicity, but this is not so.

We note situations where West Indian women, on seeking entry for their children after having found employment, etc., are asked to 'prove' that they are indeed the parents. Consequently, the houses of the extended family have to be opened to intruders who impose themselves on and interrogate the members of the families, but seldom to their advantage.

There is also the notorious situation where families have, for a number of years, made applications for a permit; they are successfully delayed until the child reaches 16–18 and is no longer allowed to join the parents as dependants. These are only some of the racist practices which we have to deal with, and more ...

The evolution and consequences of current British Immigration Acts are of vital importance to every Black person in and outside of Britain.[1] British immigration controls have been declared both illegal and racialist under international law. Yet they remain the focal point for racist opinion and our greatest source of oppression. The Acts must be exposed for what they really are – and then thrown out.

The history behind the Acts

Up until the early sixties, Britain was quite content not to discriminate between Black and White members of the Commonwealth. The only distinction which the law drew was between 'British subjects' and 'aliens'. To be a British subject meant that, while remaining a citizen of a Commonwealth country, we were also

---

1   *Editor's note:* See the Commonwealth Immigrants Act 1962, the Commonwealth Immigrants Act 1968 and the Immigration Act 1971. See also 'Immigration' (*Speak Out*, no. 3), pp. 168–74 in this collection.

given the same status as English-born residents of the British Isles. The status entitled us to enter this country as we wished and, once here, guaranteed us full civil rights. Aliens, on the other hand, were anybody else and were denied the rights of subjects. Over the past fifteen years, a series of immigration controls have deprived us of our rights as British subjects by reducing our status to that of contract-labourers, while leaving the rights of White Commonwealth citizens intact. Why was this?

Successive British governments have introduced immigration controls which are designed to suit the prevailing economic needs of the country. This policy helps to explain any changes in the law. Before any immigration control, Britain was suffering from a post-war labour shortage. In order to solve the problem, Britain drew on workers from the Commonwealth. During the fifties, Enoch Powell personally ran to parts of the Caribbean and Asia, begging Black people to come over here and save the country!! But by the 1960s, Britain was entering an economic crisis, so the demand for immigrant labour fell. Overnight, Black people became a 'problem'. It was from this point onwards that racist immigration acts were introduced, eating away the rights of Black people according to a system of work vouchers.

The last immigration act was passed in 1971 by the Conservatives. It contains the notorious 'patrial clause'. A patrial is any Commonwealth citizen who has at least one parent or grandparent born in England. In other words, a patrial is someone who has White English ancestors, and non-patrials are Black. Disguising its racism behind the patrial clause, this Act *removed all controls* from the White Commonwealth while stipulating that no one else has an automatic right to enter Britain. Ireland, incidentally, proved a problem. Its people were White, but like West Indians and Asians, they were legally classified as 'non-patrials' and therefore should suffer the same restrictions as us. The solution? The Act made the Irish 'exempt from exemption' – this was the fig-leaf, now ripped away, of British racism. The Immigration Acts are defended by lies which are widely publicised and made to appear credible.

People say ...

'The Blacks are taking over' – The truth is that, over the past twenty years, Britain has lost more emigrants than it has gained immigrants. Many people talk of 'immigrants' when they really mean Black people. Yet, because of the patrial clause, only about one in every three immigrants to this country is Black!

'Greater unemployment' – Yet, in the thirties, few Black people lived in Britain, but there was massive unemployment. Today, areas where unemployment is highest, like Northern Ireland, have virtually no Black residents. Also, far from depriving anyone of work, job discrimination forces Black people to take the jobs which White people don't want – like in the transport services, hospitals and catering industry.

'Over-burden social services' – Newspapers run sensational stories about Black people and the social services. Yet, on average, we contribute more and take less from the welfare state than any other section of the community. Official figures show that Black people are likely to receive only 80–85% as much as White people from state funds. And, as workers, we make a bigger contribution: without Black doctors and nurses, the Health Service would collapse.

'Cause overcrowding' – Racialists claim that we take all available council houses, but residential qualifications virtually exclude us from them. Over 33% of White Britons live in council houses, compared to only 16% of Black families.

So, who benefits from the racist propaganda? ...

It is not difficult to guess, when we remember the immigration laws have *not* cut the numbers entering Britain but *have* served to reduce the rights of settlement, citizenship and permanency of Black people ...

Politicians – By creating the myth that Black people are a 'problem', the government has provided itself with a convenient scapegoat for its own economic and social failures. The lies behind the immigration laws put the blame for unemployment and over-crowding in houses, hospitals and schools on the shoulders of Black people instead of where it really belongs – on the shoulders of politicians. It is easy enough to find a scapegoat, but this does nothing to solve the problems. In the past, the Jews and the Irish were used as scapegoats. Now, it's our turn.

Capitalist society – The racist immigration controls are an official go-ahead for open prejudice and discrimination, in the hope of maintaining the status quo. Racism deflects the anger of White workers suffering from the economic crisis away from employ-ers and politicians and redirects it against the Black community. Racial hatred sets worker against worker – to the bosses' benefit. It is no more than the old trick of 'divide and rule'.

Consequences of the acts for Black people ...

As a result of the Immigration Acts, Black people are now sub-jected to restrictive and often inhuman conditions of entry and settlement. It is common practice for anyone over eight years old who applies to come to this country to be interviewed for up to six hours at a time. Medicals are made to check the details given by applicants. Procedures include the notoriously unreliable bone X-rays to determine age and the internal examination of women and girls to check virginity. Any discrepancies can mean that a family is permanently separated.

On arrival to Britain, a similar vetting procedure is adminis-tered. If an Immigration Officer is not satisfied with somebody, the person can be put into a detention centre for an unspecified period of time, until their case is dealt with. Early this year, a pregnant Indian woman came to join her husband. Not only was she deported, but she was so badly treated that she lost her child in the process!

If we do get through all this red tape, what kind of reception can we expect in Britain? ...

Deportation – Many of us now live under the constant fear of deportation. The Immigration Acts state that a Black person can be deported if the Home Secretary thinks deportation is 'conducive to public good', if the person is over seventeen years old and is convicted of an offence punishable with imprisonment, and if the person is undergoing treatment in a mental hospital. Furthermore, it is not just the person who suffers, but the entire family. Any wife or child under 18 years of a person ordered to be deported must go with them. It is obvious that the deportation regulations are designed to reduce the social costs of immigration by kicking out anyone who might be a troublemaker or a burden on the state. But the recent case of Wayne Williams shows that, if we organise against the law, we *can* win. Wayne, a 21-year-old brother from Antigua, was released after massive pressure from Pentonville Prison. He had served 12 months of an 18-month sentence and was awaiting deportation. His crime? 'Handling stolen goods' – some 20 records. The deportation order was made even though his parents live in London and he has no living relatives in Antigua. Wayne was lucky; but what about hundreds of other Black people waiting to be deported in British jails as a result of the racist laws?

The police – Under the laws, the 'muggers-in-blue' have been given the power to arrest without warrant 'anyone reasonably suspected of being an illegal immigrant'. Add to this the general powers of the police, particularly under 'Sus' ('Suspicion of loitering with intent to steal, rob or conspire to cause other criminal offences') and you begin to realise how extensive the police powers are in relation to the Black community. It seems the government, with the backing of the bosses, has decided that, if Black people are to have any kind of future in this country, we will have to fight for it. The massive powers which the police now have are trying to prevent this. But we *must* fight back. In April of this year, the government discussed new proposals for establishing two types of citizenship: 'British Citizenship' for patrials, and 'British Overseas Citizenship' for the remainder – US. The changes are designed to draw a tidy line around the immigration controls. If they become law, the complex distinctions which currently govern the right of entry to Britain would disappear and 'citizenship' would become the test. Worse still, the logical extension is that, at some point, in order to enjoy full civil rights, people would not only have to be British citizens but also *patrials*. This would mean that successive generations of Black families could live in this country but never be entitled to full civil liberties. This is the reality of the situation ahead of us now and our generations in the future. Are you going to get up and stand up for your rights?

Poems

Brixton Black Women's Group
First published in Speak Out, *no. 1, 1977, p. 11*

> I am bored with it all she said,
> luckily we go to the cote d'azur
> for a few days, or maybe we will
> try the avignon district, this
> year instead.
>
> It is so nice to get away,
> but here in Railton Road,
> and others like it may await
> their fate.
>
> Young mothers and their babes
> sit huddled in front of kerosene fires,
> kids crawl into bed with near empty bellies,
> winds howl through gaping cracks and holes,
> holes left unrepaired by uncaring council and
> landlords, who are no doubt away themselves,
> men return from domino joints and public houses,
> women ply their trade in flesh to feed the now
> sleeping mouths, mangy dogs and cats rummage half
> empty dustbins, for carefully discarded scraps.
>
> Not for them the cote d'azur
> marseille,
> avignon,
> at least not this year.
>
> Where can they go?
> Where do they go?
> Need it be?

Tower blocks or tenement flats,
H.M. prison, Brixton or Holloway,
William Hill or Ladbrokes,
The Crown and Hope, the Dog and Crown or
Le Dole Queue?
Tell me! where do they go?

❧

Lawd of mercy chile, is why you luk so?
Look what me come a England fe set eye pon
is what wrong wid yuh, what no you live in a
council flat and de pon welfare?
good lawd that you died in my womb

and no, is what you do to yuh hair?
no lawd dis could'nt be the girl I rear.

The girl I spend all mi money pon an send to
good school, and live wid in a decent house,

if you dad had seen yuh before him did ded, him
woulda ded before him did ded

What yuh no wear make up?
No wonder yuh look so mash up
and dem boots pon yuh feet me child,
back home in a New York, a only poor nigger
sport dem after welfare visit.

Come to yuh senses, come let me clean yuh
up and tek yuh home to New York,
the family would love to see yuh,
dem would'nt tink dat you'd sink so low,
get out a dis godforsaken country
come home to New Yolk.

Donald's got a new sports car,
Ever buy him second one,
Dawn on her second trip
Gloria engaged to a doctor from N.Y.
and I'm having the garage extended.

SPEAK OUT!

Me can't tell dem how me find yuh,
contented! you could never be, after
what you been used to.
Don't! ask me bout KU KLUX KLAN
A leave all dem tings to politician

REVIEW

Brixton Black Women's Group
First published in Speak Out, *no. 1, 1977, pp. 11–12*

Problems of Women's Liberation
by Evelyn Reed
Published by Pathfinder Press
Available through Sabarr Books, Railton Road, Brixton

Evelyn Reed's *Problems of Women's Liberation* (1970) is an important book for the women's movement. It is a collection of essays written in an attempt to dispel the myth that the basis of women's supposed inferiority lies in our ability to have children, i.e. the motherhood trap. In the essays 'Women and the Family' and 'The Myth of Women's Inferiority', she shows that in primitive classless society women reigned supreme. They bore children but remained free and independent. In fact, childbearing was a chief source of power, because it was through the women that ancestry was traced.

In primitive society, women worked closely together in and around the home. Because of this, they became the innovators in those important 'homely' activities that are now seen as the work of men. Women were paramount in the development of architecture – they built their own houses; in agriculture – they discovered the first tools; in medicine – they experimented with herbs; and even animal training – the domestication of goats and cats, etc., was due to their initial efforts. At this time, the men were confined to the solitary and often unrewarding job of hunting.

However, if women had this important place in society as its cultural leaders, equal to and in many ways superior to men, how did their downfall come about? How was the woman robbed of her place in society? Ms Reed is quite clear: 'It is not nature, but class society, which robbed women of their right to participate in the higher functions of society and placed the primary emphasis upon their animal functions'.[1] In the essay 'How Women Lost Control of Their Destiny and How They Can Regain It', she explains how the development of class society and the emphasis on surplus wealth negated the position of women.[2] Her child-bearing and child-rearing functions were without any 'surplus value' and therefore lost their importance. Then, free of the 'ties' of childbirth, men took over the reins of society and the patriarchal family based on the father-line became dominant. Women now were dependent on men and were forced to compete as chattels for economic society.

And so, not only did women lose their power through the development of class society, they became dependent on men and antagonistic towards other women. This is developed in the essay 'Cosmetics, Fashions and the Exploitation of Women'.[3] Ms Reed shows how the fashion and cosmetic industry have exploited this dependence on men. They have inverted primitive social activities like painting one's face until it has become no more than a way that women, by competing, can capture a man.

Even though the book is historical, it still has a lot of importance for us today. It is particularly important for us as Third World women, because many of the characteristics of the mother-centred family that she describes are still applicable. Black women are often the main provider in the home, running the house and looking after the children. Yet, because of capitalism and class society, they have not the freedom and independence of primitive women.

1   *Editor's note:* Evelyn Reed, 'The Myth of Women's Inferiority', in *Problems of Women's Liberation* (New York: Pathfinder Press, 1970), 23.

2   *Editor's note:* This essay is not included in the first edition of *Problems of Women's Liberation* but appears to be included from the second edition onwards.

3   *Editor's note:* This essay is also not included in the first edition of *Problems of Women's Liberation* and also seems to be included from the second edition onwards. It appears to have later been expanded into (and to be more readily available as) a book: J. Hansen, E. Reed, and M.-A. Waters, *Cosmetics, Fashions, and the Exploitation of Women* (Atlanta: Pathfinder Press, 1986).

BLACK WOMEN AND NURSING: A JOB LIKE ANY OTHER

Brixton Black Women's Group
First published in Race Today, *August 1974, pp. 226–30*[1]

In the present struggle, nurses, for the first time, have come out on strike in support of their demands for more money. They have acted in opposition to the myth that women administering to sick, young and old should not behave in this way. Nursing is traditionally women's work, especially black women's. In the following article, widely illustrated with interviews, we maintain that the presence of black women in the health industry has been

---

1   *Editor's note:* The Race Today Collective (so named after the journal they produced) was central to many struggles for racial liberation in Britain. Its members included Jean Ambrose, Barbara Beese, Farrukh Dhondy, Patricia Dick, Leila Hassan, Darcus Howe, Gus John, Linton Kwesi Johnson, Akua Rugg, and Mala Sen. From 1973 to 1988, the collective's journal was home to the work of leading Black British intellectuals and activists of the time. C. L. R. James lived above their squatted Brixton offices (at 165 Railton Road) in his later years, until his death in 1989. See A. Donnell, 'Race Today', in *Companion to Contemporary Black British Culture*, ed. A. Donnell (London: Routledge, 2002); P. Field, R. Bunce, L. Hassan, and M. Peacock, eds, *Here to Stay, Here to Fight: A Race Today Anthology* (London: Pluto, 2019); A. Vasudevan, *The Autonomous City: A History of Urban Squatting* (London: Verso, 2017).

crucial in bringing the struggle to its present stage. This is not a comprehensive statement in that most of the nurses who participated in writing it work in London hospitals, and we know that the most militant action has come from outside London. Also, all of the nurses are of Afro-Caribbean origin. We concentrate here on nurses. Because of space limitations, we do not deal with the situation of ancillary workers, not because we see them as subsidiary to the hospital structure (as do the nurses' unions). However, we point out that it was these workers, recruited from Southern Europe, Ireland, the Caribbean and Asia, who first brought the strike weapon to the hospitals in Britain.

–Black Women's Group

Nursing is a 'caring profession', and traditionally the work of women – to be of service not only to their own men and children, but to other people's. No woman is more identified with service work than black women, especially the black women with a slave or colonial past. The relationship between the black woman and nursing, wet nursing or dry nursing, of other people's children and other people's husbands and wives, dates from before any National Health Service. Whether working in hospitals as auxiliaries, SENs [state enrolled nurse] or SRNs [state registered nurse], in the head of the black nurse from the Caribbean is the echo of slavery; in the head of the Asian nurse is the servitude to Sahib and Memsahib.

The colonial legacy expresses itself today in the young woman who, from very early on, knows she must take disciplined responsibilities in her own family – for example, for younger sisters and brothers. This legacy is alive in another sense: often the only waged jobs open to women in the ex-colonial world is in the kitchens of the middle and upper classes.

From their traditions in the family and in waged employment, in this country and 'at home', flow easily the tradition of black women in hospital work.

We believe that we can show that there is a connection between the nationalisation of the Health Service (1948) and the immigration of these workers with this tradition. A health service which was intended to see after the *whole* working class, and not just those who could afford it, would need a tremendous injection of workers who would not expect too much in wages and would not be in a position to challenge their working conditions.

During the last 20 years, the class composition of nursing has changed. A hundred years ago, this was said of nurses: 'Many gentlewomen were recruited because it is the belief that this type of nursing required the highest type of women who were well-educated' (Report of the National Association for Providing Trained Nurses for the Sick Poor, 1874). This is not a picture of nurses today, and certainly not a description of the recruiting policy of the National Health Service. What used to be a vocation for women of the middle class is now a *job* for women of the working class, and particularly for black and other immigrant women.

Overseas nurses: Cheap labour

The number of overseas student nurses coming into the British Health Service increases rapidly each year. In 1959, approximately 6,000 came in; in 1970, just under 19,000. They come mainly from the Caribbean, Hong Kong, Mauritius, Malaysia (which is now the highest sending country) and Ireland. We cannot analyse in depth who these women are, and the specific conditions that exist in their own countries which force them to come to Britain for training as a way out.

For a way out it certainly is. Few come with the desire to nurse. But whether the desire is there or not, the National Health Service ensures that they will work here for at least five years. Many of them are deliberately directed to take the SEN qualification, which is of no use to them outside of Britain but which guarantees a trained, low-paid workforce on the ward floor. One way of pushing women from overseas into SEN training is by demanding educational standards which overseas students are less likely to have.

During their stay here they have to renew their permits through the hospital every six months. They have also to give an undertaking that they will stay for a certain period of time after they have trained, so that Britain can benefit from 'the training she has paid for'. Yet since most of her training is spent working on the ward, the SEN pupil nurse repays for her training a million times over by the cheap labour she provides. The NHS need for this labour as opposed to skilled labour is shown by the fact that, in 1972, only 120 qualified nurses were allowed into the country.

Grace Jenkins, SEN, Trinidadian:
'I came to England to train as a nurse in 1970, when I was 22. I applied to the Trinidad Health Service and they sent me a list of hospital addresses in England. I chose one in Birmingham. I went for an interview in Trinidad and took a sort of intelligence test. I was accepted by the hospital. I came direct to the hospital. I didn't really want to nurse but I wanted to leave Trinidad. I have never had a job there.

'I did eight weeks' training and then went straight on the ward working – that is, changing bed pans, cleaning lockers and generally fetching and carrying. At first I got £45 a month after deductions. It took me a week to realise that I didn't like England and not much longer to realise I didn't like nursing, but I have to stay five years; that is the condition under which I came.

'From Birmingham I went to Nottingham to do a special theatre training – it's more money once you are trained. I find nurses are very conscious of what position they hold – even some of the black ones.

'When I was in Birmingham in 1970, they told two black trainee nurses that they would have to leave because they had failed three times a test you take after your eight weeks' initial training. About 50 of us [black nurses] went on strike, some for half a day, some for two or three days, and demanded that they be re-instated. We got the help of the local West Indian Association and we got them back in. I'm doing agency work now – during my holiday period. I need the money.'

Labour in the hospital is devised according to sex, race and age. Different jobs are done by people in different uniforms, getting different wages, and having different degrees of power. Those who work the hardest have the least status and the least wages. These divisions are further reinforced by the division between those who are 'professionals' and those who are not. 'The specific way this hierarchy functions, which is different from other waged work, is that every student nurse has a chance to be second year, and every second year a chance to be third year, and every third year a chance to be Staff Nurse, and every Staff Nurse the chance to be Ward Sister, and Ward Sisters become Matrons, and a few Matrons become ...' ('Wages for Housework and the Struggle of the Nurses', Power of Women Collective, 1974, p. 3).[2]

There are two types of training from the beginning – a two-year course leads to an SEN (State Enrolled Nurse) qualification which cannot lead to a promotion. A large number of Asians, Irish and West Indians are deliberately directed to SEN.

'When you are interviewed, they ask you if you want to do the course in two years or three, and all of us said we would like to do the two-year course. It's only when you get here that you realise that if you do two years, you will be an SEN'. The SRN (State Registered Nurse) goes through a three-year training and it is she who has the potential for promotion.

On the ward floor, black women are invariably to be seen in the lower trades, servicing doctors, 'professional' nurses, and patients. Few black nurses enter the National Health Service as a vocation, in the hope of becoming a matron – and to even those who do, it soon becomes clear that this is not what they have been recruited for. For black women, nursing is a *job*, nothing more, and by refusing to treat it as a vocation they are not only exposing the real nature of nursing in the health service but are undermining the hierarchy which depends on them wanting to be a part of it.

Agency nurses

We believe that the agency nurse has represented the spearhead for the force for change in the National Health Service. The attempts to victimise her are racist and anti-working class. A significant

---

2 *Editor's note:* The text this quote is taken from can be found online at bibliotechecivichepadova.it/sites/default/files/opera/documenti/sezione-5-serie-2-55.pdf. The text is dated 27 June 1974 and is marked as a draft. It is unclear whether a final version was ultimately published (perhaps as a pamphlet?), but reference is made to it in an issue of the Power of Women Collective's journal – see Bernadette, 'Welcome to Britain', *Power of Women: Journal of the Power of Women Collective* 1, no. 2 (July/August 1974), 12.

Mrs. Andrews, Nursing Assistant (psychiatric hospital equivalent of an auxiliary in a general hospital):
'But this is what I think was wrong from the beginning, by giving us the name of nursing assistant, this "nursing" – it shouldn't be, it should be workers ... To me it is just a job like any other, if I was in a factory or anything like that.

'All of us have to do a lot of things they [nurses] do, except we don't give injections and write reports. We have to admit the patient, we have to make beds, take them to ECT treatment, we do everything they do ... only they sit in the office. We are the ones outside with the patients all the time.

'People ask me why I have stayed so long. Come December, I will have been there for eight years. But I can defend myself. I know I am not liked by them and I can't really say that I want to hug and squeeze with them. I just want them to accept me as I am, and I accept them as they are and do their work.

'The majority of the staff are black here, they are mostly nursing assistants. For example, on the children's ward, I counted that they had 12 nursing assistants, two sisters, a charge nurse [male equivalent of a sister] and a staff nurse and an SRN. All the nursing assistants were black. It's little things that I check up on.

'Some people ask me why I don't want to go further. I don't want to because I have fulfilled my goal by bringing up my two children on my own. I don't want any status behind my name because it is a bloody racket ... I can't see where they are going anyway, they have more heartaches than anything else. Just where I am is where I want to stay and I will be just on the outside looking in at them fighting. They don't have time for their husbands; it's just position, position. It doesn't help the patients recover, it's only themselves ... Now they have a new badge. When we were first there, all they put on it was Nurse Andrews or Nurse Brown. On this new badge, everybody has their status on it – T.T. Andrews, which is my name – and this is causing some dispute from those who feel that their years of service mean they are more than just workers – and want recognition of it. I am pleased, because once they see it they know exactly who I am and they can't ask me to do certain things and I can refuse to do a lot of things.'

number of black nurses are doing agency work. Nursing agencies have mushroomed in the last two years, and more and more nurses, particularly those who are married, are doing agency work as a flexible alternative to working in the Health Service. In the London area, especially, the teaching hospitals rely heavily on agency supply easing their labour problems. For example, the last available figures from the DHSS show that, on 30 September 1971, 'the equivalent of 2,720 agency nurses and midwives working the whole time were being employed in the area of central London and the four Metropolitan Regional Hospital Boards ... 54% were employed in the teaching hospitals, which employed only 11% of NHS nursing and midwifery staff' (Report of the Briggs Committee on Nursing, 1972).[3]

The agency nurse has been singled out and made a focus for attack. The attack has come from within the 'profession', from the union executive of COHSE, and from so-called revolutionary organisations.[4] All have said that NHS nurses should refuse to work with agency nurses. At the time of writing, COHSE has withdrawn use of the strike weapon by its members, pending the Halsbury Committee Report, but their ban on working with agency nurses remains and is to become permanent. The National Rank & File Organising Committee, who produce *Hospital Worker*, have also called for a complete end to the use of agency nurses, and a recent report in *Women's Voice*, the paper of International Socialist Women, said: 'At our first meeting we decided that the best action would be to ban working with agency nurses. There's 300 in King's [Hospital] and £12,500 a week is spent on them – the hospital would collapse without them. Of course, it's hard on them, but if they're bothered about the state of nursing they should be in the NHS fighting with us'.

The reality is that the National Health Service wage rises with seniority, from grade to grade. If a nurse breaks her service, for example to have children, she loses all seniority and the wage that goes with it, and when she re-joins she must begin over again working her way up the pay ladder. This kind of penalisation excludes almost all black nurses who are mothers from re-joining, because whether or not there is a man in the house, the woman must work. So, they do agency work more and more, because

---

3   *Editor's note:* The Department of Health and Social Security (DHSS) was a ministry of the British government, in existence from 1968 until 1988.

4   *Editor's note:* The Confederation of Health Service Employees (COHSE) was a trade union representing workers primarily in the National Health Service.

that is their only choice. Furthermore, having children raises the question of child-care facilities, which are not available on the scale needed and certainly not at a price black nurses could afford. So, many work the night shift and see after the children and housework by day. The question of how much money the agency nurse earns is wildly exaggerated, and some agencies operate a pay scale for white nurses and a lower one for black nurses. We were told: 'At the agency they said you were never to discuss your wages. I did and I discovered that Australian nurses were getting more.'

At critical points in struggle, when the interests of two different sets of workers seem to clash, the stronger often win their case temporarily by excluding the weaker. The trade unions were formed in Britain to exclude women from skilled trades. The trade unions in the US were formed to exclude white women, all 'foreigners' and blacks from skilled trades. The nursing work force *appears* to be divided by different unions and professional bodies, but they are not. In this case, the divisions between unions need not divide workers and may even be helpful, since nurses are getting together across trade union barriers. Non-trade union workers (and that includes agency nurses) are therefore not excluded by the workers' own way of organising. The divisions that are dangerous are between, first, nursing and non-nursing staff, and, second, NHS and agency nurses – divisions among hospital workers. They must come together and refuse these divisions that the government, unions and the Left are trying to deepen. Racism and sexism are not about abstract moral attitudes, but about whether you take position with black women, agency or non-agency, auxiliary, SRN or SEN.

The agency nurse is the first refusal to be tied to the hospital hierarchy, thereby confronting the blackmail that faces all nurses, that they are caring 'professionals' and not workers. The issues which have created the agency nurse are fundamental to all nurses and in fact to all women. But the unity necessary to make a fight will come only when NHS nurses join with agency nurses to raise these issues.

Patricia Mathews, SRN, Barbados:

'I came to this country in 1962, when I was 17. I went to look for a job and the Youth Employment Officers suggested that I go for a job in the factory. I didn't want to work in a factory, but I didn't know what I wanted to do. I didn't really want to do nursing as such. I went to a London Teaching Hospital to train as a nurse. They said I would have to work as an auxiliary first, because of my age. I now know this isn't true; they could have taken me on as a cadet. So I worked as an auxiliary doing bed pans, washing babies' woolies, cleaning lockers, etc.

'When I first started, it was so depressing, I was one of the only black girls there. Then more and more black girls came into London, and it wasn't so bad. I remember one incident: I was living at the nurses' home, and at that time I was wearing clothes I had brought with me from home. As I was going out while living at the nursing home, the matron said to me, "Where are you going dressed like a tart?" They used to do things like going through your clothes and then ask how you could afford certain things. I remember that the first pay I got was £9 a week. In 1963, I started training for an SRN, and I felt so isolated. There would be times when I would sit in the canteen all by myself, with no one to talk to. I was unhappy, but I didn't want to work in a factory and my family and friends all felt nursing was better than that, so I stayed. It was during that period of my life that I saw I was being victimised. To me, it has always just been a job. I trained because I couldn't see what else there was; now it is a way of earning a living. When I finished training and was on the wards, the doctors especially wouldn't recognise black nurses then. Many is the time I was asked to fetch a nurse. But this has changed; they can't do without black nurses at all now.

'In 1964, I qualified and left the Health Service immediately, and I went to work for an agency. I will never work for the Health Service, because of what I went through during my training. The patients are not being looked after properly, and the nurses have no say in the way the patients are looked after – and the money is disgusting. Everyone on the ward is divided by what status they are. In the NHS, you have to put up with things that as an agency nurse you don't have to. Matron doesn't rule you anymore. When I first started agency work there were not many agencies around, and in those days it was mostly private nursing that they catered for. Many times I have gone to a job and the person has said that they didn't want me to nurse them. If they were desperate, they would say, "Oh, you could look after me today, but I would like someone else tomorrow". I don't particularly like working for an agency, either, but you get more money and more freedom. If my daughter is sick, I just ring up and say I am not going in. Whereas in the Health Service they would try and persuade you to come in, saying how short-staffed they were, and if you didn't you would lose a night's pay. But I do feel that they are making a big business out of us. You get different rates from different agencies, and some take up to 12% commission. I work nights all the time because I have a child. I chop and change agencies to get more money. I work 4 nights a week, from 8.30 p.m. to 7.30 a.m., at a London hospital where the majority of nurses are from overseas. I find that whenever people talk about agency nurses they mean black nurses, but there are nurses from all over the world working for agencies. I feel very sorry now for the girls, say, from the Philippines and Malaysia, who don't speak English very well and who are being exploited. They remind me of when I first started training.'

Marilyn came to England at the age of 16, from Trinidad. She has been nursing for 12 years, the last 5 of which have been spent working for agencies. She says:

'I left school in Fulham when I was 18 years with no qualifications except CSEs, and I went straight to nursing. I had always wanted to be a nurse from home in the Caribbean, since I was young. There were four of us, three girls and one boy. The three of us were going to be nurses and the boy was going to be a doctor. I got £12 a month after they had deducted for board and lodging. After two years I got pregnant, so I left. I went back to work 6 weeks after I had my child and I did a year of SEN ... I really started agency work for 6 months only and because it's a job I can leave whenever I want to, if I feel like leaving. I've worked for about six agencies. The first one paid the same as the NHS, so I didn't stay ... I worked nights so I could be with my child in the day. That's why a lot of women work nights ... I don't care, really, because I've had so many different experiences nursing, it has made me sick. Even if you have qualifications, you have to work so hard to prove yourself as good as they [white nurses] are, or even better. It's not handed to you on a plate. With white nurses, it's just handed to them. Black nurses get most of the dirty jobs. Say you have one white trained nurse and one black trained nurse on the ward, you will have the white one in the office and the black one on the ward. Doctors treat you terrible, and the black ones are just as bad. They just completely ignore black nurses once there's a white nurse there. The last hospital I worked in, there were more agency nurses than NHS nurses ... There should be some arrangement by the hospital to provide nurseries. Some hospitals have crèches but they're no use because you have to work odd hours. It might be open 9-5, but if you're working until 8 it's no good. Or they close on a Saturday or Sunday, so what happens then, or on a Bank holiday?'

General Nursing

SRN (3-year course)

Student Nurses' Training Allowances		Training Allowances	Lodging charge where resident
Aged under 21 on entry	Age 18	£ 816.00	£ 29.40
	Age 19	£ 891.00	£ 58.80
	Age 20	£ 936.00	£ 58.80
Aged 21 or over on entry	First year of training	£ 1,065.00	£ 120.00
	Second year of training	£ 1,098.00	£ 120.00
	Third year of training	£ 1,131.00	£ 120.00

(A single payment of £5 is made on passing the Preliminary or intermediate qualifying examinations)

Qualified Nurses' Salary Scales		Salary Scales	Lodging charge where resident
	Staff Nurse	£1,338 – £1,725	£ 192.00
	Ward Sister/Charge Nurse	£1,632 – £2,202	£ 225.00
	Lower scale	£2,070 – £2,523	£ 312.00
	Higher scale	£2,160 – £2,610	£ 324.00
	Senior Nursing Officer		
	Lower scale	£2,328 – £2,814	£ 366.00
	Higher scale	£2,460 – £2,949	£ 384.00
	Principal Nursing Officer		
	Lower scale	£2,667 – £3,195	£ 402.00
	Highest scale	£3,222 – £3,810	£ 501.00

Higher salary scales are applicable to the senior nursing staff of Regional Health Authorities and Area Health Authorities

SEN (2-year course)

Student Nurses' Training Allowances		Training Allowances	Lodging charge where resident
Aged under 21 on entry	Age 18	£ 816.00	£ 29.40
	Age 19	£ 891.00	£ 58.80
	Age 20	£ 936.00	£ 58.80
Aged 21 or over on entry	First year of training	£ 1,065.00	£ 120.00
	Second year of training	£ 1,098.00	£ 120.00

(A single payment of £5 is made on passing the Preliminary or intermediate qualifying examinations)

Qualified Nurses' Salary Scales		Salary Scales	Lodging charge where resident
	Enrolled Nurse	£1,203 – £1,455	£ 162.00
	Senior Enrolled Nurse	£1,380 – £1,755	£ 192.00

Qualified Nurses' Salary Scales		Salary Scales	Lodging charge where resident
Nursing Auxilliaries	Age 18	£ 816.00	£ 58.80
	Age 19	£ 855.00	£ 58.80
	Age 20	£ 900.00	£ 58.80
	Age 21 or over	£1,053 – £1,293	£ 120.00

Black nurses have been accused of not participating militantly in the present struggle. Such accusations, like those against agency nurses, are based on the racism inherent in the hospital hierarchy. Black nurses cannot know if the unity for which white nurses are calling is any guarantee that their specific grievances will be dealt with. They, more than white nurses, face the indignities of the ward from patients and doctors, and the entire history and experiencee which they bring to nursing causes them to proceed with caution. The attack on the agency nurse has confirmed that they have been right to be cautious so far about joining the struggle when they are not leading it.

For further information on the Black Women's Group, contact 65 Railton Rd., Brixton S.W.2.

Mrs. D., who comes from Jamaica, started off as a nursing auxiliary and after some years trained as an SEN. She is now doing agency work and explains why:

'Well, I wanted to go home on a holiday. I hadn't seen my mother for over 10 years. I went to the matron and asked her if I could have my five weeks' holiday, plus three weeks without pay. She said, "No", I would have to resign and then re-join. So I resigned ... It's not that you have to start training again, but after you're qualified, each year you're a year up, and when you get to three years you're a Senior Enrolled Nurse and you get a higher pay than when you are first or second year. If you break your time before your three years are up you have to start back at Grade 1, which is what happened to me. I tried to re-join but I couldn't get in, so I decided to go to the agency ... I don't know why I couldn't get back in – they're supposed to be short of nurses. I don't know if it was the reference or what ... I work for Mrs. H. in Streatham – she doesn't pay top rates, but you can always get jobs as long as you want to work ... I work the night shifts ... it suits me and fits in with my housework ... I'm working now in Battersea. Most of the night staff are black. Night nurses are black because they have children and it's more convenient for them to be at home in the days to see after the children. If you work days you're not there to send them off to school, you're not there to receive them when they come back, and you have to get somebody to look after them. With nights, you can actually put them off to bed before going to work.

'I support the strike wholeheartedly. Nurses are saying they won't work with agency nurses and I think they're being silly, because, number one, they should find out why nurses have to go on the agency, because in my case it's not because I wanted to but because I was forced to ... I can't do without working. If I could have got back into the hospital, I would have, because there is more security and there are periods with the agency when I can't get work at all, like in the winter when the nurses are not on holidays. If you are ill on the agency, you get no pay and no looking after.'

'I joined the Union COHSE since the strike for protection. I have been to two meetings, one at the Maudsley and the other at Bethlem, and the things Mr. Spanwick told us were different than from what he said on television. "STRIKE", he said to us, and when I saw him on the television, I said, "Look at that bitch". He was saying that he thinks that nurses are dedicated, and that if they walk out on the patients they will lose their reputation. We haven't raised the question of discrimination, because at the first meeting it was said that it wasn't a meeting for that, only for money.'

'... AND WHAT DID WE FIND?'

Brixton Black Women's Group
First published in Red Rag *13, 1978, pp. 16–18*

This is a contribution made by the women from the Brixton Black Women's Group to the rally 'Women All Over the World in Struggle for Liberation', held at Conway Hall on International Women's Day, March 8th, 1978.

Caribbean women today, and Black women in general, remain an exploited class. We are the poorest internationally and throughout history. We were a substantial part of the labour force in Britain, imported to meet its economic needs, and we remain a significant part of that force.

Britain's relationship with the Caribbean (in fact, it is the relationship of any metropolis with her colonies) has always been that of active underdevelopment.

What I mean by active underdevelopment is that *our* labour power and natural resources was always at the disposal of Britain; economics was the decider in our relationship.

So that Enoch Powell, when he toured the Caribbean in the late fifties and early sixties and invited the people of the Caribbean to come and work in England, was no less racist then than when he made his 'Rivers of Blood' speech, or now when he voices his fear that we might spoil the British culture. Racist and imperialist motives are one and the same thing, they are not at all opposed. Imperialist decisions run with the economic tide.

Caribbean women who came to Britain at the time of the call were to staff the National Health Service with Black nurses and auxiliaries, British hotels and restaurants with chambermaids/ washer-ups, and Greater London Transport with conductresses.

Other Caribbean women who came independently of the campaigns were forced to leave because of near-starvation, unemployment for their men and themselves, and little prospects of education for their children. *Near-starvation* because the countries were geared to producing for the metropolis, *unemployment* because one Black person could reputedly perform the task of five white men (even if it would mean that their life expectancy would be only 30 years) and few schools, because what indeed would a colonial government do with educated Blacks? To make it to Britain, regardless of the economic need, we had to pay our way. We had to pay to come to work, and at such cost! It certainly does not compare with tube fares.

Women had to depend on relatives (members of the extended family) to club together and raise the fares to send to Britain the most educated, aspiring member of the family. They in turn were obliged to repay and to assist the members of the family remaining in the West Indies. In order to fulfil these commitments, Black women were forced into the most low-paid jobs and exploited sections of the community (even this compares well to situations in the West Indies); whatever the skills, the opportunities were severely limited.

Black women came to reap some of the economic joy that they knew was Britain's to regain, albeit by sweat and blood what was rightly theirs and had been misappropriated. Things were rather more difficult than had been anticipated; it was taking so long to accumulate anything that would significantly affect our lives in the Caribbean should we return, and rather than maintaining 2 homes – one in Britain, one in the Caribbean – we had our families join us to struggle together.

We came here for better opportunities – What, in reality, did we find? On arrival, Black families were faced with appalling housing conditions, we were unwelcomed by racist landlords, and those landlords who did rent to us were to exploit us with overly high rents and inadequate facilities.

3–4 families were to occupy a couple of rooms where individuals slept in shifts. The slums were *already* existing then. Black women had become the new underdogs, we were to replace the lower working class. The government were complacent, since any immediate threat from the indigenous working class was delayed and also because, historically, their interest had always been in the labour power of Black people, not in their social welfare.

In employment, we were to fill the worst-paid jobs with long and unsociable hours and poor working conditions. They were also the kinds of jobs that were non-unionised, and where unions existed, the interest of the Black woman worker remained unheard and went undefended. Despite all these odds, Black women have fought heroically to resist exploitation. Examples of this can be seen in the Night Cleaners' Strike of 1972.[1] Black women were to contribute in the fight to obtain an increase in pay – and union recognition.

The Ancillary Workers' Strike, also of 1972, brought the struggle into the hospitals where nurses were later to strike for more money and better conditions.[2]

---

1   *Editor's note:* The Cleaners' Action Group was set up by women who worked as cleaners (often through the night) in office blocks and other buildings, in order to organise for better pay and working conditions as well as for union recognition. Among other actions, they organised a strike which began in the Ministry of Defence building in July 1972. May Hobbs, one of the driving forces behind the Cleaners' Action Group, recounted her experiences in her book *Born to Struggle* (1973). See also Judith Weinraub, 'London's Night Cleaning Women Arise', *New York Times*, 24 July 1972; and the 1975 documentary *Nightcleaners* by the Berwick Street Collective (Marc Karlin, Mary Kelly, James Scott and Humphry Trevelyan).

2   *Editor's note:* The Ancillary Workers' Strike referred to here lasted six weeks over 1972 and 1973 and affected 300 hospitals. In support of the strike, a December 1972 demonstration organised by the Confederation of Health Service Employees (COHSE) and the National Union of Public Employees (NUPE) saw NHS workers from across Britain march in London. Sister marches also took place in Glasgow, Birmingham, Manchester, Cardiff, Liverpool, Leeds, Newcastle, Brighton and other major cities. For more, see D. Widgery, 'Unions and Strikes in the National Health Service in Britain', *International Journal of Health Services* 6, no. 2 (1976), 301–8; and J. Saunders, 'Emotions, Social Practices and

In the sphere of education, children came into schools that were not prepared for their arrival. Consequently, there were language and cultural barriers that contributed to the alienation of West Indian children. Teachers reflected the racism of the society, and many children, regardless of the difficulties that they were experiencing, were labelled *educationally sub-normal*. These miseducated youths were to provide a new source of cheap labour for the economy. Britain no longer had to import labour; here was a secure reserve, purpose-built. The harsh realities of racism, then, manifested in employment, housing, education and social life, served to entrap Black workers yet further. Any hopes of returning home were now shattered.

Britain's response has been to implement a series of immigration controls to deprive us of our rights as British subjects by reducing our status to that of contract labourers, while at the same time leaving the rights of white Commonwealth citizens intact. As Britain began to feel an economic decline, Black people became more and more of a 'problem', the Acts became increasingly restrictive and repressive, and Black women faced particular violation of their home and privacy. For instance, Black women were asked to prove that they were indeed the parents of their children. This meant that the homes of the extended family had to be opened to intruders who imposed themselves on the interrogated individual members of the family.

The lack of status that these Acts gave to Black people have meant increased harassment of Black people by the police. Now they have a right to arrest you on suspicion – in fact, for any arbitrary reason. Many a Black mother has come under attack of the police when she rose in defence of her children. Recently, there has been a change in the 1977 Finance Act which means that Black women who work in this country and have children and other dependants abroad will soon be unable to support their family, either through tax claims or child benefits. This has been necessary, they say, because of the number of false claims

---

the Changing Composition of Class, Race and Gender in the National Health Service, 1970–79: "Lively Discussion Ensued"', *History Workshop Journal* 88 (2019), 204–28.

that are made! This is practically impossible with all the evidence and documents that we have to provide before the claim is recognised.

The media and other institutions continue to make attacks on Black women. We are projected as perverted sex objects. Like the idea that every Black person is a potential mugger (as the police said on the TV), the Black woman is a potential prostitute, and we could go on ...

Black women have been victims of forced sterilisation. The desire to decrease the Black race, and thus 'the problems', has meant that we go into hospitals for simple operations and find ourselves sterilised. Even though in principle we believe in a woman's right to choose, we realise that Black women in Britain do not have this choice; in fact we are encouraged to abort!

Pretty raw deal

So yes, we are having a pretty raw deal and I suppose the questions in your mind include – What are we doing about it?

How can you support us? All over Britain where Black people have settled, we have soon enough realised that institutions play a negative role in our lives. As a result, we have sought to form self-help groups to provide alternative education geared towards a questioning of the system and the influencing of our community in a positive way. There are numerous Black groups interested and geared towards supplementary education in the form of Saturday and summer schools – notably Ahfiwe in Brixton, which has dealt with children who are reputedly ESN [educationally sub-normal] and have later sat and passed GCE exams.[3] There are

---

3   *Editor's note:* The Ahfiwe ('All for We') supplementary school was established by Ansel Wong in 1974. It was based at 1 Gresham Road in Brixton and had strong links with the Abeng Centre (the location of the first OWAAD conference) at 7 Gresham Road. See this book's afterword for more; see also Rob Waters, 'Student Politics, Teaching Politics, Black Politics: An Interview with Ansel Wong', *Race and Class* 58, no. 1 (2016), 17–33. A photo of the cover of issue 2 of *AHFIWE: Journal of the Ahfiwe School and Abeng* – part of the Ansel Wong collection at

various groups, like the West Indian Parents Action Group, who are actively seeking to influence the education of their children and to be recognised by the decision-making process. There are Black students' action groups, also, who reach out to the Black community to help in a practical and advisory capacity.

Neighbourhood law centres have been set up to defend the rights of Black people. *Black women's co-operatives* have been concerned with the politicisation of adults and with involving them in skills like the printing of news sheets, etc. There are also women's study groups attempting to raise our own consciousness so that we can be active politically and in other projects, now and then highlighting issues that we feel the community need to know about.

Black women have found the need to become more autonomous from Black (often male-dominated) revolutionary groups. Still, the revolution is important to us. We would only betray our own experiences if we did not link our struggle with the struggle of the proletariat. We face a triple jeopardy; as workers, as women and as Black people. The fight for freedom and self-determination in the Third World; for the abolition of capitalist society and therefore the freedom of the working class; the fight against racism and for the liberation of women are all our struggles.

We have enough on our hands without the National Front. We need to form a broad anti-racist and anti-fascist front.

Brixton Black Women's Group

the Black Cultural Archives – can be seen online as part of a collaboration between the Black Cultural Archives and Google Arts & Culture, artsandculture.google.com.

Issue No. 2   15p

SPEAK OUT

BRITISH PASSPORT

NO ENTRY

CONTENTS

BLACK WOMEN'S GROUP BRIXTON

EDITORIAL

Brixton Black Women's Group
First published in Speak Out, *no. 2, c. 1979, pp. 2–3*

Over the last year to eighteen months, many local campaigns against racism and fascism have sprung up all over the country. In London alone, there were approximately 30 committees affiliated to the now defunct All London Anti-Racist Anti-Fascist Co-ordinating Committee. These included local groups, Women Against Racism and Fascism, Gay Activist Alliance and some trades councils. These organisations also attempted to *redefine* racism. For them, racism is embodied in the National Front, which is regarded as a cancer that contaminates the non-racist. Therefore, if it goes, racism will also disappear. This attitude is especially true of the Anti-Nazi League, which has undermined the positive contributions made by a few local committees.

Misconceptions ...

These campaigns fail to recognise that the National Front only represents an extreme version of the national ideology which runs strongly through the whole of British society, including the working class. By adopting this position, they fail to attack the *real* breeding ground of racism and fascism (e.g. schools, housing, police and trade unions). The anti-fascist movement has not taken up the issues of racism that affect Black people's lives *daily*, and as such has failed to understand the true nature of racism in Britain.

This over-simplification of racism becomes more disturbing when people who claim to be fighting racism and fascism describe the reaction of Black people to racist oppression as racism in reverse. These 'anti-racists' arrive at this position because they do not understand that racism derives from the ruling class ideology, and, by its practice, benefits only the ruling class. The refusal to accept *our* definition of racism is part and parcel of their arrogance and chauvinistic behaviour towards Black people all over the world. This arrogant and chauvinistic attitude grew out of their history of colonial and imperialist exploitation.

We know

Racism is ... labelling Black children as educationally sub-normal; denying them the opportunity of 'higher' education; miseducating them out of the labour force.[1]

Racism is ... police harassment under 'Sus'; our young people rotting in borstals, prisons and mental institutions; breaking into our homes without warrants and searching for 'illegal immigrants' to arrest, brutalise, and detain indefinitely.[2]

Racism is ... being forced into low paid jobs; working under intolerable conditions, or, more frequently for our youths, having to face frustration, degradation and humiliation in the Social Security and unemployment offices.

Racism is ... having no choice in where we live, and so being forced into ghettos or deliberately being dispersed.

It is impossible to name one British institution which does not practice racism! *This* is what the White left refuses to understand – the greatest threat to Black people is the organised attacks, physical and psychological, by the British state. By this refusal, the White left is failing to educate the British working class, which has gained much from our oppression both here and abroad.

---

1   *Editor's note:* See 'What Are They? Disruptive Units' (*Speak Out*, no. 3), pp. 194–7 in this collection.

2   *Editor's note:* For more on the 'sus laws', see 'Scrap Sus Now' (*Speak Out*, no. 2) and 'Scrap SUS Conference' (*FOWAAD!*, No. 1), pp. 76–9 and pp. 110–11 in this collection.

The British working class

Since the latter part of the nineteenth century, the British working class has benefited from and taken part in the imperialist plunder and exploitation of developing countries. Imperialism enabled British workers to enjoy a constant rise in their standard of living at our expense. But once the rising consciousness and active struggles of developing countries for liberation from capitalism began, there were fewer possibilities of capitalist exploitation. So, capitalism has now been forced to squeeze White workers more than before.

The logical step is for the British working class to align with workers worldwide. But what has been its record so far? The White working class has proved to us time and time again that they feel they have more in common with the ruling class and royalty. This is the real problem that the White left should be tackling, rather than fighting Nazis or Skateboards!

White workers have persistently refused to give our unions recognition. They have crossed our picket lines for racist reasons. They have organised against our organising in the trade unions – for example, Standard Telephone Cables, Mansfield Hosiery and Imperial Typewriters, where White trade unionists and union officials put skin colour before the overall interests of workers. Furthermore, they have often physically attacked Black workers.

Then there was Grunwick. The only basis on which the trade union movement and the White left would support the struggle of Black workers was on the condition that they subordinate the main issue of racism to trade unionism, which is of importance, but not sufficient to ignore the racist issue. Grunwick offered a unique opportunity whereby the labour movement could confront and deal with the issue of racism. But, instead, it was turned into one big jamboree and no one, especially the White working class, learnt anything from it.[3]

---

3   *Editor's note:* For more on the Grunwick Strike, see Pratibha Parmar, 'Gender, Race and Class: Asian Women in Resistance', in Centre for Contemporary Cultural Studies, *The Empire Strikes Back: Race and Racism in 70s Britain* (London: Routledge, 2005 [1982]), 235–74; A. M. Phizacklea and R. Miles, 'The Strike at Grunwick', *Journal of Ethnic and*

Racist violence is not new

The physical attacks on Black people did not commence in 1977, contrary to popular White left beliefs, but for as long as we have lived in this country. In 1971, petrol bombs were being thrown into Black people's homes and clubs. In Coventry, a young sister lost her life as a result of fascist attacks. In London, petrol bombs were thrown into a party at Forest Gate, and many people were injured. Bookshops were burned to the ground. People on housing estates came under attack from fascists. Skinheads were roaming the streets beating up newly arrived Asians. The racist and fascist attacks we have faced, physically and psychologically, from all quarters since we began arriving in this country have been numerous.

Fighting back

Black people have always fought and will continue to fight racism and fascism. We have organised supplementary schools. We have clubbed together and bought our own houses to house each other. We have organised our own clubs and recreational facilities. We have formed political organisations, gone on strikes, pickets and demonstrations, signed petitions – the lot. Today, we resent criticisms from the British left who sit on their backsides accusing us of nationalism, emotionalism and acute paranoia.

Right from the start, many Black newspapers and journals warned against the threat of open fascism in Britain. This had been manifested in the Labour and Conservative parties' immigration policies, and in the police's repressive activities towards Black people. Where was the White left then? Some were busy shouting their empty phrase of 'Black and White unite and fight', empty because of their political short-sightedness.

Migration Studies 6, no. 3 (1978), 268–78; L. McDowell, S. Anitha, and R. Pearson, 'Striking Narratives: Class, Gender and Ethnicity in the "Great Grunwick Strike", London, UK, 1976–1978, *Women's History Review* 23, no. 4 (2014), 595–619.

The White left in this country has always refused to face the fact that the working class is racist and therefore needs ideological education. Instead, it attempts to trivialise the issue of racism so as not to upset the 'great' British working class. To take the issue of carnivals, this is just an opportunist attempt by the White left to jump on the bandwagon of *our* Notting Hill Carnival, using the idea to trivialise the issue of racism. The White left herds people together without attempting to educate them about racism. Rather, they are miseducating them and perpetuating racist ideology. It is not enough to like reggae and jump around the streets wearing badges. Racism and fascism have to be tackled from their roots – institutional racism: the police force, the education system, the trade unions. It is for these reasons, and others, that Black people are reluctant to get involved in the present anti-racist/anti-fascist charade. We refuse to be told when, where and how to organise!

SCRAP SUS NOW

Brixton Black Women's Group
First published in Speak Out, *no. 2, c.1979, pp. 4–5*

What is Sus?

Sus is being a suspected person loitering with intent to commit an arrestable offence – you haven't actually done anything, but the police say they think you are going to and, before you can, arrest you for Sus. It is an abuse of police powers.

Sus comes from section 4 of a Vagrancy Act of 1824.[1] The act was so old that it was dropped – that is, until recently. It has been given a new lease of life to break Black people's fighting spirit.

How does Sus work?

As told by the police, a typical example of how Sus works is where two or three Black youths join a crowded bus queue. When the bus arrives, the youths are said to jostle a woman getting on the bus. They are supposed to be trying to steal from the woman's bag, but, since it is empty, they get nothing. The youths then go to a couple of more bus queues and the same thing is said to happen. At this point, the police, who have been watching from a van parked nearby, arrest the youths for Sus. Recall the Lewisham 24, Islington 18 and now Kensal Rise 10.

---

1   *Editor's note:* See 'Vagrancy Act 1824' at legislation.gov.uk.

But the *real* story is different. The youths are simply walking down the street passing, as you do in any large city, crowded bus queues on the way. With almost 18% of Black youths out of work, there is simply nothing else for them to do but walk the streets. So, the real purpose of Sus is to isolate Black youths by frightening them off the streets. The police hope this will break Black people's resistance to unemployment and racism.

Magistrates' courts are police courts

Sus charges are always tried in magistrates' courts. This means you are convicted on the 'evidence' of the police alone. It's always your word against the police's. The magistrates nearly always believe the police – after all, they don't lie! The woman you are supposed to have tried to steal from is never called as a witness. The purse you are accused of stealing is never produced. It is obvious magistrates' courts are police courts.

It is almost impossible to prepare a proper defence against a Sus charge. And this explains why so many cases are lost. You never know what the police's story will be until you get in court. Anyone found 'guilty' of Sus can be imprisoned for 3 months, but after two convictions you can be sent down for a year. The idea is to spread fear, and so obedience to racists, by the constant threat of being put in prison (and mental institutions) *for doing nothing*.

We are all 'suspected persons'

Normally, Black youths are singled out for harassment under Sus. In 1976, some 1,000 White people were convicted under Sus, and over 800 Black youths. But, by 1977, whereas the number of White people convicted stayed the same, the number of Black youths had shot up to *over* 1,000.

From what has been said, you might get the idea that only Black youths suffer under Sus. This is not true – we are *all* 'suspected persons'. Many older Black people have been harassed. Take, for example, the case of a 38-year-old Black man in Brixton. He was picked up for Sus after getting a prescription from Boots. His 'crime'? Standing on the street trying to decide whether to go home immediately or to visit his sister. So, *parents*, take note!

The makings of a police state

Not content with the present abuse of police powers, the Metropolitan Police Commissioner, McNee, wants to increase them. His wishes include that:

1. The police should be allowed to arrest and hold people for 3 days, *without charge*.
2. The police are given greater powers to search people and raid their homes, *without a warrant*.
3. If taken to a police station, people should no longer have *the right to make one telephone call*.
4. People's *right* to remain silent before being charged with an offence should be removed.
   and
5. The police should be allowed to finger-print and photograph people, *without a court order*.

If accepted, these suggestions would *legalise* the present *abuse* of police powers. This should leave no-one in doubt that Britain is a *police state*. It is a threat not only to Black people, but to White people also.

What is to be done?

Action against Sus and McNee's ideas has already begun. We call on all Black women, youths and men to join it!

... Force the withdrawal of Sus!
... Demand an independent investigation into police powers!
... Contact:

Black People's Organisations Campaign Against Sus (BPOCAS)
C/O 206 Evelyn Street
Deptford
London SE8
Tel (01)692 7568

Black People Against State Harassment (BASH)
Black People's Information Centre
301-303 Portobello Road
London W11
Tel: Ricky (01)671 3459
or
Cecil (01)969 4123/969 9825

The All-Party Select Committee on Immigration

Another Attack on Black People

Brixton Black Women's Group
First published in Speak Out, *no. 2, c. 1979, pp. 5–6*

Threat of institutional racism

In the first edition of *Speak Out*, we exposed the debate around immigration for what it is – a means of legalising racism in order to blind people to the constant failure of *governments to stop unemployment and improve social services*. We also warned that if Britain's economic problems did not improve, the debate would get more vicious. We were right. In March 1978, the Conservative, Labour and Liberal Parties got together to agree upon one common policy on immigration. As a result, an All-Party Select Committee on Immigration was set up, which suggests that repatriation should now become *the* 'respectable solution' to Britain's problems.[1] The Committee is further proof that all the political parties are racist.

---

1   *Editor's note:* The resulting report was published by the Select Committee on Race Relations and Immigration in 1978.

Sexism as a tool of racism

The Select Committee recommends that immigrants should be divided into two types. These are 'primary' immigrants, which means people who come to Britain to look for work, and 'secondary' immigrants, which means people who come to join their family. The idea is to put an end to both types of immigration.

Most Black people came to Britain during the fifties and sixties, when there were more jobs available than people to fill them. Once Britain no longer needed Black workers, immigration controls were introduced to stop 'primary' immigrants coming in. So, the Select Committee is *not* concerned about the number of people entering Britain, but the presence of Black people here.

Since the Immigration Acts have already stopped 'primary' immigration, most immigrants to Britain are now of the 'secondary' type only – the wives, fiancé(e)s and children of those settled here. The Select Committee recommends that only a restricted number of wives or fiancé(e)s should be let in, and that the age limit for some children allowed to join their parents should be cut to twelve. If accepted, these proposals would mean families permanently divided between Britain and other countries. The Committee wants to discriminate against Black women and children to encourage so-called 'voluntary repatriation'. Sexism is now being used as a tool for racism.

A threat to us all

Since Asians came to Britain after West Indians, the Select Committee singles out 'secondary' immigrants from the Indian sub-continent for racist and sexist immigration controls. But this does not mean that the Committee excludes other Black people from attack.

In order to tighten controls against 'illegal immigration', the Select Committee recommends that the Department of Health and Social Security (DHSS) and police should be given greater powers to trace illegal immigrants. The Committee also recommends 'internal controls', by which it means identity cards for non-whites. Since the government has admitted that the number of illegal immigrants to Britain is actually very small, the real purpose behind these proposals is to increase the harassment of *all* Black people through greater spot-checks, police raids and a pass-law system. It is obvious that this kind of harassment is really meant to force all Black people out of this country.

Sisters – unite and fight!

With the brutal murders of Gurdip Chaggar, Kenneth Singh and Altab Ali in London and the shooting of Black brothers in Birmingham, there has been growing anti-racist activity in recent months.[2] Much of it has been directed against the National Front and other racist/fascist organisations. Of course, this anti-racist activity is important. But we also see its limitations. In attacking the National Front, the white left has tended to ignore racism that is built into the British way of life *through law*. It is Britain's immigration controls that remain one of our greatest sources of oppression. This must be brought home to Black and white alike – especially to Black sisters, since immigration controls have become yet another attack on women's rights.

2   *Editor's note:* See Anandi Ramamurthy, *Black Star: Britain's Asian Youth Movements* (London: Pluto, 2013).

THE CHILD BENEFIT ACT

Racist Legislation
Against Black Families

Brixton Black Women's Group
First published in Speak Out, *no. 2, c. 1979, p. 7*

The Child Benefit Act of 1975 was first set in motion in April 1977. Under this Act, Child Benefit is payable only to mothers whose children live in Britain. It replaces the old system of Child Tax Allowances, whereby any parent living in Britain could get tax allowance for children living abroad.

Lies and myths

How is the government defending the abolition of Child Tax Allowances and their replacement by Child Benefit?

The government claims that withdrawing Child Tax Allowances will help improve 'community relations'. It suggests that Child Tax Allowances caused resentment amongst White tax-payers when they saw Black tax-payers with different wage-packets from themselves. It *is* true that Black people have different wage-packets – they are almost always lower! By now denying us the right to support our children abroad, in reality the government is bent on worsening 'community relations', not on improving them.

The government also claims that Child Tax Allowances are expensive to administer and that abolishing them will save money. But it refuses to say how much will be saved. Also, the cost of Child Tax Allowances is not new, but a long-standing *right* which is now being taken away.

Finally, the government claims that there was much abuse of Child Tax Allowances. But in view of the amount of information needed to satisfy the 'authorities' that a claim is valid, this is difficult to believe. In any case, even if there were abuses, this is *no* reason to deny genuine claimants of their right to tax allowance. Just as the government uses the myth of 'illegal immigrants' entering this country to justify racist immigration controls, they are using the myth of abuses in Child Tax Allowances to introduce racist child benefit schemes.

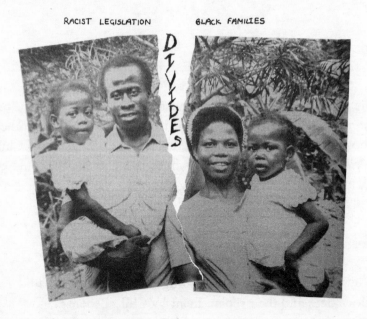

RACIST LEGISLATION · BLACK FAMILIES · DIVIDES

Permanently divided families

Only women are eligible to claim for Child Benefit, but, traditionally, fathers have come to this country before wives and children. So, under the new system, men like these could find it impossible to maintain children abroad or to save enough money to bring them over here. The Child Benefit Act, then, is meant to deprive

Black parents of the ability to support their children overseas and is likely to result in many families being permanently divided between Britain and elsewhere. Of course, there are reasons for this racist policy.

'Voluntary repatriation'

There can be no doubt that the Child Benefit Act is aimed at Black people. There are more Black parents than White ones with children living abroad. Also, White people from the Common Market, civil servants and members of the armed forces working abroad will *not* be affected by the abolition of Child Tax Allowances. By singling out Black families for this inhuman treatment, the act is obviously designed to encourage us to leave this country.

Act now

The decision to withdraw Child Tax Allowances signals another stage in the whittling away of Black people's human rights – in this case, the basic right to support our children or have our families with us. Other legislation affects our freedom of entry to Britain and conditions of life once here. The Child Benefit Act was passed in 1975, but will only be fully operative in 1979. In future, we must strangle any such racist proposals as they come up.

... Fight for basic, human rights!
... Repeal the Child Benefit Act!

The Green Paper on Nationality

An End to Black Civil Rights

Brixton Black Women's Group
First published in Speak Out, *no. 2, c. 1979, p. 8*

The racist chain

In April 1977, a Green Paper on Citizenship and Nationality was introduced.[1] It is meant to strengthen the present racist attacks on both Black people's right to enter Britain *and* civil rights if settled here.

'Patriality'

The 1971 Immigration Act is built on the idea of 'patriality'. A 'patrial' is someone who has at least one parent or grand-parent who was born in Britain. A 'non-patrial' is someone whose parents

---

1 *Editor's note:* The Green Paper referred to here was issued in April 1977 by James Callaghan's Labour government. Titled 'British Nationality Law: A Discussion of Possible Changes', it was followed in 1980 by a Conservative government White Paper (under Margaret Thatcher) which closely followed the Labour proposals. This became the British Nationality Act of 1981, which came into force on 1 January, 1983. Both parties were in agreement on the new law.

or grand-parents were not born here. In other words, a patrial is White and a non-patrial is Black. Under the 1971 Immigration Act, only patrials can enter Britain freely. It is non-patrials alone who suffer immigration controls. Patriality draws a tidy, racist line around British immigration laws.

Citizenship and nationality

The Green Paper on Citizenship and Nationality wants to link patriality with citizenship. It proposes that there should be *two kinds of citizenship*. These are: *British Citizenship* for patrials (White people) and *British Overseas Citizenship* for non-patrials (Black people). British Citizens would be given *full* British citizenship, but British Overseas Citizens would be given *second-class* citizenship. Full citizenship is important because of the *civil rights* it gives a person. So, the Green Paper is really suggesting that a person's historic right to become a full citizen of the country where they were born should be taken away. If it becomes law, it means that generations of Black people born here would be labelled British Overseas Citizens, and so denied their civil rights.

Civil rights

What are the civil rights the Green Paper wants to deny Black people? They include:

... The RIGHT to free education and health treatment.
... The RIGHT to unemployment and Social Security payments.
... The RIGHT to vote.
... The RIGHT to form a political organisation.
... The RIGHT to enter and leave the country without immigration controls.

The civil rights taken away from Black people classed as British Overseas Citizens would be numerous. It is obvious that the Green Paper is meant to do two things. First, encourage 'voluntary repatriation' by forcing any Black person who wants full civil rights to leave Britain and become a citizen of another country. And second, if we stay here, to weaken our fight against racism by making it difficult to organise in the ways in which we do at present.

Lessons for action

The Child Benefit Act was passed in 1975, but will not come fully into force until 1979. This is deliberate. Such delaying tactics are meant to blind people to seeing the need for *immediate* action. The Green Paper on Citizenship, as well as the Select Committee Report on Immigration, are not yet law. So, the lesson to be drawn is that we must fight these racist proposals now. We owe this not only to ourselves, but to every Black child in a pram and to those as yet unborn.

Sickle Cell Anaemia

Organisation for Sickle Cell Anaemia Research
First published in Speak Out, *no. 2, c. 1979, pp. 8–10*

This condition should be understood by all members of the Black community, as it affects approximately 1 out of every 400 Black people. It must be stressed that it also affects other races, e.g. Saudi Arabians, Turks and people from the Mediterranean and Asia. However, it is rarely seen in certain races, e.g. the British.

Why?

Before describing sickle cell anaemia, it is essential to understand why this condition is mainly seen amongst the Black community, as there is a lot of guilt and embarrassment about such a situation.

It is an inherited condition passed on to people by their parents who have either got the condition or who are sickle cell carriers (to be explained further on). Nobody has definitively answered the question of why sickle cell anaemia mainly affects Black people. However, one important clue is that many sickle cell carriers seem to have some protection against one form of malaria. This may explain why only certain parts of Africa have a high incidence, e.g. Ghana and Nigeria. The condition can be passed on from generation to generation, and therefore Blacks in the Caribbean, U.S.A. and Britain are still affected by a condition that may have developed to protect their ancestors in Africa.

What's the difference between a sickle cell carrier and a person with sickle cell disease?

A person who has sickle cell trait does *not* have the signs and symptoms of sickle cell disease. They will not realise that they are carriers until they have a blood test. 1 in 10 of the Black population have the sickle cell trait and are perfectly healthy. However, it is important for Black people to have a small blood test to see if they are carriers for the following reason.

If two people who have sickle cell trait have children, there is a 1 in 4 chance that each child might have sickle cell anaemia. Later on, I will explain how this can happen in more detail, after describing sickle cell anaemia.

Sickle cell anaemia

This condition affects the red blood cells of the body. Normally, they are round-shaped and contain a substance called haemoglobin, which carries oxygen in the blood and takes it to all parts of the body from the lungs.

When a person has sickle cell haemoglobin, it causes the red cells to change from a round shape to a sickle shape when the oxygen level drops in the blood. In addition, the red cells do not last as long as normal ones. These two features cause the following signs and symptoms found in people with sickle cell anaemia:

ANAEMIA	Which cannot be helped by taking iron tablets. It is harmful to do so.
CRISIS	These are painful episodes caused by the sickle-shaped cells blocking the blood vessels.

Pains can occur all over the body and can be every week or just once a year. They may also be jaundiced. It may have to be treated by admission to hospital.

Infection

Because of the anaemia, people with this condition are more likely to have chest infections, for example.

These are the main symptoms, but there are many other problems that can affect people with sickle cell anaemia. There are several types which can be milder types. One type, SC disease, is particularly relevant to Black women. This is a milder condition, but a woman may experience her first crisis (pains in the joints, stomach and chest) during pregnancy.

How is it treated?

There is no cure for sickle cell disease, and therefore it is only possible to give drugs for pain, infections and preventing a worse type of anaemia. Women affected by sickle cell anaemia should not normally take the pill. In the past, it was thought that people died at a very early age if they had sickle cell anaemia. Nowadays, with better knowledge, it is possible to see people living into their 40s and above. However, there can be certain complications that may lead to the death of young children and adolescents who have the condition.

It is important for Black people to know about sickle cell anaemia so that:

1. It can be diagnosed early.
2. Children affected can have proper health care (e.g. protected from extremes of temperature and receive prompt treatment for infection).
3. The incidence can be reduced by understanding which couples are likely to produce children with the condition.

How is it passed on?

In order for somebody to be born with sickle cell anaemia, either:

1. Both parents are sickle cell carriers, or
2. One is a carrier and one has sickle cell anaemia.

If one parent is a carrier and one has normal haemoglobin, it is not possible to produce a child with sickle cell anaemia.

Example

A person who is a carrier has some normal haemoglobin (HB A) and some sickle haemoglobin (HB S). Therefore, in medical terms, they have HB AS.

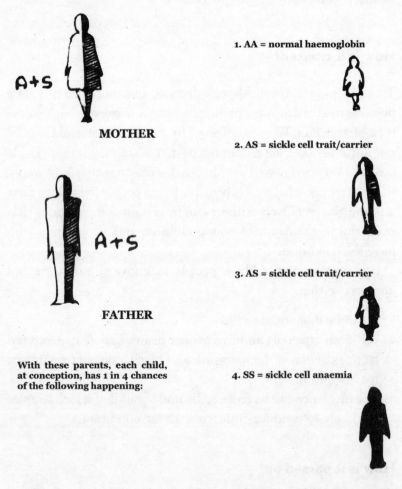

A+S

MOTHER

A+S

FATHER

With these parents, each child, at conception, has 1 in 4 chances of the following happening:

1. AA = normal haemoglobin

2. AS = sickle cell trait/carrier

3. AS = sickle cell trait/carrier

4. SS = sickle cell anaemia

The above diagram shows what can happen when two people who are carriers produce a child, depending on how the father's normal or sickle haemoglobin links up with the mother's normal or sickle haemoglobin.

Conclusion

Most Black people are not aware of sickle cell anaemia until it affects their family. Even then, most have not had it explained how their child acquired it. It is essential that more information is given to the Black community about this condition. There is now an organisation called OSCAR (Organisation for Sickle Cell Anaemia Research), which has been set up to educate the Black community and health workers, as well as raise funds for research into a cure.

I am the Public Relations Officer and go around the country showing slides and discussing the condition. Any group interested in such a talk should contact:

OSCAR
200A High Road
Wood Green
London N22
Tel. No. 01 889 4844

It is now time that the condition is given more attention to reduce the suffering amongst our community. We are hoping to set up small local groups where affected families can meet and discuss areas of action. At the moment, there is the group meeting in Brent, and we hope to set more up in North and South London as well as in Birmingham and Manchester. Other Black groups need to be involved and support our aims.

Elizabeth[1]
21 Gunnersbury Court
Bollo Lane
Acton Town
London W3
Tel. No. 01 992 3258

---

1 *Editor's note:* Elizabeth Anionwu – see Elizabeth N. Anionwu, *Dreams from My Mother* (London: Seven Dials, 2021).

Poems

Brixton Black Women's Group
First published in Speak Out, *no. 2, c. 1979, p. 10*

I dont wanna be a heartache,
I dont wanna be a pinup,
I dont wanna be the decorative
   posey, which
you wear tucked beneath your
   arm, a symbol of your
male pride.
I dont wanna be no good time
   gal, to whom you turn
when the lights are out.
No, I just want to be me.
The me that shatters the image
   enshrined within
virgin and whore.
The me that sings songs of pain
   and joy.
I'm letting myself go,
pimples, flatchest, mind and all,
discovering the me the adverts
   destroy.
Stop me if you can!

Watch her move
whom centuries have dealt with
   in anecdotes
wrinkles upon her face,
the sinewy arms which cradled
   young bones
helped them grow strong.
Flabby breasts which dripped
life's first sustenance deep
   contours
upon her taut face, life's sorrows
   pains and joys.
Black, solid, granite.
Whose oxen qualities once
   moved mountains
ensuring our survival, so
   precarious it could've
been put to sleep before it began.
Watch her move
through us who have not
   forgotten
and remembering, won't allow
   you to forget.

꿍   꿍

White Rule Not OK
South Africa 2/12/77
Justice Minister Kruger
cleared of charges.
Steve Biko's inquest. Death by
Misadventure ... while in police custody.
Bermuda 3/12/77,
Larry Tacklyn, Erskine Burrows
taken to the gallows,
their appeal against death sentences,
refused ...
What is the connection you might ask
I might reply none, or say,
their crimes lay dormant in the color of their skins,
or I could recount the history of their race,
my race.
Maybe I could explain
white rules and white justice,
from Bermuda to South Africa.
Would that do! maybe not.
Coincidences or separate events.
No, regularities. Malign growths,
stretching from east to west,
north and south, washing the shores
of continents ... miles apart.

A SISTER'S VISIT TO CHINA

Women in China

Brixton Black Women's Group
First published in Speak Out, *no. 2, c. 1979, p. 11*

This article is a continuation of a series of reports made by sisters who visited China in the summer. In the last issue, a sister from the group dealt with China's relation to the Third World. In this issue, a young student gives her impression of the developing women's movement.

Women in China have gone a long way towards winning equality with men. But it has been, and continues to be, a long, hard struggle.

In old China, both sexes suffered heavily under class oppression. Women, however, had to cope with the additional burden of being victimised by rampant sexism. Within the patriarchal family structure, women were subject to the Confucian ethics of the 'three obediences' – to the father when young; the husband when married; and to the sons when widowed.

It was a repressive tradition that was strictly adhered to, and it kept Chinese women under the yoke for centuries. A young girl would be betrothed by her parents, and upon being married lost all semblance of her identity. For instance, at meals, she could not sit at the table, but had to serve her husband and parents-in-law. In addition, her husband could beat or scold her at will.

Economically, women were also at the bottom rung. Most were peasants. As such, they lived in poverty. Constant indebtedness to the landlord was a fact of life. Some women found themselves in the unenviable position of having to beg or sell their children in order to survive. Other women worked in factories for the colonialist. The hours were long, and the conditions poor. What's more, foremen could insult and humiliate the workers, and had whips to make sure the young ones worked hard.

When the revolutionary movement began to sweep through China, the idea of equality spread and the women's movement grew up. There were two schools of thought as to what its focus should be. One view saw the movement's main task as being to struggle against male domination. The other view held that organising women to join in the revolution was the most important thing. This latter view came to be accepted, with the rationale that, otherwise, women would never be free from oppression and exploitation.

With their new-found strength, women supported the soldiers in the anti-Japanese war and formed their own self-defence units. When the men left for the front, it was the women who looked after the land and livestock. Women also played a major part in land reform and, for the first time, their names appeared on land deeds. In these ways, they gained self-confidence and, as a consequence, men began to change *their* ideas.

In 1949, China was liberated – the working class and its allies had seized power. The following year, the new Marriage Law was instituted – men and women were given legal equality. Marriage [took place] by mutual consent only, and practices like child betrothals and having concubines were done away with. Divorce became legal. Wives had the right to share in the ownership of family land, and to keep their own surname. This was a great step towards equality, and one which continued to grow during the years of new democracy and socialism.

Now, women do all kinds of work, as we saw when we visited China. In the countryside, there are women tilling the fields and looking after livestock. In the cities, women can be found working in small neighbourhood factories [and] engineering works as builders, and as shop assistant cadres.

With so many more women working, better childcare facilities had to be, and were, provided. This was not as much of a problem as it could have been, however, because the Chinese practice what they call birth planning. This means that not only do women use some type of birth control method, but, in addition, they marry later and thus have children later. Also, in most parts of the country, they are encouraged to have no more than two children so they can give them adequate care. The result is that, when a worker is pregnant, she is given light work, and she also gets 56 days paid maternity leave. When she returns to work, the child is looked after in a nursery at her workplace. She is given breaks for feeding until the child is weaned. Alternatively, the child may be cared for by the grandmother.

Women also fare much better when it comes to chores in the home. Today, the whole family shares the housework.

Traces of the past still remain, however. One thing we noticed was that there are still certain jobs which are more or less reserved for women. For example, in a visit to a printing plant, we noticed that the workers checking magazines were mainly women. Also, there are no male nurses, except in mental hospitals. It was explained that women were more meticulous! Additionally, there are fewer women leaders than might be expected.

Women in China have achieved a lot. However, if the full impact of the late Chairman Mao's words that 'women hold up half the sky' is to be grasped and taken to heart, there is still much to be done.

Reviews

Brixton Black Women's Group
First published in Speak Out, *no. 2, c. 1979, p. 12*

Book

For Colored Girls Who Have Considered Suicide /
When the Rainbow Is Enuf
by Ntozake Shange

After some years of being a closet feminist, I decided, not long ago, that it was time to 'come out'. I am still discovering and adapting to the implications of that decision.

In that respect, Ntozake Shange's *for colored girls who have considered suicide when the rainbow is enuf* speaks to me as a black woman, and, to some extent, reinforces my feelings about the rightness of my decision.[1]

Ms Shange's choreopoem (a series of poems which has been done as a play in New York with dance and music) embraces themes common to all women. Rape, abortion, broken relationships, growing up and out are all honestly and sensitively explored. Her poem 'latent rapists', which emphasises that rapists are more often than not people we know, is particularly compelling.

Shange has allowed herself a free reign with the language (as evidenced by the book's title), which at times obscures, but more often refreshingly illuminates, her points.

---

1   Editor's note: Ntozake Shange, *For Colored Girls Who Have Considered Suicide / When the Rainbow Is Enuf* (Berkeley, CA: Shameless Hussy Press, 1976).

The added bonus for me is that, as it's told from a black perspective, I read her poems, written in the dialect of my culture and felt, 'That's me; those are my experiences; I've felt the same things'.

While I realize that one of the ultimate aims of the women's movement is to unite all women in sisterhood, I feel that such a coming together is strengthened if the individual components have sound bases from which to emerge. *for colored girls ...* goes a long way towards providing that base for black women.

film

Blacks Britannica
by David Koff

One of the most important points made by this film is in its emphasis on the fact that institutional racism poses a much greater threat to black people in Britain than does the National Front.[2]

The 57-minute film illustrates the black (primarily West Indian) community's understanding of and response to racism in Britain, and presents an analysis of racism within the context of British history and the post-war crises of the British economy.

It makes its statement through the technique of montage – intermingling comments by black people (e.g. teenagers describe how they are victimised by the Sus law), with speeches by Enoch Powell and Margaret Thatcher, and footage of clashes with the National Front and police. The result is that the sinister implications of institutional racism and immigration controls become all too apparent.

The fact that the film does make such a powerful statement, however, makes it all the more difficult to understand why it has ignored another equally oppressed group – the black woman. Its treatment of the problem is done very much within a masculine

2 *Editor's note: Blacks Britannica*, directed by David Koff (US, 1978), documentary.

framework; and apart from one or two isolated and secondary appearances by black women, the film consistently fails to present a realistic picture of their role in fighting racism.

Perhaps its producers should have listened more closely to the words of one male speaker, who said, *'I learned my politics in my mother's kitchen'*.

BLACK WOMEN AND ABORTION

Brixton Black Women's Group
Leaflet distributed by the Brixton Black Women's Group, c. 1979

A woman's right to choose means:

- the right to abortion on demand
- the right to free and **SAFE** contraception given on the basis of **INFORMED** consent
- no forced sterilization

Once again, an attempt is being made to restrict a woman's right to safe, legal abortion. As feminists and socialists we believe that this, and any other attack on our democratic rights, should be resisted. But the position of Black women in England means that we cannot separate the issue of abortion from the other issues that affect our lives.

Attack on the Black family

The slogan 'a woman's right to choose' refers to the right of women to decide if, when, where and how many children to have. All too often it is used in its narrow sense to refer to the right to abortion alone.

Black women are being denied the right to choose in its broad sense by:

Immigration laws	–	which prevent families being together in this country. Also, not infrequently, Black women seeking contraceptive and/or abortion advice are asked to prove their 'immigration status' before they can obtain advice and/or treatment.
Use of Depo-Provera	–	along with some white working class women and our sisters in the Third World, we are given Depo-Provera without any information of the possible dangers; and sometimes without our knowledge at all!
Withdrawal of child tax allowance	–	We are not eligible for child benefit for our children in our home countries. At the same time, there are proposals to withdraw the child tax allowance we can claim for those children we support abroad.

Reduction of the Black population

The British state is attempting to reduce the number of Black people in this country. At the same time, the idea that 'the fewer there are, the better race relations are' pervades most of English society. Because of this, many Black women are suspicious of abortion because on a gut level we know that sometimes it is used by 'well-meaning doctors' against us. Similarly, a Black woman is often only offered an abortion if she agrees to undergo sterilization at the same time.

The Brixton Black Women's Group and the campaign against Corrie

The B.W.G. supports a woman's right to safe and legal abortion and any campaign that seeks to safeguard and/or extend this right. At the same time, we expect such a campaign to include in its information and propaganda the position of Black women vis-à-vis abortion. This is rarely the case. For example, the 'conscience clause' allows doctors and nurses to opt out of performing an abortion for any reason at all. Yet its vagueness could easily make it possible for it to be used as yet another attempt to control the numbers of Black people here, whilst still being used in a restrictive way against white women. After all, all it needs is a 'concerned' individual to want to do her/his bit for 'racial harmony'. Despite this, we have yet to see this type of statement in any of the literature arguing why we must defeat Corrie's Bill.[1]

The Black Women's Group says, **YES**, defeat the BILL – but also defeat **ALL** the other attempts to deny Black women their right to choose.

This means:

- fighting the use of Depo-Provera
- fighting the enforced sterilization of Black women
- fighting tax legislation that specifically discriminates against **BLACK PEOPLE**
- fighting the **IMMIGRATION LAWS.**

A WOMAN'S RIGHT TO CHOOSE MEANS OUR RIGHT TO CHOOSE AS WELL!!

Black Women's Group – Brixton

---

1   *Editor's note:* The Corrie Bill was introduced in the House of Commons in 1979 by John Corrie (Conservative MP for Bute and Northern Ayrshire) to restrict abortion rights that had been granted under the 1967 Abortion Act. The bill was withdrawn in March 1980, before its Third Reading, following widespread criticism and demonstrations. See also 'Abortion Bill: Fight the New Proposals' (*Speak Out*, no. 3), pp. 160–4 in this collection.

FOWAAD!

15 pence
no 1. july '79

NEWSLETTER OF THE ORGANISATION OF WOMEN OF ASIAN & AFRICAN DESCENT (OWAAD)

In this first issue of *FOWAAD* we hope to achieve many things:

- We hope to give you plenty of information about OWAAD, especially if you're hearing about us for the first time.
- We hope to give you all some feedback on the National Black Women's Conference, which we held last March, including what you thought of it.
- We hope to give you as much up to date information as we can get hold of about the issues, campaigns and concerns which are affecting us at the moment, either because we are Black workers or because we are Black women, or both.
- We hope to provide sisters everywhere with a space where you can air your views, pass on your information and call on other sisters for support in your everyday struggles.
- We hope to provide sisters throughout the country with a forum where we can form and voice our opinions, exchange our ideas and devise our strategies.
- Finally, we hope that sisters will relate to the contents of this newsletter, so much so that you will begin to see it as your paper – for it is your letters and articles, your news and reviews, your ads, cartoons and poems which will make *FOWAAD* into the genuine mouthpiece of Black women in Britain.

All contributions to *FOWAAD* – which we plan to produce every 2 months, to begin with – should be sent to:

OWAAD Newsletter Committee,
OWAAD,
c/o 10 Cambridge Terrace Mews,
London NW1

FIRST NATIONAL BLACK WOMEN'S CONFERENCE (Organised by OWAAD. Photo of bookstall by Sindamani Bridglal.)

EDITORIAL

Organisation of Women of Asian and African Descent (OWAAD)
First published in FOWAAD!, *no. 1, 1979, pp. 2–3*

The National Black Women's Conference, held at the Abeng
Centre in Brixton on March 18th, 1979, was an important and
unforgettable occasion for many sisters, particularly for those of
us who organised it.[1]

For the first time, nearly 300 Black women got together from
places as far afield as Birmingham, Brighton, Leeds, Coventry,
Manchester, Sheffield, Bristol and London to discuss some of
the many issues which concern us because we are Black, female,
working-class or all three.

But it was not the number of sisters who attended, or the
distances they had travelled, or the wide age range (from 15 to
65) of the sisters who came which impressed us most. It was the
achievement of bringing Asian sisters, Afro- and Indo-Caribbean
sisters, African sisters and Black sisters born and brought up here
together, for a day, to really get down and discuss some of the
many issues which unite us.

We discussed a wide range of subjects: our immediate history;
the experiences we had upon first arriving in Britain; the types of
job we are doing and the ways Black women are being exploited
and discriminated against in employment; the housing conditions

---

1   *Editor's note:* The Abeng Centre was located at 7 Gresham Road,
Brixton, in what is now the Karibu Education Centre. Photographs of
the conference – in the Stella Dadzie collection at the Black Cultural
Archives – can be seen at artsandculture.google.com as part of a collaboration between the Black Cultural Archives and Google Arts & Culture.
These include a photo of a panel discussion ('OWAAD Conference') and
a photo of BBWG and OWAAD member Sylvia Ome Erike delivering a
paper titled 'Black Women and the State' ('Papers and Photographs from
the National Black Women's Conference').

we face and the education that we and our children are (not) getting; the many health issues which concern us; the different forms of state harassment we are facing daily in the guise of SUS, passport raids and intimidation by police and immigration officers; and the situation of our sisters in the Third World.

We tried to touch on all the important issues, but inevitably we left many of them out. We hope that sisters will continue to tell us what they were. It was probably inevitable, too, that we ended up by focusing our attention on just one issue of major importance – education – recognising that we will need to hold a series of regular, single-issued conferences if we are to effectively and collectively take up any one of the many issues we touched upon in the course of the day.

We are including, on the letters page, a few extracts from the mail we received after the conference. Many sisters simply wanted to tell us how high they felt when they went home that evening, others wanted to let us know what mistakes thy felt had been made. We agreed with a lot of the criticisms and hope to learn from them in time for the next conference.

However, although the conference was an important achievement, we do not feel that it was an end in itself. In the weeks since then, we have been involved in a lot of activity in the hope that OWAAD will go now from strength to strength.

We have edited and updated the conference talks, which will be published in pamphlet form by the end of July.

We have also had a number of lengthy discussions about how to create a workable structure for OWAAD, so that it can really develop into the national umbrella organisation we want it to be.

We have held a call-back meeting for all sisters in London who came to the conference, to discuss this structure and to set it up. Although we wished more sisters had attended this meeting, we were nevertheless able to set up a number of working committees to deal with a variety of activities.

All of these committees have now met at least once. They are open to any sisters in London who genuinely wish to get involved in a constructive and creative way in building OWAAD into an effective, fighting Black women's organisation.

Outside London, we are hoping that sisters will organise similar call-back meetings of sisters in their areas (we will gladly supply regional address lists to any authentic Black women's groups or organisations which let us know of their intention to do this). Such call-back meetings could set up working committees of sisters, similar to the ones now established in London, which can be involved in a practical way in the running of OWAAD or in the campaigns and issues we are involved in.

We also intend to print, on a regular basis, a list of Black women's groups already established throughout the country, and we hope that sisters will use this page as a way of contacting other sisters in their areas if they are trying to set up a group there.

We hope to have regular features, articles and reviews, WRITTEN BY YOU, which will keep us all informed and up to date with the things that Black women are involved in and concerned about.

We invite all Black women's groups (especially those outside London whom those of us here don't see so often) to contribute articles on a regular basis, which will talk about the campaigns and issues they are involved in locally. This is one way, we hope, of ensuring that our paper in future reflects what we are doing nationally, rather than simply concentrating on what sisters here in London are doing. We look forward to plenty of feed-back from you on this, our first issue of *FOWAAD*. What should be changed or improved? What else would you like to see in the newsletter?

OWAAD IS ALL OF US!
FOWAAD BELONGS TO ALL OF US!
MAKE IT <u>YOUR</u> MOUTHPIECE, SISTERS![2]

◆━━◆━━◆━━◆━━◆━━◆━━◆━━◆━━◆━━◆━━◆━━◆

2   *Editor's note:* For more on OWAAD, see Julia Sudbury, *'Other Kinds of Dreams': Black Women's Organisations and the Politics of Transformation* (London: Routledge, 1998); Tracy Fisher, *What's Left of Blackness: Feminisms, Transracial Solidarities, and the Politics of Belonging in Britain* (New York: Palgrave Macmillan, 2012); Nydia A. Swaby, '"Disparate in Voice, Sympathetic in Direction": Gendered Political Blackness and the Politics of Solidarity', *Feminist Review* 108, no. 1 (2014), 11–25; and Natalie Thomlinson, *Race, Ethnicity and the Women's Movement in England, 1968–1993* (Basingstoke: Palgrave Macmillan, 2016).

CAMPAIGNS

SCRAP SUS CONFERENCE

Organisation of Women of Asian and African Descent (OWAAD)
First published in FOWAAD!, *no. 1, 1979, p. 3*

The first ever national Scrap SUS Conference was held on Saturday 16th June at Aklam Hall in Ladbroke Grove, London.

The SUS law is the notorious section of the 1824 Vagrancy Act, under which so many Black youths are harassed. This law makes it an offence to be a suspected person, loitering with intent. Not only is it unnecessary to commit any crime to be convicted of SUS – you don't even have to attempt to commit a crime. There is no right to trial by jury, and policemen are always the only witnesses. There is a mass of research which shows the racist way in which this law is being used, particularly by the Metropolitan Police.

The conference was organised by the Black People's Scrap SUS Campaign. This campaign started 18 months ago, with a handful of Black parents in Deptford, and has grown into a national movement.

In the morning, there were a number of speakers, including Black mothers and youths who have suffered as a result of the SUS law. At lunch, patties and curry goat and rice were served. And in the afternoon there were workshops on 'Black people, Police and the Courts', 'SUS and the Black Family', 'Setting Up Local SUS Groups' and 'The Role of National Organisations in the SUS Campaign'. The conference was well-attended, with over 150 people in the audience.

The issue of SUS is, of course, not the only aspect of state repression of Black people, but it is an important issue because it has politicised so many Black people who were not interested in politics before. The campaign believes that there is so much authoritative evidence of what a bad law SUS is that they can get it repealed. And it is important that the Black community be seen to be organising and fighting for something on its own behalf, instead of relying on white 'liberals' to fight its battles for it. As Basil Manning (Steering Committee member of the Scrap SUS Campaign) said in his closing speech: 'No power on earth can suppress a people intent on being free.'

HACKNEY SCHOOLS STAY OK!

Hackney Flame
First published in FOWAAD!, *no. 1, 1979, pp. 3–4*

The Hackney Flame group decided to join the 'Hackney Schools Stay OK' campaign, because these types of cutbacks in education will affect mainly Black children and also children of other ethnic minority groups living in Hackney.

We gave out leaflets in Ridley Road Market, Dalston, on Saturday, giving many of them to children since the names of their schools were printed on them. They could pass the message on to their parents.

This campaign is important for the Black parents and children in Hackney because most of these schools are majority Black. If ILEA's plans are carried out, the children will have much bigger classes, which will add to the problems of being labelled 'under-achievers' by racist intelligence tests.[1]

The campaign is fighting for smaller classes (supposedly ILEA's aims, too) so that each child receives individual attention. It will also give teachers more time to teach basic skills and prepare lessons and courses which will really suit the experiences and needs of our children. We also want to improve nursery provision. All these aims will benefit Black children in Hackney.

The closure and amalgamation of seven schools was threatened to take place in May '79. ILEA put this plan into action at a time when the children were on holiday. Therefore, it was difficult for parents and teachers to organise in such a short period of time. A public meeting was held, and we have now been given until September.

For more information, contact:

Hackney Schools Stay OK Campaign,
c/o Centerprise,
136 Kingsland High Street,
London E8

---

1 *Editor's note:* 'ILEA' refers to the Inner London Education Authority, which was established in 1965 and abolished in 1990.

SUSPENSIONS AND SIN BINS

Haringey Black Pressure Group on Education
First published in FOWAAD!, *no. 1, 1979, pp. 4–5*

On Sunday 24th June, a public meeting was held in Haringey to raise and discuss some of the worrying trends affecting our kids' education in the borough.

The meeting was the result of moves made by sisters in the United Black Women's Action Group (UBWAG) who were anxious to take up some of the demands which came out of the OWAAD conference, while at the same time tackling the more immediate problems affecting Black children in Haringey schools.[1]

Such problems include exclusions, which have been taking place at an alarming rate. Black children have been finding themselves asked to stay away from school, often unofficially (i.e. without the schools following the official procedure of informing the parents and governors) and frequently just before the children concerned are due to sit public exams.

One Black mother told the meeting how her son had been sent home from school with no attempt made to inform her. She only discovered that he had been suspended when she decided to contact the Education Office to find out why he had not been collected at the start of the new term to take him back to the residential school for deaf children which he had been attending.

The meeting also heard how a Black schoolgirl, who was frequently subjected to racist abuse by her teacher, was suspended for slapping her. No attempt was made to look into the girl's claim that she was provoked; no investigation was made of the teacher, who was renowned for statements such as "Black people look like gorillas" and "Black people should go back to where they came from" and "Rastas look a disgrace and should have their hair forcibly cut".

---

1 *Editor's note:* For more on UBWAG, see 'Have You Heard about the Head Count?' (*FOWAAD!*, no. 1) and OWAAD's "Black Women Together: The Need for a United and Autonomous National Black Women's Organisation" (pp. 116–18 and pp. 135–44 in this collection).

Recently, a newly-appointed headmaster of a Haringey secondary school is alleged to have excluded around 20 youth from the school – all of them Black. When questioned, he only admitted to five of them being suspended officially. Even the governors of the school knew nothing about it, when asked.

Another cause for alarm in Haringey is the rumour of a plan to attach disruptive units to every secondary school. These 'sin bins', as they are called, are simply dumping grounds for all the unwanted 'disruptive' pupils whom the schools cannot handle. A disproportionate number of the children attending them are Black. The effect of setting up more sin bins can only result in even larger numbers of Black youth being deprived of their right to education, and their right to an educational system which caters for their particular cultural, linguistic and social needs.[2]

The meeting discussed the need for a local Black Pressure Group on Education, which can take up both the issues in Haringey and the more general educational issues such as racism in textbooks and the curriculum. The objectives of this group will be decided in the course of the next few meetings, as well as what sort of practical suggestions the group should be making. For example, will the training of more Black teachers help to solve the dilemma our children are facing? Many felt that this could only prove successful if the Black teachers concerned were of the type who would identify and sympathise with the problems our children are facing in school. Would the introduction of examinable Black Studies courses enable Black youth to identify more fully with what they are being taught? Some felt that such courses were often abused by the schools, which use them as an excuse to segregate Black children and keep them occupied while the white kids are getting on with their exam courses. Others expressed the view that a more radical change in the subject matter of the whole curriculum is needed, since a Black Studies programme cannot compensate for the biased Geography teacher who portrays the Third World as being dependent on Western generosity for its development and as populated with 'savages'; or the biased Home

---

2 *Editor's note:* For more on 'sin bins', see 'What Are They? Disruptive Units' (*Speak Out*, no. 3), pp. 194–7 in this collection.

Economics teacher who spends hours teaching the class how to make Christmas cake, but would never dream of attempting a curry or patties!

A lot more discussion is needed on these and many other issues. However, the fact that Black parents, teachers and students have begun to take action can only serve to encourage others to try to set up similar pressure groups in their own areas. Moves have already been made by sisters in Hackney and Camden to organise public meetings, not to mention the West Indian Parents' Action Group (WIPAG) based in Brixton, who have been making their voices heard in Lambeth for some time.

The next public meeting in Haringey organised by the group will be devoted to suspensions and exclusions. It is hoped that a video film about suspension procedure, made by UBWAG, will be shown, and that speakers (both Black youth who have been excluded from school and their parents) will be invited to come and talk.

For more information about this meeting and for general information about the Haringey Black Pressure Group on Education, please contact:

Avril (01-272-2784), Pat (01-802-7805) or Katja (01-888-3755)

ISSUES

HAVE YOU HEARD ABOUT THE HEAD COUNT?

United Black Women's Action Group
First published in FOWAAD!, *no. 1, 1979, pp. 5–6*

On April 1st this year, 65,000 households – many of them Black – were asked to fill in a Test Census form, in preparation for the compulsory National Census which is to take place here in 1981.

The purpose of the Test Census was to 'sound out public opinion' on the questions which the government plans to include.

Haringey was chosen because it was considered to have living in it a 'typical' mixture of people – the well-off, white middle class, the 'socially deprived', plus a wide variety of members of ethnic minority groups.

The last consideration was particularly relevant to the government, given the nature of some of the questions they plan to force us to answer in 1981.

These include a question about the country of birth of our parents, a question (on an alternative form) requiring us to tick a box to indicate which racial or ethnic group we belong to – the groupings being: English, Welsh, Scottish or Irish; Other European (please specify); West Indian or Guyanese; African; Indian; Pakistani; Bangladeshi; Arab; Chinese; Any other mix (describe). In addition, we were expected to answer the question, 'Have you registered or naturalised? If not, state the country where your passport was issued.'

The (Labour) government attempted to justify these questions on the grounds that they need such information in order to enable them to introduce schemes which "positively discriminate" in favour of ethnic minority groups!

Black people in this country have for many years now been experiencing the <u>negative discrimination</u> of the British state. We have always been 'last hired, first fired'; we have always been the first to suffer from cuts in public spending, since we were thrown into the worst homes, the worst schools and the lowest-paid jobs when we arrived here.

We should remember, too, that little has been done to improve the poor living conditions of most Black people, despite the fact that many of us filled in the housing question ten years ago in the 1971 census, in the misguided belief that the government would actually DO SOMETHING to improve the slums. We are <u>still</u> living in damp, decaying homes with no bath rooms, no inside toilets, no running hot water and no effective heating!

How, then, can we be expected to believe the government's claim that the 1981 census questions on race are only going to be used to our advantage? They have already compiled accurate statistics, at local government level, about where we live, how many of us there are in any given house or neighbourhood, and how fast we reproduce. An organised and nationwide headcount of Black people can do nothing to improve our situation, nor will it help the government to move more quickly to meet our many housing, educational and community needs.

What this carefully planned headcount is actually for can be better understood if we look at the proposed contents of the latest Government White Paper on Immigration.

These proposals are likely to make official the two distinct categories of British citizen – those with citizenship 'of the blood' (i.e. whites, patrials or British citizens) and those with citizenship 'of the soil' (i.e. Blacks, non-patrials or British overseas citizens).

Which type of citizenship future generations of Black people can claim will be based <u>not</u> on the number of years we have lived and worked here, and paid our taxes and propped up the economy here. It will be based instead on whether we can prove that we are directly descended from a white father or grandfather (mothers and grandmothers don't count).

This proposed change in the definition of nationality will bring Britain more into line with EEC policies on citizenship and nationality, where migrant workers rather than immigrants are far more common. It will also bring some welcome advantages to the government closer to home, enabling racist measures to be carried out more effectively. Forms of state harassment like SUS and passport raids, political and police intimidation, and the control of the size of the Black population through the use of dangerous drugs like Depo-Provera will all be easier to implement once this massive and compulsory headcount in 1981 has taken place.

When rumours about the Test Census began to circulate in Haringey earlier this year, the Tottenham-based United Black Women's Action Group (UBWAG) quickly got involved in a campaign against the census.

We got together with a number of other anti-racist groups and held a public meeting to inform people in the borough why we are so concerned about the questions on race. We produced and distributed a leaflet to every household due to receive the Test Census form, in which we explained the dangers of such questions and urged people to boycott questions 10 and 11 (the questions on race). We wrote letters to the local and national newspapers. And we even attracted the curiosity of BBC TV News.

The Test Census forms have long ago been collected and fed into a computer somewhere. But that is by no means the end of our campaign. We have to begin to take action NOW if we are to ensure that the same questions on race do not appear in the 1981 census, which will be distributed to every household in the country and will be compulsory – meaning that we face a fine or imprisonment if we fail to fill in all the questions truthfully.

All those interested in joining our campaign to rid the 1981 census of the questions on race, please contact United Black Women's Action Group, care of OWAAD.

◆━◆━◆━◆━◆━◆━◆━◆━◆━◆━◆━◆━◆

SHADES OF BLUE?

Black People Against State Harassment
First published in FOWAAD!, *no. 1, 1979, pp. 6–7*

Early in May 1979, London's Police Chief David McNee told the press that the Metropolitan Police are going to pay for a study into what is going on between Black people in London and his policemen. And it is about time, you might think, when, like on April 23rd '79, the police operation to 'protect' the National Front in Southall resulted in a death, scores of injuries and over 350 arrests among the demonstrators; when the brutal presence of the Special Patrol Group (SPG) on the streets of London threatens the physical safety of Black people; and when Black youths have been barred from certain 'no-go' areas in London by the racist use of the SUS laws and police malpractices. It seems clear, therefore, that there is something seriously wrong with current police behaviour, which might well need investigating.

But don't be fooled! It is not the growing body of evidence of day-to-day police brutality and malpractices which concerns McNee. His interests lie not with the well-being of Black people, but with our effective control by the British state. So we say DO NOT co-operate in the biased police 'immigrant' enquiry.

The team of so-called 'academics' chosen for the police study comes from Cranfield Institute of Technology. This place is nothing more than a training ground and spying centre for the police and army. The Institute is mainly concerned with controlling the lives of ordinary people and it searches for ways of getting the community to spy on itself. It represents the interests of the rulers in this country.

The man personally chosen by McNee to head the study is John Brown (God bless his soul!). McNee claims that Brown is a 'respected, independent figure, acceptable to all' – but is he? It was John Brown who was responsible for a study called 'SHADES

OF GREY' done in 1977 in Handsworth, Birmingham.[1] A lot of Black people live there, and the police have a long history of brutality against them. We know that 'SHADES OF GREY' was a biased, pro-police and racist report, providing a blue-print for informers.

'SHADES OF GREY' attacked Black people and our way of life. In Handsworth, Brown said, 'the inheritance of the Caribbean plantation comes home: a lack of strong family and community structures and values'!!! The report was also misleading. Brown claimed to find 'little evidence of racist attitudes' among CID officers, and suggested making 'vigorous residents' associations' into spy centres for the police.[2] Since 'SHADES OF GREY', the Birmingham police force has taken up Brown's advice. With the help of lots of police money, they now boast of having tied and tied up the West Indian community there. So be warned!

While trying to sell us Brown, McNee has personally kept very busy. In August 1978, McNee and the Metropolitan Police submitted 'evidence' to the Royal Commission on Criminal Procedure. He recommended that the police should be given 'additional powers' to those they already have. McNee is trying to turn Britain into an open police state in which people have no defence against police attacks. Then, in March '79, he secured an agreement with the BBC. This is the first step towards police control of the media. And now, in May '79, the police 'immigrant' probe has been ordered, under the guidance of McNee's carefully chosen man.

We urge the Black community not to co-operate with Brown or McNee in this misleading 'police study'. If there are to be studies or inquiries, let them be truly public and independent – not called by and appointed by the police! A good starting point for Brown and McNee, we suggest, would be to listen to what Black people have already said through the Scrap SUS Campaign and Black People Against State Harassment (BASH).

---

1   *Editor's note:* John Brown, *Shades of Grey: A Report on Police–West Indian Relations in Handsworth* (Cranfield, Bedfordshire: Cranfield Institute of Technology, 1977).

2   *Editor's note:* CID = Criminal Investigation Department.

We say, refuse to co-operate with John Brown in Hackney, Brixton or anywhere else – to do so would be to become police informers. After all, McNee's solution is quite simple – 'stay off the streets and behave yourselves'. But let him know, we intend to fight for a different solution!

Black People Against State Harassment (BASH)[3]
Black People's Information Centre, 301-303 Portobello Road, London W11.
Tel: 01-671-3459 or 969-4123 (or 9825)

---

3   *Editor's note:* For more on BASH, see Colin Prescod, 'Black People against State Harassment (BASH) Campaign – A Report', *Race and Class* 58, no. 1 (2016), 94–100.

OWAAD
WORKING COMMITTEES

Organisation of Women of Asian and African Descent (OWAAD)
First published in FOWAAD!, *no. 1, 1979, p. 7*

The following OWAAD sub-committees have been set up and are open to any Sister living in London:

ORGANISING COMMITTEE responsible for linking and supporting Black women's groups. We meet monthly on Wednesdays.
Contact: Gerlin (01) 274 1542

NEWSLETTER COMMITTEE responsible for producing and distributing *FOWAAD!* We meet every second Thursday.
Contact: Katy (01) 226 8654

VISUALS COMMITTEE responsible for producing and distributing the video on the first OWAAD National Conference.
Contact: Katja (01) 341 0682

STUDY COMMITTEE responsible for providing a study guide for any interested Black women's groups or individuals.
Contact: Pat (01) 673 4085

REVIEW
D.P. on T.V.

Campaign Against Depo-Provera
First published in FOWAAD!, *no. 1, 1979, p. 8*

If you were up fairly late a few Fridays ago, you may have seen the London Programme on ITV, which chose Depo-Provera as its concern of the week.

Depo-Provera is a 3-month injectable contraceptive drug with some very nasty side effects, including an increased risk of cancer of the breast and the cervix, irregular or heavy periods (or none at all), weight gain, depression, migraines, hair loss and the possibility of permanent sterility.

It is manufactured by UPJOHN, an American company which has used thousands of Third World sisters first as guinea-pigs and then as recipients of this dangerous steroid contraceptive. The drug's convenience, both in the way it is given and its absolute reliability in preventing pregnancy, has proved highly attractive to population control programmes which are prepared to inject thousands of Third World women with the drug, despite the fact that it has not yet been approved for wide-scale use on European or American women.

In Britain, DP is being given mainly to Black and working-class white women by doctors who are ignoring the recommendations of the Committee for the Safety of Medicines. The CSM has only approved two short-term uses of DP – by women who have just been vaccinated against rubella (German measles) and women whose partners have recently had a vasectomy.

The London Programme investigated a few of the cases uncovered by sisters working in local campaigns against DP. They looked at the case of the 14-year-old West Indian girl who went into hospital to have her tonsils removed, was discovered to be pregnant, asked to have a coil fitted after the termination, and only discovered some days after the joint operation that she had been injected with DP. The surgeon justified having given her DP with neither knowledge or consent, while she was still under the anaesthetic, claiming that she was 'ESN' (educationally sub-normal) and that it was his moral duty ('as a citizen of this country') to make the decision for her.

They also interviewed a Black mother who had been given DP by the Domiciliary Family Planning Service shortly after the birth of her third child. She was not told what the drug was, nor was she warned of the possible side effects. She subsequently gained a huge amount of weight and suffered from severe depression. Only when the same doctor decided (once again without consulting her) to take her off the drug, a year later, did she realise that the drug was responsible for all the unpleasant side effects she had been experiencing.

No real attempt was made by the London Programme journalists to investigate more thoroughly the allegation that DP is being given to large numbers of Black women, particularly to Asian sisters in the East End of London, although they did broadcast the alarming figures. Nor was the racist use of DP genuinely exposed, despite frequent references to 'the particular type of women' who are getting it.

The programme did not serve as a genuine warning to all women not to allow ourselves to be given any drug without first questioning what it is and what its side effects might be. And they even ended up by plugging a less concentrated version of DP which is now on the market and has to be injected more frequently.

The Campaign Against Depo-Provera still has a lot of work ahead if it is to succeed in its stated aim of getting DP banned and demanding free, safe, reliable contraception for all women.

For more information, contact:

Campaign Against Depo-Provera,
c/o ICAR, 374 Gray's Inn Road,
London WC1.

REVIEW

First published in FOWAAD!, *no. 1, 1979, pp. 8–9*

Second Class Citizen
by Buchi Emecheta

Buchi Emecheta is a Nigerian author. She has written several books, but to my mind the most capturing of all those I have read is *Second Class Citizen* (1974). This is because it relates to the position of many Nigerian and possibly other Black women in this country, and tells of their struggle and bitter realisation of what 'Great' Britain is really like.

The story describes a Nigerian girl who had a dream of going to the UK, which she believes (like many others who live in the neo-colonies) will be paradise.

The girl fights for her right to education, which was something an African girl just didn't do. To further her education, she marries young. This marriage proves to be the root of all her problems when she fulfils her dream and arrives in the UK with her two children to join her husband.

This story not only shows the struggle of Black women, but also their oppression by men.

This book makes easy reading, and Buchi Emecheta's style makes it accessible to all women.

Many Black women, when reading this book, will, I'm sure, find parts where they can say, 'This happened to me'. The book is, in fact, Buchi Emecheta's life story, written through the eyes of the girl Adah. It is published by Fontana.

LETTERS ...

First published in FOWAAD!, *no. 1, 1979, p. 9*

Dear OWAAD,

This is just a short note to say thank you for all your efforts in making the conference last Sunday such a success.

It must have taken a lot of hard work on everybody's part to organise such an event and I am sure, like myself, everyone who attended appreciated it.

I left at about 6.30 because I was feeling a little tired mentally, so I did not see the film which I would have liked to have seen. I felt it would have been better for the group to go into workshops to discuss what positive action we could take, but at the time the meeting thought we should stay together, which I realised later was a mistake.

Thanks again, and I look forward to attending the next one. At least I hope to have more notice of it so I will be able to help to get more people to attend.

Keep up the fight.

Best wishes,

K.G.

Dear OWAAD,

I enjoyed the conference last Sunday very much and wish to congratulate your initiative.

However, I did feel that the best part of the conference was discussion and questions from the floor. I felt too many papers (too many subjects) were read. Also, I don't think speakers should read their papers – they should talk to the audience. It's very dull being read to. I just felt frustrated that there was no time for the most important items – the workshops and discussion for further action. I think people only learn through discussion – by having their attitudes challenged – and that they learn very little through the lecture method.

It did feel very good to meet up with other Black women and I hope there will be a follow-up.

Best wishes,

B.T.

Hair Today – Where Tomorrow?

First published in FOWAAD!*, no. 1, 1979, pp. 9–10*

Dear sisters,

Before I go on to the main point of my letter, I must just say how I enjoyed the Black Women's Conference. It was really great to see so many Black sisters together, expressing their opinions on some of the major topics affecting them and those around them today.

I really felt high after the conference and, after attending the London call-back meeting, I decided to join the Newsletter Committee in order to be able to voice a few of my views as regards our appearance as Black women.

I begin at the top, with our hair. Not merely what the latest hairstyle is, or what is in the heart of the fashion world – NO!

A point of fact is that hair, whether regarded politically, psychologically or even sociologically, is a sensitive issue, and for the Black Woman a very serious issue indeed, since the <u>imposed</u> psychological (and sometimes physical) burden of being labelled as inferior is manifested in the pathetic attempts to be acceptable (i.e. in someone else's image – the white man and woman's).

PHEW! That was a mouthful – but it had to be said.

We go around pulling, stretching, creaming, tying, pressing, scorching and chemically treating our locks because we believe it improves our image in some way. We are so insecure with our beauty and our capacity to attract that we go to unbelievable 'lengths' to conform.

I decided about ten years ago that I was through with the humiliation/ridicule I received in secondary school and later still whilst I attended college. I still hate to see the sight of some of our Black sisters wearing wigs when I know of the striking images of African hairstyles and those from the West Indies.

However, I am encouraged by the fact that Black people have started their own 'thing' with their hair – it implies steps in the right direction – but the 'route' is difficult.

I have concentrated initially on 'Afro' type hair, since it is the one I possess and would therefore be glad to hear from my Asian sisters about theirs. Along with our struggle for liberation from the bottom of the heap in society, we must be together 'body and soul'.

Write and tell me – where do we go from HERE?

Ama.

GROUPS

First published in FOWAAD!, *no. 1, 1979, pp. 10–11*

<u>THE EAST LONDON BLACK WOMEN'S ORGANISATION
(ELBWO)</u> was set up after the first OWAAD conference in March
'79.

Some members of the group who met each other there agreed
that there was a need for a self-conscious Black group in the
East End of London, which, as many are aware, is a traditional
working-class area.

This area has been a gateway for some of the ethnic groups
which came to settle in Britain – the Jewish people, for example
– partly because of its economic history. As is common to many
traditional communities, a fair amount of reactionary politics
exists among the white population. In the last election, the
National Front got nearly 5,000 votes, and racial attacks and
harassment are common.

No one can doubt the vulnerability of Black people in this
area. ELBWO has been meeting since April, and its members have
attended in encouraging numbers. In our struggle, we hope to
pool our resources and join in action with other groups. We, like
them, have to concentrate on the emergencies among priorities –
education, SUS 1 & 2 and the new nationality laws.

We meet at a temporary address, but hope to have a permanent
meeting place in East Ham soon.

For further information, contact:

Ms Thomas at 01-471-8226

THE NORTH PADDINGTON BLACK WOMEN'S GROUP

On the whole, North Paddington is a very deprived area, with mainly Black and Moroccan residents. Because of the deprivation, over the last few years a number of 'welfare' agencies have been set up, but somehow these agencies are not really making a good job of sorting out the problems facing the different ethnic groups in the area. So we decided to get together to try and create a better life for the Black families here.

The North Paddington Black Women's Group was formed in April 1979, as an information and action group. We collect information to help deal with the pressures created by bad housing, poor education, unemployment, police harassment and health problems. We also act upon information. The first action we took was on 6th June, when we demonstrated outside St Marylebone Housing Association. Members of our group had been served with notices to quit their homes. Why? – because they had complained about repairs that needed to be done!

On a lighter note, we hope to form a cricket, netball, rounders or basketball team so that we can play friendly matches with other teams – so form a team now! For the children and male members of our families, we plan outings, socials, parties, dances and concerts.

We welcome all Black women wishing to join our group, whether they live locally in North Paddington or afar.

Interested sisters should contact:

Celia Payne,
North Paddington Black Women's Group,
115 Portnall Road,
London W9
Tel: 01-969-8897

OTHER GROUPS

BRIXTON BLACK WOMEN'S GROUP
c/o 121 Railton Road,
Brixton, London SE24.
Meetings every Sunday from 3
to 5pm at the above address.

**UNITED BLACK WOMEN'S ACTION
GROUP**
c/o 2 Chacewater, Boyton
Road,
Hornsey, London N8.
Meetings every 3rd Sunday of
the month at:
West Green Community Centre,
Stanley Road, Tottenham,
N15.

AWAZ
Asian Woman's Organisation
Meetings every month.
For details contact:
Ravi Randawa at 01-767-3631

**Manchester Black Women's
Co-operative**
Moss Side People's Centre,
St. Mary's Street,
Moss Side, Manchester M15
5WA
Tel: 061-226-6837

ZANU WOMEN'S LEAGUE
c/o 34 Chalcot Crescent,
London NW1.

SWAPO WOMEN'S CAMPAIGN
c/o 188 North Gower Street,
London NW1 2NB
Tel: 01-388-2080/89

**BLACK/BROWN WOMEN'S
LIBERATION NEWSLETTER**
c/o 43 Grosvenor Terrace,
Bootham, York.
Tel: 0904-39330
At the moment, only two
sisters are involved in
putting the newsletter
together. Offers of help
would be gladly received.
Also, financial assistance
and contributions (from
Black sisters only).

LATIN AMERICAN WOMEN'S GROUP
c/o Latin American Centre,
16 Hoxton Square,
London.

SCRAP SUS CAMPAIGN
c/o 206 Evelyn Street,
London SE8.
Tel: 01-692-7568

in memory of OLIVE MORRIS

Organisation of Women of Asian and African Descent (OWAAD)
First published in FOWAAD!, *no. 1, 1979, p. 12*

All over the country, Black groups, organisations and individuals, along with countless white comrades and friends, are mourning the loss of our dear sister Olive Morris, who died in the early hours of Thursday July 12th.

As one of the founder members of OWAAD and a longstanding member of the Brixton Black Women's Group, our sister Olive was known and loved by a great many of us. We grieve her at her death, at the age of 27, and pledge ourselves to continue the struggle to which she devoted her short life.

For ten years, Olive was known as an active and committed sister in the Black community. She was an early member of the Black Panthers in the '60s. She fought for the right to squat and the right to better housing for Black people living in the slums of Brixton. In 1974 she helped set up the first Black bookshop in Brixton, Sabarr Books. She was at the head of many a Black protest demonstration, raising her voice against police harassment and brutality. She was also well-known in Manchester, where she worked with the Manchester Black Women's Co-operative. More recently, she was involved in the Sus campaign and in the campaign by the Brixton Black Women's Group to set up a Black women's centre there. We intend to call the centre after her. She was also totally committed to the struggle against imperialism.

Everyone who came into contact with Olive was touched by her honesty, her humour and her passionate love of her people. We will remember her until long after the struggles to which she committed her life have become tomorrow's victories.

...

For further information, contact: Brixton Black Women's Group, 121 Railton Rd, Brixton, London se24.

Black Women Together

The need for a united and autonomous National Black Women's Organisation

Organisation of Women of Asian and African Descent (OWAAD) /
AWAZ, Brixton Black Women's Group & United Black Women's
Action Group
First published in Spare Rib, *no. 87, October 1979, pp. 42–5*

For us Black women, the National Black Women's Conference
held at the Abeng Centre in Brixton, London, on March 18 this
year was an historic occasion. For the first time, nearly 300 Black
women got together from places as far apart as Birmingham,
Brighton, Bristol, Coventry, Leeds, London, Manchester and
Sheffield to discuss some of the many issues which concern us
because we are Black, female, working-class or all three.

But it was not so much the number of sisters, the distances
travelled, nor the wide age range (from 15 to 65), as the achievement of bringing together Asian, Afro- and Indo-Caribbean,
African and Black sisters born and brought up in Britain which
we regard as historic.

The conference marks an important stage in the development
of an autonomous Black Women's Movement in Britain. It was a
living witness to our conviction that if the voice of Black women
in this country is to be heard, we need to set up a separate and
independent organisation of Black women in which we ourselves

lead the struggle against the specific type of oppression that we face. For too long, the fact that as Black women we suffer triple oppression has been ignored – by male-dominated Black groups, by white-dominated women's groups, and by middle-class-dominated left groups. This continual lack of interest in the situation of Black women created a vicious circle, so that many of us who wanted to speak out were reluctant to do so. But, by contacting each other and working together, we have now broken this circle.

Moreover, the fact that the conference took place testifies to our belief that our common experience as second-class citizens in contemporary Britain, as well as our joint history as victims of colonialism and imperialism, represents a bond between us which far outweighs ethnic and cultural differences which may exist.

The conference was organised by the Organisation of Women of Asian and African Descent (OWAAD). This was set up in February 1978 and, although at the moment largely based in London, we already have strong links with sisters in the North West and Midlands. Our ultimate ambition is to establish a national Black women's umbrella organisation made up of local groups and individuals who are active in anti-racist, feminist and community campaigns. In the weeks since the conference, we have been involved in a lot of activity in the hope that OWAAD will now go from strength to strength. We have edited and updated the conference talks, which will shortly be available for general sale. We have completed a video of the conference and we have started a newsletter, called *FOWAAD!*, to help forge national links between Black women's groups and individuals.[1]

Here are the perspectives and corresponding activities of some

---

1   *Editor's note:* For more on OWAAD, see Julia Sudbury, *'Other Kinds of Dreams': Black Women's Organisations and the Politics of Transformation* (London: Routledge, 1998); Tracy Fisher, *What's Left of Blackness: Feminisms, Transracial Solidarities, and the Politics of Belonging in Britain* (New York: Palgrave Macmillan, 2012); Nydia A. Swaby, '"Disparate in Voice, Sympathetic in Direction": Gendered Political Blackness and the Politics of Solidarity', *Feminist Review* 108, no. 1 (2014), 11–25; and Natalie Thomlinson, *Race, Ethnicity and the Women's Movement in England, 1968–1993* (Basingstoke: Palgrave Macmillan, 2016).

of the member groups within OWAAD who took an active part
in making the conference possible.

AWAZ – Asian Women's Movement

Coming to Britain from a village in India which has been
impoverished by colonialism; having your family split up by the
immigration laws; being responsible for the whole household but
not being given credit for it by anybody; having your young children bussed miles away from home; having to work all day in a
sweatshop and then going home to wait on your family hand and
foot; never being safe on the street and never knowing when your
family will be beaten up by the police or civilian racists; having
your self-image distorted by a racist culture – these are some of
the experiences which are the genesis of our politics. The racism
we face every day places us at the bottom of the class structure.
The fact that we or our families come from Third World countries
makes imperialism something we can't forget about, and our
oppression as women is so acute that if we are to be involved in
politics at all we have to be feminists.

AWAZ was formed just over a year ago. It consists of women
of all ages and different economic backgrounds, either directly, or
by descent, from the Indian sub-continent. A few of our members
had been involved in the predominantly white women's movement in Britain. Their experiences have led us to believe that, at
present, our political direction is very different from that of most
white feminist groups. The roots of our oppression in the family,
and hence our views of the family, are very different from those
of white women in Britain. Also, we see racism as a class issue,
not a moral issue. So we think that groups which lack an understanding of racism and imperialism also lack a class analysis, and
we can work with them only on a very limited basis. However,
although we are an autonomous women's organisation, we do
not believe in isolating ourselves as women while fighting racism.

AWAZ's current campaigns are against state racism – against
passport raids, deportations, police brutality and the forthcoming
nationality law which. according to the recently published Green

Paper, will designate a large proportion of Black people in Britain as British Overseas Citizens. This would mean they would have no right to work or vote here – a system of induced repatriation. We are also involved in supporting the Black workers at Futters (a factory in Harlesden in London). Later this year, we shall produce a pamphlet on racism in the National Health Service and launch a campaign around this. The first issue of AWAZ's newsletter will appear later this year. We meet weekly, but in addition there are open general meetings every month.

Brixton Black Women's Group

Our group was set up in 1973, in response to the lack of interest in women's issues displayed by male-dominated Black organisations. Over the years, experience has shown us that, if we are to be liberated as women and as a subjugated people, we must both raise our own level of consciousness and lead our own campaigns. Since that time, we have been active in programmes and projects which we believe are fulfilling those aims.

AS ANTI-RACISTS, we work with Black groups involved in community affairs. In the field of education, for example, we work with the West Indian Parents' Action Group and the Black Educational Action Group. These groups are actively seeking to influence the education of our children and to be recognised by decision-making bodies.

We also work with Black People Against State Harassment (BASH).[2] BASH is active in the campaign against police malpractices such as the use of Section 4 of the 1824 Vagrancy Act ('Sus'), whereby a disproportionate number of Black people are being picked up, beaten and locked away on the charge of being a 'person *suspected* of loitering with intent to commit an arrestable offence', as well as any attempts to extend such malpractices – like the proposals recently put forward by the Metropolitan Police Commissioner, David McNee. And on June 3 this year, along with

---

2 *Editor's note:* For more on BASH, see Colin Prescod, 'Black People against State Harassment (BASH) Campaign – A Report', *Race and Class* 58, no. 1 (2016), 94–100.

AWAZ and the Indian Workers' Association (IWA), we helped organise the demonstration Black People Against State Brutality – an initiative largely taken by Black women as a reaction to police brutality in Southall (*Spare Rib* 84).[3]

AS FEMINISTS, in conjunction with the Mary Seacole Crafts Group, we are opening a centre for Black women. (Mary Seacole was a Black nurse who travelled by herself from Jamaica to the Crimea, where she did important nursing work alongside Florence Nightingale).[4] The centre will have a crèche and meeting rooms, as well as facilities for craft-making. It will be a place where Black women can come to meet one another.

We also work with white women's groups on international women's issues. Most recently, for example, we have been working with white women to get the contraceptive Depo-Provera off the market. Depo-Provera is an injection mainly used on Black and Third World women. It lasts up to three months and has side effects which are definitely unsafe (*Spare Rib* 80).[5]

We are also working on a study programme. We are drawing up a bibliography of writings by and about Black women, and we have formed a study group which concentrates on issues that affect women in general, such as women's rights, sexuality and contraception, as well as those affecting Black women in particular, like immigration laws and practices, Black girls in the education system, Black women in prison, and Third World women in struggle. From this, we hope to work out a coherent political perspective.

AS ANTI-IMPERIALISTS, we help spread information through our newsletter, *Speak Out*. We feel that such a newsletter is necessary because too little is known about the history of Black women. To expand on this theme: it is not widely appreciated that Black women started to come from the West Indies to Britain in the '50s

3 *Editor's note:* See P. Dhillon, "'They're Killing Us in Here": Black Women and the State', *Spare Rib*, no. 84 (July 1979), 32–3.

4 *Editor's note:* See Mary Seacole, *Wonderful Adventures of Mrs Seacole in Many Lands*, annotated edn, ed. S. Salih (London: Penguin Classics, 2005 [1857]).

5 *Editor's note:* Campaign against Depo-Provera, 'Organising against 'the Jab', *Spare Rib*, no. 80 (March 1979), 9–10.

and '60s, either because we were duped by an invitation from the British government to help staff the National Health Service and London Transport, or because we were forced by the ravages of colonialism, which had left us near starvation, unemployed and with little prospect of education in the Caribbean. We came to Britain in search of better opportunities or to get some of the wealth which had been misappropriated from the Caribbean, but what in reality did we find?

On arrival to Britain, Black women became the new underdogs. We faced racist and exploitative landlords and the least desirable and lowest paid jobs, many of which were non-unionised. Where unions did exist, they were not interested in defending our rights. The British government, meanwhile, was complacent, since it was interested in the labour power of Black people, not in their social welfare.

Moreover, once our labour power was no longer needed, the British government began to label Black people as a 'problem' and to deprive us even of the rights that we had. The immigration laws, the Green Paper on Citizenship and Nationality, the Child Benefit Act of 1975, police harassment, and the use of Depo-Provera to control our numbers are just a few examples.

It is against this background that the Brixton Black Women's Group was born and remains active. We will continue to fight for our rights both as women and as Black people; fight for the overthrow of class society and the liberation of women and Black people world-wide. It is all one struggle. We need the support of all Black women.

United Black Women's Action Group

WHO ARE WE? This Tottenham-based group got together to bridge the widening gap between us. We are from different parts of the world, yet have many things in common. This gap was holding us back in the struggle against the issues that concern us most. We started off with meetings, talking about our common problems and experiences. Top of the list were, and still are, housing, education and employment, and police mistreatment of

Black youth. So we decided to do something about the pressures on us and our children.

WHAT HAVE WE DONE? We believe in action, and since we started we have done a lot. We are active in the campaign to publicise the facts about sickle cell anaemia, an hereditary blood disease which mainly affects Black people but which is widely ignored by the National Health Service. We believe that until Black people know the facts about sickle cell; until medical staff, social workers, health visitors, teachers and others learn about it as part of their training; until there is a national programme for screening children in schools and expectant mothers in clinics; until the government puts enough money into sickle cell anaemia research ... Black people will continue to die from it unnecessarily. We have set up the Organisation for Sickle Cell Anaemia Research (OSCAR) in Haringey, which organises public meetings and slide shows on sickle cell.

We are also involved in the anti-Sus campaign. We are calling for a review of the Vagrancy Act and the repeal of Section 4. We have held public meetings and public hearings. Most recently, we helped organise the first ever national Scrap Sus Conference held in June of this year in London.

In addition, we were active in the Tony Anderson Campaign. One night, Tony was walking home when a policeman called out to him, 'Hallo sunshine'. When Tony said his name was not 'sunshine' he was punched in the kidneys by the policeman's mate. When he eventually got home, obviously in great pain, his mother took him to the police station where he was examined by the police surgeon and found to have severely bruised kidneys. His mother filed a complaint. Attempts were made to frustrate her complaint, which was eventually dismissed. From that time onwards, Tony was the victim of constant police harassment, until he was finally sent down for 'assault'.

We decided to press for an inquiry into Tony's case, which we publicised widely. Whilst gathering information, it became obvious that Tony's case was not unusual. It is clear that, if we want to protect Tony and other Black youths in Haringey, we need the support of all sisters and brothers.

We were also active in the campaign to remove Questions 10

and 11 from the Haringey trial census of April this year. One question asked us about the country of birth of our parents, a question requiring us to tick a box to indicate which racial or ethnic group we belong to. The other asked, 'Have you registered or naturalised? If not, state the country where your passport was issued'. The (Labour) government attempted to justify these questions on the grounds they need such information so they can introduce schemes which 'positively discriminate' in favour of ethnic minority groups. But we know better! Black people have for many years now been experiencing the negative discrimination of the British state. How then, can we be expected to believe that such questions are only going to be used to our advantage?

The test census forms have long ago been fed into a computer somewhere. But that is by no means the end of our campaign. We are taking action now to ensure that the same questions on race do not appear in the 1981 national census. Whereas it was not compulsory to fill in the test census, it will be to fill in the national one.

Most recently, we have begun a campaign around education. In response to some of the demands which came out of the OWAAD Conference, in June of this year we held a public meeting to raise and discuss some of the worrying trends affecting our children's education in the borough. Such problems include suspensions, which have been taking place at an alarming rate. Black children have been finding themselves asked to stay away from school, often unofficially (i.e. without the schools following the official procedure of informing the parents and governors) and, frequently, just before the children concerned are due to sit public examinations. Recently, for example, a newly-appointed headmaster of a Haringey secondary school is alleged to have excluded around 20 youth from the school – all of them Black. When questioned, he only admitted to five of them being suspended officially. Even the governors of the school knew nothing about it, when asked.

Another cause for alarm in Haringey is the rumour of a plan to attach 'disruptive units' to every secondary school. These 'sin bins', as they are called, are simply dumping grounds for all the unwanted 'disruptive' pupils whom the schools cannot handle.

A disproportionate number of the children attending them are Black. Setting up more 'sin bins' can only result in even larger numbers of Black youth being deprived of their right to education, and their right to an educational system which caters for their particular cultural, linguistic and social needs. As a back-up to the campaigns, we have run courses on 'know your rights' when it comes to the courts and police, housing, women's issues and schooling. We have also made a three-part video called *Late One Evening, Truth Makes You Free in the End*, and *Suspended, Expelled and Kicked Out*. These cover arrest, troubles at school, and the dangers of not knowing your rights.

Finally, we have linked up in joint meetings with other Black women who share our experiences. For example, we met with the Afro Caribbean Women's Association in Deptford, who made a video on 'Sus' and Black youth/police relations called *Hands Off Our Kids*. We exchange videos. We believe there is strength in unity!

OWAAD will put Black women wishing to form local groups in touch with each other, inside and outside London. For information about *FOWAAD!* (newsletter) and the conference papers/video, contact OWAAD, 10 Cambridge Terrace Mews, London NW1.

Groups named in this article:
AWAZ, Asian Women's Movement, 57 Trinity Road, London SW17.
Tel: 01 767 3631

BRIXTON BLACK WOMEN'S GROUP, c/o 121 Railton Road, Brixton, London SE24. Meetings every Sunday from 3 to 5pm at the above address.

UNITED BLACK WOMEN'S ACTION GROUP, c/o 2 Chasewater, Boyton Road, Hornsey, London N8.
Meetings every 3rd Sunday of the month, at: West Green Community Centre, Stanley Road, Tottenham N15.

MARY SEACOLE CRAFTS GROUP, c/o St. Matthews Meeting Place, Brixton Hill, London SW2.

Other contacts:

Manchester Black Women's Co-operative, Moss Side People's Centre
St. Mary's Street, Moss Side, Manchester 15 M15 5WA.
Tel: 061-226 6837.

ZANU Women's League, c/o 34 Chalcot Crescent, London NW1.

SWAPO Women's Campaign, c/o 188 North Gower Street, London NW1 2NB.
Tel: 01-388 2080/89.

Black/Brown Women's Liberation Newsletter, c/o 43 Grosvenor Terrace, Bootham, York. Tel, 0904-39330.

Latin American Women's Group, c/o Latin American Centre, 16 Hoxton Square, London.

Scrap SUS Campaign, c/o 206 Evelyn Street, London SE8.
Tel: 01-692-7568.

'SPEAK OUT'

ISSUE 3   20p

The cuts hit women harder

Hospital closures 'mean deaths'

Joseph links regional decline with arrival of immigrants

Corrie Abortion Bill gets by

Immigration Laws- 'are subversive

NO to housing cuts

to do will depend upon his judgment of what is in the best interests of the patient." it states.

BIRTH JAB BARRED

Are West Indians top of the form?

AXE FALLS ON HOSPITAL

ug watch-
y refused
ntroversial
ntracept,ve
women to
ral use.
follows pro-
MPs and
women's groups who say
possible side effects of
the drug Depo-Provera
—have not been fully
investigated.
The Committee on the
Safety of Medicines was
expected to grant a full-
product licence at its
meeting yesterday.

BLACK WOMEN'S GROUP BRIXTON

EDITORIAL

Brixton Black Women's Group
First published in Speak Out, *no. 3, c. 1980, p. 1*

We enter into the 1980s headlong into a world crisis that has been deepening since the 1970s and, as a result of which, Britain's response has been savage attacks on working people. As Black women, we will suffer most from these attacks. Therefore, we ...

SPEAK OUT

against the cuts in education, in the health services and in the social services ...

SPEAK OUT

against measures designed to foster class inequality through race and sex measures ...

SPEAK OUT

through campaigns in the community, some of which we outline in this issue.

We must fight these cuts with the determination shown by the late OLIVE MORRIS, who was an inspiration to all BLACK WOMEN who knew her.

All these events are significantly linked with many Third World countries which are successfully waging their struggle for self-determination and are beginning to exercise power over their own resources.

NEWS

Brixton Black Women's Group
First published in Speak Out, *no. 3, c. 1980, p. 1*

The Black Women's Group and Mary Seacole Craft Group –
Brixton, will shortly be opening a Black Women's Centre at 41
STOCKWELL GREEN, SW9.[1]

---

1   *Editor's note:* When the Brixton Black Women's Group first began
meeting at 41 Stockwell Green sometime in 1979, it was a squat – see
G. Lewis, interview, 15 and 18 April 2011, Sisterhood and After: The
Women's Liberation Oral History Project, British Library, London. The
official opening referred to here likely marks the eventual combination of
three developments which occurred at different stages: first, the Brixton
Black Women's Group having obtained a 'short-life licence' from Lambeth
Council, granting it a relative measure of permanence at 41 Stockwell
Green; second, the Brixton Black Women's Group's partnering with the
Mary Seacole Craft Group to offer a range of resources and activities;
and third, the group's successful bid for funding from the GLC's Inner
Area Partnership Scheme to run these.
    Initially named Mary Seacole House, the centre was later re-named
the Brixton Black Women's Centre and formally opened in September
1980 – see S. Scafe, 'Brixton Black Women's Group', in *Companion to
Contemporary Black British Culture*, ed. A. Donnell (London: Routledge,
2002), 80–1; Tracy Fisher, *What's Left of Blackness: Feminisms, Transracial Solidarities, and the Politics of Belonging in Britain* (New York:
Palgrave Macmillan, 2012); K. Laybourn, *Marxism in Britain: Dissent,
Decline and Re-emergence, 1945–c.2000* (Abingdon: Routledge, 2006);
see also 'Brixton Black Women's Centre: Organising on Child Sexual
Abuse', pp. 315–19 in this collection. The centre offered a regular welfare
and legal rights advice and referral service run by BBWG member and
lawyer Clover Graham. For more on Graham, see the *Guardian*'s obituary
at theguardian.com.
    'Short-life licensing' – sometimes known as 'licensed squatting' –
refers to the permitted short-term use of empty property owned by local

MARY SEACOLE HOUSE

41 STOCKWELL GREEN, SW9.

authorities. At the time, such empty properties were overwhelmingly
in very poor condition and not up to the required standard for human
habitation (and thus were unsuitable for officially housing those on
councils' housing waiting lists). Short-life licences were often issued so
that councils received some level of money from occupants – crucially,
however, while avoiding the creation of official tenancies (which would
have entailed tenants' rights). Such arrangements granted occupants some
measure of security from sudden eviction; occupants, however, committed
themselves to vacating properties licensed to them when required to by
local authorities, even at relatively short notice – see A. Bowman, *Interim
Spaces: Reshaping London: The Role of Short Life Property, 1970 to
2000* (Bristol: University of Bristol, 2004).

Sometime between 1985 and 1986, as a result of local authority budget
cuts, the Brixton Black Women's Centre lost its funding; during this
period, the centre also lost its short-life licence, and 41 Stockwell Green
was condemned by Lambeth Council – see Julia Sudbury, *'Other Kinds
of Dreams': Black Women's Organisations and the Politics of Transformation* (London: Routledge, 1998); 41 Stockwell Green was demolished
sometime during or after 1996. It can be seen still standing in a 1996
photograph by Horst Friedrichs, viewable online at 'Black Women's Centre

The aim of the Black Women's Centre will be to give support and help to Black women in the community in different ways. We will be dealing with some of the specific problems we face as Black women, such as racism, sexism and class oppression. In addition, we will be running a craft workshop and playgroup.

The Centre will further be developed to provide up-to-date information on all aspects of women's rights and benefits. Our programme of work will include our political development through discussions, seminars and exchange with other women's groups.

These are some of the uses to which the Centre will be put. We hope to establish a permanent base where women with different experiences can become involved in the Centre and make their contributions.

At present, work is being carried out on the house and we will let you know well in advance when the Centre will be officially opened.

The Black Women's Group now meets at the house (41 Stockwell Green, SW9) at 3:00pm on Sundays for weekly meetings.

For further information, phone 274-9220.

Mural, Stockwell Road, Brixton', boroughphotos.org. An apartment complex called 'Draymans Court' now stands in its place (Land Registry documents – title number: 197064 – appear to suggest it has stood there since 2006).

Background to the CUTS

IT'S OUR TURN AGAIN

Brixton Black Women's Group
First published in Speak Out, *no. 3, c. 1980, pp. 2–3*

BACKGROUND TO THE CUTS

When British imperialism was at its height, the ruling classes were able to finance public welfare schemes because control of our countries of origin meant expansion of their industries.

Since 1973, Western countries have been experiencing a progressively worsening economic crisis. This is due, in part, to the fact that these countries are finding it increasingly difficult to keep economic and political control of the Third World. The political crisis in countries like Zimbabwe and parts of the Caribbean, the decline in oil supplies and oil profits (as a result of policies such as Nigeria's nationalisation of British Petroleum), the cessation of millions of barrels of oil from Iran, the increased prices forced by the OPEC countries – are all examples of this fact.

The response of successive British governments has been to make the working class pay by making bigger and bigger cuts in public expenditure. The areas where these cuts are taking place, such as health, education and housing, will systematically deprive the already disadvantaged, i.e. all working class people, and especially Black women.

CUTS IN EMPLOYMENT – what it means to us

Because of our position in this country, many of us work outside the home and we are often the sole providers for our families. We work in the Health Service, on public transport and in factories or as cleaners – in fact, in most areas of the service sector which are state-financed. Because of this, cuts in public expenditure not only affect us in essentials like housing and effective health services, but also by reducing our employment opportunities.

London Transport, for example, has announced that it intends to cut 35,000 jobs. Because so many Black women work in London Transport as conductors, ticket collectors, cleaners, and canteen and clerical workers, these cuts, if carried out, would mean that we would be disproportionately affected. The same is true of cuts in the Health Service. The Health Minister has told London Area Health Authorities that they must cut £38m off their budget. In the Merton, Sutton and Wandsworth areas, this means the closure of four hospitals plus specialist units and wards, and, of course, a cut to all staffing sectors (except, not surprisingly, managerial and administrative). This would include nurses, domestics, and porters, to name a few. Since many Black women work in all sectors of the Health Service, the effect on our employment chances will be devastating. It also means that more and more student nurses will be herded into being State Enrolled Nurses (SEN) as opposed to being State Registered Nurses (SRN).

To make matters worse, the Conservative government is suggesting that there should be changes in the Employment Protection Act, especially those sections which protect women – for example, a woman's right to return to her job after taking maternity leave. Also, the introduction of new technology will increase unemployment many times over. One such introduction which will affect women the most is the micro 'word processor'. This will affect secretaries, shorthand typists, audio and copy typists. Since Black girls are pushed into the lowest levels of secretarial courses in schools and colleges, and given that these are precisely the skills the word processor will replace, Black women will once again be the worst hit.

The cuts in public expenditure will also affect us in other ways. The closure of nurseries, particularly in poor areas where they are needed most, i.e. where WE live, will prevent women with children getting a job even when we have the chance of one. This will force women back into the home and, as a result, will increase our isolation and the tension and frustration we experience because of constant money worries.

In situations where Black women are the major or only breadwinners, and even when we are not, we shall be forced into an even greater dependency on childminders. This could have a detrimental effect on our children, since one woman cannot hope to provide the range of facilities that children need for their proper development. It can also be detrimental to the childminder herself. Childminders are often forced into childminding as the only source of getting money. So, with alternative sources of employment becoming less and less available, women will have to take larger numbers of children in order to make ends meet.

EDUCATION – what cuts will mean to our children

Black children will be forced to go to schools with bigger classes, fewer facilities and materials, and increasing teacher frustration. At the same time, any special provisions that our children might need will also be cut, or more probably never be provided in the first place. This new round of cuts in education can only make matters worse. Yet, whilst the government is forcing local authorities to implement massive cuts and punishing those authorities which refuse to carry them out by withholding the already greatly reduced Rate Support Grant, it is increasing expenditure on things like 'disruptive units'. These are used as means of 'deskilling', isolating and controlling our youths. Already, Black school-leavers' rate of unemployment is much greater than that of white school-leavers. For example, in one London borough,

Black school-leavers' chance of unemployment was three times that of white youths, whilst for Black female school-leavers it was four times!! And all in the name of getting Britain back on its feet!

The government – and some local authorities, we might add – are also toying with the idea of cutting the cost of education by reorganisation of the school day. The proposal is that school should finish at about 2pm. Obviously, this would mean that school-age people would have longer time to roam the street, since any provision of youth clubs and/or facilities are also being cut.

Given the way the 'police' already harass our youth under the 'SUS' and immigration laws, any shortening of the school day will only increase this. Also being discussed is a proposal to shorten the summer holiday and lengthen the winter one, with the idea that it may lead to cheaper heating bills for the education authorities. It will mean more expense for us, because our children will be at home for longer periods. This comes at a time when we can least afford it, because the Gas Corporation also proposes to increase the cost of heating by 40–60 per cent.

However, whilst the government is reducing the amount spent on providing and extending the basic education system, at the same time it is going to spend £62m in direct grant schools, which will mainly benefit middle class children in schools where you hardly ever find Black children except the odd one or two whose parents can just about manage that income range.

How they intend to back up the cuts

This is a consistent pattern throughout the expenditure cuts. Whilst the situation of Blacks as well as the white working class worsens, the shift of resources in the health sector in favour of management increases, as does the rise in wages for the police and army. The immediate wage increases for the police and army is the Tory government's incentive to these 'forces' to strengthen them, as the State will need their services in order to deal with the increases to resistance that these cuts will create.

HOUSING

Housing has not been exempted, either. Since we have been in this country, we have been forced into the worst housing conditions. Whether in the private or public sector, our housing needs are given least priority. Now, even those authorities which take our needs into account will be prevented from taking any positive action because of these unreasonable cuts.

For example, Lambeth Borough Council recently decided that 30% of new and recently converted accommodation should go to Black people, since that is equal to our numbers in the borough. However, the cuts, if implemented, will mean that there will be virtually no new houses or conversions, so our housing conditions will not alter.

Similarly, the proposal not to directly employ maintenance staff for local authority housing will affect not only the conditions of council housing accommodation but also increase the unemployment figures. At the same time, however, private construction firms will receive a boost, since they will be given contracts to carry out repairs, conversions, etc. on council houses and flats.

NO MORE SOCIAL SERVICES

All the cuts in public expenditure will act in such a way to make the situation of Black people, especially Black women, increasingly worse. To add insult to injury, there are even proposals to reduce our rights to Social Security benefits. Proposals are to tax 'dole' money and sickness benefit, and to deny young unemployed people in part-time education their right to claim supplementary benefit. This will only add to the already high degree of intimidation that claimants have to endure. A perfect example of this is to be found in a new policy introduced by Wandsworth Social Security offices. In order to cope with the ever-increasing numbers of people who are having to claim one benefit or another, Wandsworth now have a 'phone by name' scheme. This means that they will only deal with an individual query on the day assigned for the names beginning with a certain letter, so that if your day is Monday and you need 'help' on Wednesday – TOO BAD!

OVERVIEW OF THE CUTS

Government and local authority spending cuts are an attack on our rights to a decent life. As Black women and men, we must organise ourselves against any implementation of cuts in all areas. In 'fight-back' campaigns, we must be sure that the specific ways in which we shall be affected are taken into account. For example, we should organise against the introduction of 'disruptive units' and the increase in university fees for overseas students. If we live in an area where the local authority is refusing to implement cuts, then we must give them our full support.

CUTS WILL KILL

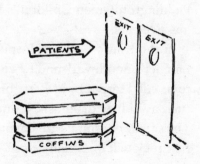

Brixton Black Women's Group
First published in Speak Out, *no. 3, c. 1980, pp. 4–5*

Once again, cuts are being instigated in an already ailing but much needed institution, the Health Service. Plans are to cut £90–100 million out of the NHS national budget of £5.9 billion. The cuts are being made as part of an overall economic strategy to curb public spending, which the government considers to be far too high. Apparently, this stance is taken without regard as to whether such cuts will have a detrimental effect on the community.

The policy seems to be to sacrifice services which will benefit, and are indeed necessary, for the health and welfare of the public. They argue that these measures will strengthen the economy and increase Britain's standing in the Western World. This in turn leads to further exploitation of the working classes, and specifically black women and children.

The health cuts in London Area Health Authorities [AHA] alone will amount to £15 million:

Lambeth, Southwark & Lewisham AHA – £5¹/²m.
Ealing, Hammersmith & Hounslow AHA – £4m.
Merton, Sutton & Wandsworth AHA – £3–4m.
Kensington, Chelsea & Westminster AHA – £2m.
Paddington & North Kensington AHA – £10,000.

Several hospitals are due to close, including St Olave's and St John's in Lewisham, St Mary's, St Charles, Gordons and St Stephen's and the Emergency Department at St Mary Abbotts in the Kensington and Chelsea AHA. Beds in children's hospitals are diminishing, also. The Belgrave Hospital at Kennington and Paddington Green Children's Hospital are both scheduled for massive cuts.

In the King's College Hospital health district, situated in the Lambeth, Southwark and Lewisham AHA, many services are due to be cut. Hospital wards are being closed for essential treatment such as kidney diagnosis, kidney transplants and heart surgery. The smaller hospitals are having ward shut-downs at such a rate that they will eventually close. Emergency services and casualty departments are being forced to shut down, either at weekends, temporarily or for good.

At present, the health service is characterised by long waiting lists, complaints of shortage of beds, chronic shortages of staff because of ridiculously low wages and overwork, outdated hospital equipment and antiquated wards in many hospitals.

Apparently, the cash limits for the various health services have not been reduced as such. However, because of a substantial rise in the costs of medical supplies due to VAT increases in the Tory budget (doubled to 15%), the government has now said that it will not subsidise the health service against the effects of VAT increases, and that local authorities must implement wide ranging economies to accommodate this. If a particular local authority refuses to make a cut in services, the government simply 'sacks' them and appoints its own Commissioners instead, as happened in the Lambeth AHA last year. The normal informal consultative procedures with bodies such as the Community Health Councils are being disregarded. In an effort to ensure the cuts are hurriedly implemented – that is, before the financial year – management is pursuing a policy of informing staff of changes as late as possible. Therefore, they are unable to effectively resist such changes.

The reduction in services is especially going to hit women, because many services seen as 'extras', such as Community Health Clinics for women and abortion facilities, are being put on top of the list of non-essentials. St John's Hospital in Lewisham, which is due to be closed, specialises in abortion and treating venereal diseases. Paddington AHA, which runs the school nurse facilities, chiropody and cytology services (tests for cervical cancer) and is situated in one of the poorest areas of London, is having £10,000 cut off its Community Health budget.

Another area in which women will be affected is in the care of elderly and infirm relatives at home, because a further effect of the cuts will be to reduce the number of old people's hostels and day care facilities. Consequently, the cutback measures will effectively force many women back into the home and to be dependent upon their husbands' income and state benefits which are far from adequate.

Women also suffer in the area of employment within the health service. The majority of those who work in the health service are women, and it is they who will bear the brunt of the cuts as economics erode their jobs. For example, domestics and nurses, many of whom are black, will face unemployment with the closure of wards. Often, no advice concerning alternative employment is given. Vacated posts, especially those of staff nurses, are frozen to cut expenditure. This leads to a staff shortage and thus the excuse to close down more wards and departments.

Cutbacks on ancillary services such as engineers and technicians will mean that, besides creating unemployment, vital hospital equipment is not maintained. This leads to inefficiency and jeopardises lives.

Staff training will also be affected. Because of the inequalities in education that currently exist in this country, many black women and men are denied the opportunity of attaining the high qualifications required for entry to a three-year State Registered Nursing course. The further effects of the cuts will be that even more students will be forced into the two-year State Enrolled Nursing course, thereby enabling the health authorities to economise even further.

Some campaigns are being initiated against the cuts by those unwilling to passively accept government cutbacks, as they recognise that this will inevitably lead to a fall in patient care and probably even an undue rise in patient mortality.

ABORTION BILL
Fight the new proposals

Brixton Black Women's Group
First published in Speak Out, *no. 3, c. 1980, pp. 5–6*

Fight the new abortion laws

We have decided to outline the 1967 Abortion Act because, with amendments and the more recent debates about Corrie's Anti-Abortion Bill, the issue has become somewhat clouded.[1]

Under the 1967 Abortion Act, a woman is legally entitled to an abortion if she can persuade two doctors that:

(a) continuing the pregnancy involves a greater risk to her life than an abortion;

(b) continuing the pregnancy involves a greater risk of injury to her physical or mental health than an abortion;

(c) continuing the pregnancy involves a greater risk of injury to the physical or mental health of the existing children in the family than an abortion; or

(d) there is a substantial risk that the child will be born seriously deformed.

---

1 *Editor's note:* The Corrie Bill was introduced in the House of Commons in 1979 by John Corrie (Conservative MP for Bute and Northern Ayrshire) to restrict abortion rights that had been granted under the 1967 Abortion Act. The bill was withdrawn in March 1980, before its Third Reading, following widespread criticism and demonstrations. See *Parliamentary Debates*, Commons, Abortion (Amendment) Bill, 13 July 1979, vol. 970, cols. 891–983, api.parliament.uk. See also 'Black Women and Abortion', pp. 102–4 in this collection.

In deciding whether the mental or physical health of the mother or existing children are at risk by the pregnancy, doctors may take present or future circumstances into account.

We are not saying the above 1967 Act was fool-proof. Even with legal rights, many women can't get abortions because the National Health Service clinics don't exist in many parts of the country, or they can't find sympathetic doctors.

In 1971, the Lane Committee was set up by the government to look into the working of the 1967 Act.[2] After 3 years, it concluded that the Act had 'relieved a vast amount of individual suffering'. The Report also showed the need for wide-spread provisions of contraceptive advice and facilities. It is now filed away somewhere in the bowels of Parliament.

Since 1975, two male MPs, James White and William Benyon, have tried to amend the 1967 Act; not to update it, or to put more money into research or facilities, or anything favourable like that – far from it. Now, under the new Tory Government, John Corrie wants to make his name on the anti-abortion wagon.

Let us not fool ourselves. If the Corrie Bill becomes law, abortion will only be allowed if:

(i) the woman's life is in 'grave danger';
(ii) there is a 'substantial' risk of 'serious' injury to the woman's physical or mental health, or that of her children.

Under these conditions, most of the abortions carried out now will become illegal, because most abortions are carried out on grounds (b) of the present Act.

The words 'grave', 'substantial' and 'serious' are so broad they can be too easily interpreted to fit individual doctors' preferences.

In addition, John Corrie wants to reduce the upper time limit from 28 weeks to 20 weeks. In practice, a 20-week limit will mean that doctors could not perform abortions after the 16th week, even if they wanted to. Therefore, will doctors put themselves at risk and possibly lose their practising rights? A woman would literally have to be dying to get an abortion after

---

2 *Editor's note*: The Lane Committee was also known as the Committee on the Working of the Abortion Act, 1971–1974. It was chaired by Justice Elizabeth Kathleen Lane.

this stage; the only exception will be if the foetus is severely handicapped.

This proviso would particularly affect young girls who don't know what to do about their pregnancy; menopausal women who don't realise until very late that they are pregnant and whose existing children are already grown up; and women who only discover late in their pregnancy that they are very likely to have a handicapped foetus.

At present, only one per cent of abortions take place after 20 weeks, and these are among the most desperate cases. Sensational newspaper stories about 'crying foetuses' have been investigated by the National Health Service and found to be grossly distorted or completely untrue. Corrie also plans to widen the 'conscience clause' so that anyone in the health service who just does not want to have anything to do with abortion can claim a moral objection. There is no evidence at present to suggest that doctors and nurses are being forced to perform abortions. However, after Corrie's amendments, Area Health Authorities may use 'unsympathetic staff' as an excuse for inadequate abortion services.

The Corrie Bill aims to destroy charities the British Pregnancy Advisory Service (B.P.A.S.) and the Pregnancy Advisory Service (P.A.S.), the two largest agencies, which not only fill the gap left by the National Health Service but also provide sympathetic services at a reasonable price. Corrie's proposals aim to intimidate them and other similar agencies in that they would have to obtain licences to carry out these services. However, a licence would not be issued by the government if there were any connections, whether financial or impersonal, between the agency and the abortion clinic, or if the agency is not managed by a qualified doctor or nurse. The work done by charities will be impossible under this new clause, and the twenty-five per cent of women who receive abortions and advice through these charities will be subjected to the unscrupulous money-makers of the private medicine market.

If this bill goes through, it means a return to the back-street abortionist – in one door and out the other, with us footing the bill. In any one year, 100,000 women decide to terminate an unwanted pregnancy. Women will be forced to return to the terrors of the back-street abortionists or forking out vast sums of money. Hundreds died each year.

If this bill goes through, people in the 1980s will be reading true stories in the newspapers about 'Women found dying in pools of blood', 'School girl said: "I did it my way ..."', 'They said I was too late, but I couldn't go on with my pregnancy, that's why I let him do it' ...

'A woman's right to choose' means: A Woman's Right to Choose:

- the right to abortion on demand
- the right to free and safe contraception given on the basis of informed consent
- no forced sterilisation

Attack on the Black family

The slogan 'A Woman's Right to Choose' refers to the right of women to decide if, when, where, and how many children to have. All too often, it is used in its narrow sense to refer to the right to abortion alone, but since the British state is bent on reducing the number of Black people in this country, many Black women are often suspicious, since we know in our case it can often mean forced sterilisation.

Black women are being denied the right to choose in its broad sense by:

- Immigration laws – which prevent families being together in this country. Also, not infrequently, Black women seeking contraceptive and/or abortion advice are asked to prove their 'immigration status' before they can obtain advice and/or treatment.
- Use of Depo-Provera – along with some white working-class women and our sisters in the Third World, we are given Depo-Provera, which is a 3–6-month contraceptive injection, without being informed of the possible side-effects and sometimes without any knowledge at all.
- Withdrawal of Child Tax Allowance – the Tory government

intends in due course to phase out Child Tax Allowance, which we can at present claim for our children abroad, replacing it with the Child Benefit Scheme, which is only payable for children resident in this country.

We have to fight to make the government and medical profession provide detailed, honest, research into providing safe contraception, free abortions on demand and no forced sterilisations, so that we can go forward instead of backward.

WE MUST FIGHT FOR OUR RIGHTS!

WHOSE CHOICE?

BAN the JAB

Brixton Black Women's Group
First published in Speak Out, *no. 3, c. 1980, p. 7*

In the first issue of *Speak Out* we wrote about the use of a contraceptive injection – Norethisterone – on Black and White working-class women in London hospitals. We pointed out the similarity between Norethisterone and Depo-Provera, a much more powerful contraceptive injection.

Since that first article, we have followed up the use of contraceptive injections in general, and D.P. in particular. What we have found out gives us great cause for concern.

There is evidence that D.P. has been associated with side effects such as weight gain and menstrual chaos; it has also been linked with increased risk of cancer in the cervix and the lining of the womb, and with malformation of the foetus in women who are already pregnant when given it. It has been shown to cause long-term infertility and possibly permanent sterility in many women, even after they have stopped taking the drug. Women have reported many other side effects, including hair loss, acne, loss of orgasm and 'sex drive', migraine, nausea and depression.

Most seriously, D.P. is passed on in breast milk at the same level of concentration as it is found in the mother's bloodstream. What does this mean for the health and safety of our children – particularly the female child?

D.P. is only approved by the Committee on Safety of Medicines for a very limited and specific use. This is for women whose partners have just had a vasectomy and for women who have recently been given an injection against German measles (Rubella). Even with these clearly limited recommendations, however, the contraceptive is becoming increasingly and widely used by doctors and health clinics.

In the earlier *Speak Out*, we pointed out the fact that D.P. is widely used in the Glasgow Domiciliary Service, where it is highly recommended and widely used. Women are referred to the service on the basis of a points system. Situations such as being on supplementary benefit, living in sub-standard housing with an unemployed consort or being a single parent are all considered high points for referral. (Remember that the Service has great faith in it as a contraceptive.) When 'low IQ' and promiscuity are added to this list, we can see the kind of context in which D.P. is dispensed.

It therefore comes as no surprise to discover that, like Norethisterone, D.P. is being prescribed to a lot of Black women. In the London hospital, it has been proved that 66% of women given the drug were Asian, when only 20% of the hospital population was Asian. On what basis can this be justified? Similarly, on what basis can a young Black girl be forcibly given D.P. after an abortion?

Obviously, there is no justification; and it is because we recognise the dangerous and racist implications of the use of contraceptive injections that we joined with others concerned about women's welfare in forming a national campaign against Depo-Provera.

The campaign has been in operation for nine months. During that time, we have tried to spread information gained about the drug's use through leaflets in local groups, articles in the newspapers, talks at conferences and two T.V. programmes. We are seeking to inform women so they can take up the issues themselves, making their own demands on doctors and the Health Service.

The campaign is calling for the withdrawal of the drug by exposing its dangerous side effects and the way it has been used on Third World women. This is NOT a side issue. In our countries of origin, our sisters are used as guinea pigs for some of the most dangerous drugs. D.P. was first tested on women in Jamaica as long ago as 1963. We have certainly not come a long way. After 16 years, it is still not recommended for use in America by their watchdog body, the Food and Drugs Administration. And, as we have said, it has a very limited recommended use here in Britain. Even so, because of the sacred principle of doctors' clinical judgement, nothing can be done to prevent them going against recommendation.

The only solution is through mounting a really effective campaign informing women of its side effects and racist use. We have had a good response from abroad, and are finding out more and more and more about why a drug banned in America can be so freely available to our sisters in the Third World.

We in the Black Women's Group support the campaign of facts and recognise that in saying no to D.P. we are rejecting the racist use of a contraceptive. We want to actively choose WHEN, HOW and WHAT we use. D.P. gives us NO CHOICE.

We are anxious to compile information about its use. If you have been prescribed D.P. or know of anyone who has, please contact the D.P. Campaign, c/o ICAR, Gray's Inn Road, WC2, or the Black Women's Centre – 41 Stockwell Green, Lon, SW9.

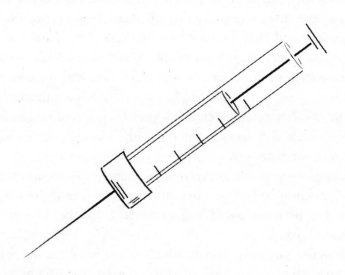

Immigration

Brixton Black Women's Group
First published in Speak Out, *no. 3, c. 1980, p. 8, pp. 11–12*

Immigration: The White Paper black-lash

The recent White Paper proposals on changing the immigration law claim to be interested in 'removing the obscurities and anomalies … and to reduce the scope for evasion'. But still the anomalies remain – in particular the distinction between Commonwealth and New Commonwealth citizens, between 'patrial' and 'non-patrial'. Patrials are people who were born here or who have a parent or grandparent who were born here, or someone who is resident in the UK and has registered as a citizen of the UK. This effectively denies Black people of the same rights as whites, unless they happen to be wealthy Blacks who can inject a lot into the economy.

A brief look at the successive immigration laws since they were first introduced will demonstrate the way in which the 'flow' has been increased and stemmed according to Britain's economic needs.

Up until 1961, any British subject could enter the UK freely. Remember that before then, Britain was experiencing a post-war situation. People as far away as Asia, Africa and the West Indies had fought on Britain's side, and later were recruited to help to reconstitute the British economy. As members of the Commonwealth and British subjects, we were required to show our loyalty.

The Conservative Immigration Act of 1962 was the first to

restrict the freedom given to British subjects to settle and take up employment.[1] After 1962, a voucher system was operated. There were three types of vouchers: category A – where a job was obtained before clearance for entry; category B – for those with specific skills and crafts (e.g. doctors, teachers, nurses, etc., constituting a drain of resources from the respective countries), and C – for unskilled workers without the promise of a job. In 1965, under the Labour Government, the total number of vouchers issued was restricted to 8,500 a year (1,000 of which were reserved for Malta) and the C voucher was abolished altogether. No controls were put on the Irish despite the fact that they came under the category of New Commonwealth, also. The 1962 Act and the 1965 White Paper were a clear statement that both Labour and Conservative regarded Black immigration as a 'problem', conveniently pointing fingers at the Black population when the economy takes a turn for the worse, and generating racism in our communities.

Fourteen years later, in 1979, after all primary immigration had been stopped, immigration became another election issue. Margaret Thatcher promises the electorate and the more extreme National Front that she will clamp down further on immigration. She accuses the Black community of 'swamping' Britain and spoiling British culture. Clamping down further will presumably help Britain out of its economic problems. But a mere 2.5 million Black people live here, in comparison with a far greater proportion of white immigrants out of a population of some 60 million.

Black people have, over the years, been the least dependent on the welfare state, firstly because a larger proportion of Black people compared with whites are of working age and are taxpayers. Even in a situation of relatively high unemployment, Black young people refuse to accept the status of scroungers meted out to them by Social Security officers and survive on little or nothing, or rely on their families' resources. Compounded with this is the fact that we hold the most low-paid jobs and live in the most run-down houses. Despite the fact that we pay taxes and

---

1 *Editor's note:* See the Commonwealth Immigrants Act 1962. See also 'British Immigration Laws: An Attack on Black People' (*Speak Out*, no. 1), pp. 37–43 in this collection.

rates, we get the least from public services – the school relegates our children to 'sin-bins', denying them a proper education and thereby serving to keep them out of the job market.

Since the passing of the 1971 Act, increasingly more people have been subject to deportation, and since 1973, when the 1971 Act came into force, 6,000 people have been imprisoned. Every day there are about 100 people who can be found in prison under the Act, the majority of whom never appear before a court. Extra time is spent in prison by people with non-immigration offences who are awaiting deportation orders. Few people are aware of the threat of deportation which faces young Black people who came to Britain as children and have grown up here. Instances of this type of deportation are still relatively rare, but the powers that exist, and increasing evidence that the Home Office are prepared to use them, make it a cause for concern. These measures must be seen for what they are: the beginning of enforced repatriation, often to countries in which the deported individuals no longer have a home.

The discretionary powers of the Home Office mean that the Home Secretary is under no obligation to disclose the basis under which people are detained, in the same way as would be required if criminal charges were to be brought.

REPATRIATION - deh ya!

In the past, police and public authorities have taken it onto themselves to ascertain whether or not Black clients or employees are illegal immigrants. There are continued raids on the homes of Black families who are suspected to be illegal immigrants. An example of this is the case of a British-born Black girl being told by a local education department to produce a passport before she could be admitted to school, despite having produced a birth certificate showing that she was born in Bristol.

The Home Office gives directions to customs officers which are not available to the public. It is, however, apparent that they have wide powers of search and arrest. Interrogation, X-rays and the notorious vaginal tests have all been used to ascertain facts. Thousands are refused entry after having passed through the bureaucracies in their respective countries. On arrival, many are detained in appalling conditions, often in prisons and detention centres such as Harmondsworth, without having the same rights as 'criminals'.

The rationale given for the recent demand for stricter controls are alleged to be a response to an increasing abuse of the laws as they stand. Arranged marriages, according to Whitelaw, are the crux of the matter. We deplore this attack on our Asian comrades and the various attempts to divert the West Indian and African communities from the other issues at hand, which clearly show that it is not simply an Asian issue but a problem affecting Black people as a whole.

It is well-nigh impossible to make a case for a 16-year-old to join his/her parents; and even when the child is younger, if the mother happens to be single or divorced, they suggest that custody of the child should be with some other person. Women who are unmarried or divorced are penalised by not obtaining clearance for their children. This sexist line runs throughout the White Paper.

If it is a parent who is applying for entry, then a catch-22 situation exists where proof has to be given that the parent is indeed a dependant – i.e. showing receipts in evidence that regular amounts of money are being sent. The British consul then estimate whether or not the living standard of the parent is significantly lower than people living in the same neighbourhood. Practically, then, the parent would need to be in rags and begging on the streets, which is unlikely to occur if one is sending regular sums of money.

A popular line throughout the White Paper is the criteria that intending visitors must prove that they can exist without recourse to public funds – what is the meaning of 'public funds'? Social Security, education, health care under the National Health Service and so on? Despite the knowledge that it is dependants who are seeking entry and that any action to deny people these rights will result in severe hardship and the break-up of families, the White Paper's declarations on the position of dependants remain unsatisfactory. A West Indian husband and father returned to the West Indies for a period of two years after having lived and worked in Britain for a long period. On seeking to return to Britain, his wife was asked to prove that she would be able to maintain him 'without recourse to public funds', without regard to the fact that his family home existed in Britain and that both he and his wife had worked and paid taxes in Britain for most of their working life. The immigration law runs contrary to the laws of a welfare state, and in the instance cited above prevents people from claiming what rightly belongs to them.

Other situations have come to light where grandparents have been admitted after the family has been forced to make such a contract; if family relationships break down, the dependant is left destitute and unaware of his/her rights as a person resident in this country.

Now that the squeeze is on and Britain has its full quota of Black people to run the hospitals and to staff London Transport, Black people are being approached daily to volunteer for repatriation, particularly by Social Security officers. Any person intending to gain entry is required to be a person of independent means, i.e. 'he/she will need to show that he has under his control and disposable in the UK a sum of not less than £100,000, or income of not less than £10,000 a year'.

Formerly, overseas students, who have always contributed a great deal to the British economy both in respect to the fees that they pay as well as the areas of research developed (often bearing much more relevance to Britain than their own countries), were allowed to have their families join them for their period of study.

So you think you are a citizen ...

Often, the wife would work and supplement the finances. The White Paper requires the student to 'without working and without recourse to public funds meet the cost of the course ... His own maintenance and accommodation and that of any dependants during the course'.

The grounds for deportation continue to be as slight as they were in the 1971 Act – 'if the Secretary of State deems the deportation to be conducive to the public good; if the person after reaching the age of 17 is convicted of an offence which merits imprisonment and the court recommends deportation'.

These new changes are scheduled to be followed by a Nationality and Citizenship Act in 1981. The Green Paper on Nationality ties in very neatly with the recent White Paper and is part of the general move to take away all civil rights from Black people resident in Britain.[2] The Green Paper proposes that there be two types of Citizenship, British Citizenship and British Overseas Citizenship for those who are patrials. British Overseas Citizenship covers those people living in a British colony which has become independent and who hold UK and Colonies citizenship, people formerly associated with a colony holding UK and Colonies citizenship granted in the name of the UK, and people living in Britain from existing colonies.

---

2   *Editor's note:* The Green Paper referred to here was issued in April 1977 by James Callaghan's Labour government. Titled 'British Nationality Law: A Discussion of Possible Changes', it was followed in 1980 by a Conservative government White Paper (under Margaret Thatcher) which closely followed the Labour proposals. This became the British Nationality Act of 1981, which came into force on 1 January, 1983. Both parties were in agreement on the new law. See also 'The Green Paper on Nationality: An End to Black Civil Rights' (*Speak Out*, no. 2), pp. 86–8 in this collection.

Commonwealth citizens are entitled to register if they have been resident in Britain for more than five years. Any work permit issued under the present White Paper is for four years, after which application can be made for an extension. In this way, people can work in Britain, pay taxes and never gain full citizenship rights. Register now, if you have not done so already.

For more information contact: The Joint Council for the Welfare of Immigrants, Theobald's Road, WC1 or – The Black Women's Group, 41 Stockwell Green, SW9.

MEMORIES OF OLIVE:
A VERY STRONG
AND FEARLESS
BLACK SISTER

Brixton Black Women's Group
First published in Speak Out, *no. 3, c. 1980, pp. 9–10*

Her fight, to the end, was symptomatic of her whole life, which
had always been a total dedication to the struggles for liberation,
democracy and socialism of all oppressed and exploited people
throughout the world.

Sister Olive's short life was in many ways similar to that of
many West Indian women living in Britain today. She came to
this country at the age of eight to live with her parents.[1] Like
many of us, she was sent to a secondary modern school, where
she experienced all the inequalities and hostilities that are so
rampant in the British education system.[2] Olive left without any
qualifications. But even at this early stage she was able to resist

---

1 *Editor's note:* Born in Harewood (St Catherine parish, Jamaica) on
26 June 1952, Olive Elaine Morris was nine when she arrived in London in
1962. She and her family lived at 7 Milford Street, Lavender Hill, London
SW8 (the street has since been demolished) – see E. Allotey, 'Morris, Olive
Elaine (1952–1979)', *Oxford Dictionary of National Biography*, 24 May
2012, oxforddnb.com.

2 *Editor's note:* Morris attended Heathbrook Primary School and
then Lavender Hill Girls' Secondary School, followed by Dick Sheppard
Secondary School for Girls in Tulse Hill – see 'Olive Morris, Jamaica',
boroughphotos.org.

the repressive forces she encountered, and when she left school she went to college to study for her 'O' and 'A' levels whilst doing a full-time job.[3]

It was during this phase of her life, when only 17 years old, that Olive carried out her first political action, which was to lead her into organised political activity for the rest of her life. This action was in 1969, when she went to the aid of a Nigerian diplomat who was being harassed by the Brixton police for having the cheek to drive a Mercedes car.[4] She herself was arrested and brutally assaulted. This incident did not dampen her fighting spirits – rather, it strengthened her opposition to injustices, manifested by racism in general and by police brutality in particular.

It was this incident, coupled with her early awareness of racism in all its forms, that led her to join the Black Panther Movement. This movement had a forceful voice in the Black communities in London, expressing their anger and demands for equality and justice.[5] It was here that Olive began to develop a political ideology

3   *Editor's note:* Morris studied at the London College of Printing.

4   *Editor's note:* According to the police, Clement Gomwalk (the diplomat in question) was arrested on Atlantic Road, Brixton, due to a parking offence – for more on the arrest and its aftermath, see chapter 5, 'The Black Elite's Experience', in Derek Humphry, *Police Power and Black People* (London: Panther, 1972). In addition to being arrested, brutally assaulted and racially abused, Morris was fined £10 and given a three-month suspended sentence for two years over charges comprising assault on the police, threatening behaviour, and possession of dangerous weapons. For reflections on Morris's erasure from accounts of Gomwalk's arrest (and on how Morris's archival traces might be engaged), see Oumou Longley, 'Olive and Me in the Archive: A Black British Woman in an Archival Space', *Feminist Review* 129, no. 1 (2021), 123–37; and Tanisha C. Ford, *Liberated Threads: Black Women, Style, and the Global Politics of Soul* (Chapel Hill: University of North Carolina Press, 2015).

5   *Editor's note:* The British Black Panthers had a base in Brixton, in a house at 38 Shakespeare Road. Morris joined their Youth Section and Sisters' Collective – see A. Colin et al., eds, *Do You Remember Olive Morris?* (London: Gasworks and Remembering Olive Collective, 2009). For more on the British Black Panthers, see A.-M. Angelo, 'The Black Panthers in London, 1967–1972: A Diasporic Struggle Navigates the Black Atlantic', *Radical History Review* 103 (2009), 17–35; R. E. Bunce and P. Field, 'Obi B. Egbuna, C. L. R. James and the Birth of Black Power in Britain: Black Radicalism in Britain 1967–72', *Twentieth Century British*

which was to help direct her future political actions. During the organisation's existence, Sister Olive gave total commitment to its work and development.

Olive was always aware of the needs of her people, and always took the initiative to act. This was certainly the case with the squatting movement in Brixton. She helped many like herself, who were forced to squat because they had nowhere to live. She was well known in the community for her willingness to assist people who were facing difficulties with schools, the police, housing, social security officials – you name it, Olive was never too busy.[6] For Olive, it was not simply 'doing things' for those who could not do it for themselves, it was her way of getting people involved in the struggle, showing by example the will to resist and to challenge.

After the decline of the Black Panther Movement, Olive worked with a few Brothers and Sisters to set up Sabarr Bookshop, the first Black self-help community bookshop in Lambeth. During this same period, she, with other sisters, formed the Brixton Black Women's Group (BWG).[7] This was a significant development

---

History 22, no. 3 (2011), 391–414; R. D. Kelley and S. Tuck, eds, *The Other Special Relationship: Race, Rights, and Riots in Britain and the United States* (New York: Palgrave Macmillan, 2015); J. Narayan, 'British Black Power: The Anti-imperialism of Political Blackness and the Problem of Nativist Socialism, *Sociological Review* 67, no. 5 (2019), 945–67; and Rob Waters, *Thinking Black: Britain, 1964–1985* (Oakland: University of California Press, 2019).

6 *Editor's note:* See Faye Harrison's accounts of squatting with Morris at 116 Dalberg Road and then at 60 Railton Road between 1974 and 1975, 'Remembering Olive Morris, Black British Activist', *knowledge-4empowerment* (blog), 21 August 2011, knowledge4empowerment.com.

7 *Editor's note:* In 1973, Morris and Liz Obi squatted a disused launderette – the former Sunlight Laundry – at 121 Railton Road. It was the first successful squatting of a private property in Lambeth (squatters usually occupied empty council housing rather than privately owned properties, as private landlords were notorious for organising swift and often violent and illegal evictions). In the face of growing police pressure and a number of attempted evictions, that same year Morris and Obi left 121 Railton Road and squatted a council property nearby, at number 65 Railton Road. Some time after Morris and Obi moved out of 121 Railton Road, Morris helped a group of men and women from the British Black Panthers and the Black United Freedom Party to re-squat the building – see

in the Black Movement. As women, we had firstly to raise our consciousness and that of other Black women by genuine involvement in the struggle against racism, sexism and class oppression.

Olive's contribution to the BWG was far-reaching on several levels. She helped the group in developing a coherent political ideology that clearly linked our struggles with the fight against Imperialism. With this understanding, we were able to form meaningful links with sisters from many Third World countries. Practically, Olive worked relentlessly to translate our ideas into positive action. This, our third issue of *Speak Out*, will be the first that will not carry the imprint of her tireless efforts. She also helped many sisters in their own personal and political development inside of the BWG.

Because of Olive's understanding of the ways in which capitalism works to destroy the individual, she was able to communicate with all the various groups which make up our communities, hence most of her political work was done at the level of the grassroots.

In 1975, Olive went to Manchester University to study for a social science degree.[8] This was an important step for Olive, who believed in education for the people. For her, going to university

---

Tracy Fisher, *What's Left of Blackness: Feminisms, Transracial Solidarities, and the Politics of Belonging in Britain* (New York: Palgrave Macmillan, 2012). This group included several members of the 'women's reading group' which would, over time, become the Brixton Black Women's Group (see 'Writing Our Own History: Talking Personal, Talking Political', pp. 321–37 in this collection). At 121 Railton Road, the new squatters opened Sabarr, 'the bookshop that turned into a movement' (Fisher, *What's Left of Blackness*, p. 83). In addition to being a bookshop, Sabarr served as a meeting place and advice centre for local Black people involved in political organising. The women's reading group (of which Morris was part) met at 121 Railton Road (an ad for the bookshop in the second issue of *Speak Out* noted that the 'Black women's group meets every Sunday 3–5 pm'). It was during this period, while meeting at Sabarr, that the reading group became a campaigning Black socialist feminist organisation. In 2016, a 1973 photograph of Morris at 121 Railton Road taken by Neil Kenlock was acquired by the National Portrait Gallery – it can be viewed at npg.org.uk.

8   *Editor's note:* As documents collected by the Remembering Olive Collective show, Morris studied for a BA in Economic and Social Studies.

was not a status symbol, but an example to many young Black people of how to fight and win against a system that tries to push us all to the bottom of the education pile, and to set one person against another.

Unlike many students, Olive did not separate her work at the university from that of the struggles that were being waged in the rest of that community. This was manifested in her work with the Manchester Black Women's Co-op, the Black Women's Mutual Aid, which she helped to form, and with the National Co-ordinating Committee of Overseas Students.[9] By being in Manchester, she provided the link between the London-based groups and those in that area.

It was also at this stage that Olive visited China. This visit was of great significance for her, because she saw China as one country that those of us who came from countries in the Caribbean, Africa and Asia could learn a lot from and use as a model in self-help and self-reliance. The lessons she learnt there she

---

9   Editor's note: See D. Watt and A. D. Jones, *Catching Hell and Doing Well: Black Women in the UK – The Abasindi Cooperative* (London: Institute of Education Press, 2015).

imparted to us on her return. This was always her practice – the sharing of knowledge.[10]

Olive has always identified the relationship between the struggles of all oppressed Third World peoples with that of the white working class against domination. This was a fight that had to be won before we could begin to work for justice and equality in any meaningful way. This awareness was one of Sister Olive's greatest contributions to the political development of those with whom she worked.

Olive's life was similar to many of ours, but in many ways she was very unique, as was testified to by so many at her memorial ceremony in July 1979.[11] In this uniqueness lie the lessons of her life. She had tremendous determination that stayed with her to the end. It was this determination that brought her to the forefront of many a fight against the system. She had a clear sense of what she saw as politically correct – basically no attack by the agents of the state on the poor should go unchallenged. For her, the fight that Black people had to wage in this country was part of the struggle that had to be waged by all working people. Every action, every incident had to be viewed in that light.

She fought selflessly against state oppression and state harassment, but it was not only that that gave her her special qualities, or rather her willingness to undertake leadership tasks in initiating and creating and carrying forward particular ideas. She could not

---

10   *Editor's note:* In 1978, Morris co-founded the Organisation of Women of Asian and African Descent (OWAAD). Upon graduating from university that same year, Morris returned to Brixton and worked in the Juvenile Unit of the Brixton Community Law Centre, where she was involved in the campaign to scrap the 'sus laws'. During this time, she lived in a squat at 2 Talma Road, Brixton.

11   *Editor's note:* Morris fell ill during a trip to Spain in 1978. On her return to London, she was diagnosed with non-Hodgkin's lymphoma. She died on 12 July 1979 at St Thomas's Hospital, Lambeth, and was buried in Streatham Vale Cemetery. At the time of her death, Morris was living at Flat 2, 182 Clapham Park Road, SW4 (a council flat). To mark the one-year anniversary of her death, the Brixton Black Women's Group held an evening in remembrance of her on Sunday 13 July 1980 at the Abeng Centre in Brixton (a centre she had been involved in establishing). See the Remembering Olive Collection in Lambeth Archives for more.

sit on the fence and shout empty slogans at injustices. Because of this, Olive achieved what we would all like to achieve, and that was the unity of theory and practice. She shared with us the vision of a society free from racism, sexism and the exploitation of man by man. Had she lived, we know she would have continued to participate in making that vision a reality. She leaves with us the inspiration to resist.[12]

OLIVE LIVES AND THE STRUGGLE CONTINUES!

12   *Editor's note:* Much of the now publicly available information on Morris was gathered by the Remembering Olive Collective (ROC), co-founded by Morris's friend and fellow squatter Liz Obi in 2008. For more information, see the original Remembering Olive Collective's website as well as the website of the second iteration of the collective, ROC 2.0, at rememberolivemorris.wordpress.com and olivemorris.org, respectively. See also the book published by the ROC – A. Colin et al., *Do You Remember Olive Morris?*, and Tanisha C. Ford, 'Finding Olive Morris in the Archive: Reflections on the Remembering Olive Collective and Community History', *Black Scholar* 46, no. 2 (2016), 5–18.

REVIEW

Brixton Black Women's Group
First published in Speak Out, *no. 3, c. 1980, p. 13*

For Colored Girls Who Have Considered Suicide /
When the Rainbow Is Enuf
Playwright: Ntozake Shange

The play was about black women, written by a black woman, but failed to reach black audiences. One of the reasons for this was that it was staged in a posh West End theatre and, naturally, with a forbidding price tag. So, white middle-class people (all dressed up for a night 'at the theatre'), saw it instead. And of course, it lost its political potential.

The play was a set of choreopoems set brilliantly to music and dance. It spoke mainly about black male violence meted out to black women in the streets and in our homes. The violence that we suffer at the hands of white society, somehow, never quite came through.

So, the main thrust was that white and black women face the same violence from all men, but the culprit of the black woman's domestic violence is the black man. And, precisely because white racism was not adequately dealt with, the response from the audience was of cutting laughter at the banal black man, the unsophisticated crude beast, arousing the laughter of middle class women. For them it simply reinforced the idea that it is the working-class 'black beast' who slugs his women.

Such a bold and generalised analysis about the oppressiveness of black men would at least merit looking at the black man in relation to the position that he holds in society, his experience being qualitatively different from that of any other oppressed group.

The play conveyed the value of women getting together independently of men to analyse their situation and to develop together. But because we are jointly oppressed by a white racist society, combined with the knowledge that black women's oppression does not stem primarily from black men, there is another area of struggle in which we need to come together to fight against our common enemy – White Racist Society.

For Coloured Girls … used the stereotyped female niceties. All seven actresses looked slick: shaven legs, tight dresses and all, and their perpetual sexy tilts of the skirts actually helped in giving a 'titillating effect', rather than the horror of the violence spoken of and well enacted.

The white audience it reached must have loved it so.

Nonetheless, the play was beautifully enacted, the words powerful and the music and dance superb.

POEM

Brixton Black Women's Group
First published in Speak Out, *no. 3, c. 1980, p. 14*

Who are you
What are you doing
Where do you come from
But Black Women
What shall you become?
I'm a woman
I'm an immigrant
I am guilty
I am she to who they say
'Your papers'
The abortion law says: Don't get an abortion!
They say to me – respect the laws!
They say to me: Shut up!
They say to me: No jobs for you!
They say to me: Go back to your country
To my country!
Military Africa
African children murdered.
Prisoners of Africa.
Starvation in Africa but whose,
Cocoa, cotton, coffee, peanuts, oil,
Uranium and aluminium make the french wealthy.
To my country?
The West Indies of hotels and holiday clubs,
of sand and markets of many colours.
The West Indies from where we export full planes.
West Indies where the french come for their relaxation.
Exploited in your country.
Put in slavery in france.
Prostituted by your family.
Renounced by your husband.
Black women, you must protest.
Black woman, we must fight together.

REVIEW

Brixton Black Women's Group
First published in Speak Out, *no. 3, c. 1980, p. 15*

*White Hero, Black Beast – Racism, Sexism
and the Mask of Masculinity*
by Paul Hoch
published by Pluto Press (1979)

So much sweat and tears have gone into the writings of politics on racism, and in feminist politics on sexism. But rarely have the two been combined to form a cohesive whole, grounded in the same analysis. And rarer, still, is the fact that it is a white male, firmly on the side of the liberationists, who has done so in this compelling book.

We saw the movements of the 1960s firmly identifying the oppressors – the white racists and the male chauvinists. Since then, the myths about white cultural superiority, and likewise of male superiority, are being steadily blown. But though this is an essential starting point, it is only the first step. For if the analysis stops here, the implications are that a white person is naturally racist, and, similarly, a man is necessarily sexist, lending itself to conservative theories of 'biological determinism' – a belief that people are impelled not so much by the ideas that exist in their environment but because they are biologically and psychologically different. Thus, Jensen and Eysenck's contention that black people are intellectually inferior to whites, and various others who maintain similar arguments about women in relation to men, are an example this.[1]

---

1 *Editor's note:* Arthur Robert Jensen and Hans Eysenck.

Race, Class, Sex

This is a serious trap which some feminists and black nationalists often find themselves in. It is important Hoch thinks to place the emergence of these ideas into a specific historical context. Then we can cite the reasoning behind why, at that particular moment in time, it was useful to spread these ideas, and also in working out who benefited most from them.

In supporting this method, he goes further to say that, in order to eliminate all oppression, 'one has to destroy its social roots, and to do this one has to have at least some idea of the precise processes, interests, fears, repressions and institutional structures which create chauvinists (or racists)'.

This 'historical materialist' approach is useful in understanding the lack of revolutionary noises in the United States since the 1960s. For Liberationist struggles to get misdirected into an attack only on 'chauvinistic ideas rather than against concrete social institutions which have produced them' can be fatal. The strongest advocates and sole beneficiaries of such misdirected movements are upper middle-class white women (or blacks), who are not interested to go all the way in overthrowing oppressive institutions but to carve out a space for themselves. What is most interesting about this work is that Hoch manages to combine the 'historical materialism' in Marx's 'Political Economy' with Freud on sexuality, instead of viewing them as two opposing poles.

His main argument is that a study of 'masculinity' in the West has to be a study of 'White masculinity'. There is a close inter-relation between the (white) Western concept of manhood and racial domination. The pinnacle of 'manhood' is the white hero (John Wayne, J. Edgar Hoover, ...) who achieves his manhood by, firstly, winning victory over the black beast. The black beast is to be found prowling around, both at home and 'out there' in the jungles of Asia, Africa, the Caribbean and Latin America. The popular media shows with great vigour the triumphs of clever

or Powerful over powerless ...

cowboys over 'dumb' Indian, hero over 'dark' villain, civilization (of course, white civilization) over underdevelopment.

Then, within this system of white masculinity, one finds class variations such as the masculinity of the leisure classes, tending to be of the 'playboy' variety, whilst the masculinity of the lower classes is expressed in 'puritan' ideas. Again, Hoch analyses all these in detail, historically. So, we see that masculinity has social class dimensions which are all related to conceptions of nationhood, race and political ideology – and all these have psychological dimensions, too.

Sexual repression is seen as part and parcel of all authoritarian structures, such as the family, school, workplace, organisations, etc., which, in turn, are important structures in a political economy. For ever since class societies emerged some four thousand years ago, these and other oppressive social structures were built on them, and with them came sexual oppression.

Hence, all ruling classes have presented themselves as either 'divine' or of superior intellects who subjugated not only masses

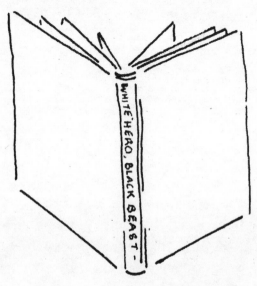

of lower classes, but 'savages', 'heathens' or 'barbarians'. And for this to have taken place, the white man has had to be sexually repressed. Sexual energy and aggression (Freud) are externalised and directed towards the enemies of 'Black Beast' and 'White Witch'. Both were thought to be hyper-sexed, so the super stud, (ever ready to destroy his 'white goddess') and the hot slut deserved to be extinguished. This was expressed in witch hunts and black lynching.

It is not only that Hoch manages to explain these complicated ideas, but he does so in a jargon-free style. Highly recommended reading.

REVIEW

Brixton Black Women's Group
First published in Speak Out, *no. 3, c. 1980, pp. 16–17*

Black Macho and the Myth of the Superwoman
by Michele Wallace

Michele Wallace's *Black Macho and the Myth of the Superwoman* is concerned with the history of Black Americans, and, although we realise that Black American history is not identical to ours, either in the Caribbean or in Britain, we regard it as important.[1]

This book is a rare example of a Black woman trying to give some insight into the social make-up of Black people, something which has often in the past been done for us – particularly by white men. Unfortunately, the book is at best disappointing, and at worst irritating. White people will be only too happy to use it as a measure of Black opinion. Ms Wallace's book is divided into two parts. The first, 'Black Macho', discusses the Black movement of the 'sixties', focusing on some of the 'leaders' like Stokely Carmichael, Martin Luther King and Eldridge Cleaver. The second, 'The Myth of the Superwoman', questions Black women in Black American struggles. Both topics are approached in terms of the sexual preferences of Black men and women – but without references to our history or our position in the economic system. The brunt of her argument is that, since the days of slavery, there has been a 'profound mistrust, if not hatred, between Black men and women that has been nursed along largely by white racism,

---

1 *Editor's note:* Originally published in 1979, Wallace's *Black Macho and the Myth of the Superwoman* was republished by Verso in 2015.

but also by an almost deliberate ignorance on the part of Blacks about the sexual politics of their experience'. And THIS explains their oppression. She correctly criticises the Moynihan Report for drawing similar conclusions to herself, for she, too, 'takes the responsibility off white shoulders – where it belongs – and places it on Blacks themselves!'[2] The suggestion is that Black men stop feeling emasculated and stop blaming Black women for their feelings of inadequacy, and if Black women stop contributing to those feelings of inadequacy and feeling guilty about it, then oppression would stop.

But perhaps such a sensationalised misinterpretation is only to be expected. The book is backed by the glossy magazine *MS*, which, despite its title, is questionably feminist and caters for a white middle class audience. Moreover, just as Ms Wallace is quick to point out Angela Davis' background, she, too, 'throughout her life has always been unmistakeably removed from the struggles of her people by education, money, and opportunities'.

Blackness comes to Harlem

She opens with a description of her early school days in the private New Lincoln School, with a mere twenty-five per cent Black children, most of whom were middle class and saw themselves as coloured. Despite her protestations that she 'did not have a solid and powerful middle-class establishment to rebel against – only an establishment of poverty thinly veiled by a few trips to Europe, a private school education, and some clothes from Bonwit Teller', it is clear that Ms Wallace is unable to identify with Black struggles at the ghetto level. She could only follow the Civil Rights and Black Power Movement through 'regular news coverage'!

---

2 *Editor's note:* Published in 1965 by the United States Department of Labor's Office of Policy Planning and Research, Daniel Patrick Moynihan's *The Negro Family: The Case for National Action* is commonly known as the Moynihan Report. For more, see Hortense Spillers, 'Mama's Baby, Papa's Maybe: An American Grammar Book', *Diacritics* 17, no. (1987), 64–81, and R. A. Ferguson, *Aberrations in Black: Toward a Queer of Color Critique* (Minneapolis: University of Minnesota Press, 2003).

Are Black women to blame?

Nevertheless, she feels confident enough to 'explain' why the Black movement of the sixties failed. She suggests it was not the result of the repressiveness of the American State, but because it was dominated by 'Black Macho' leaders – male chauvinist[s] who [were] frequently cruel, narcissistic, and short-sighted'. According to Ms Wallace, Black men and white America saw Black politics in sexual terms alone. White America, in other words, [...][3] of the Black movement stemmed from an age-long fear that the super sexual 'Black Macho' men would escape front the ghetto and gain access to his most prized possession – the white woman. White America, in other words, saw Black power as equal to sexual authority, personified by Stokely Carmichael, as 'an erect phallus ... pushing it up in America's face'. He was sexual, virile, strong, tough and dangerous. Meanwhile, since Black men inter-nalised the 'Black Macho' self-image presented to them by white America, they allowed it to foreshadow any political demands, then abandoned everything – all the traditional goals of revo-lution, money, security, the overthrow of government – in the pursuit of an immediate sense of their own power. The clarion call was for 'Black manhood', and this, Ms Wallace suggests, was why the movement failed. And the Black woman, because she, too, had absorbed an image of herself put out by white America as the achiever, and stood by and watched it happen: she was a 'Superwoman'.

---

3   *Editor's note:* Original text illegible.

Superwomen or just black women

According to Wallace, Black American women are 'Superwomen'.
They have 'inordinate strength, with an ability for tolerating
an unusual amount of misery and heavy, distasteful work. This
woman does not have the same fears, weaknesses and insecurities
as other women, but believes herself to be and is, in fact, stronger
emotionally than most men. Less of a woman in that she is less
'feminine' and helpless, she is really *more* of a woman in that she
is the embodiment of Mother Earth, the quintessential mother
with infinite sexual, life-giving, and nurturing reserves'. She therefore feels superior to the Black men, but also feels guilty about it.

This constituted a contradiction for Black women – 'the Black
Movement seemed to guarantee ... secret dreams of being male-
dominated and supported women'. In other words, Black women
failed to see the Black movement as it really was and, in this way,
they contributed to their own oppression. But this is only part of
an historical pattern, says Michele Wallace.

Ms Wallace states that, during the times of slavery, Black
women colluded with white America to get Black men's penises
to 'shrivel up into their bellies'. We Black women, she argues, 'have
a hell of a history to live down. We had been rolling around in bed
with the slave master while the black man was having his penis
cut off; we had never been able to close our legs to a white man
nor deny our breasts to a white child; we had been too eagerly
loyal to our white male employer, taking the job he offered when
he would give none to our man, cleaning his house with love
and attention while our man was being lynched by white men
in white hoods. We had not allowed the black man to be a man
in his own house. We had criticized him interminably and questioned his masculinity. We had driven him to alcohol, to drugs,
to crime, to every bad thing he had ever done to harm himself
or his family because our eyes had not reflected his manhood'.
Clearly, Ms Wallace has no conception of the realities of slavery.
Black women were raped, not the seducers; they were slaves,
not employees; and they were fighters, not passive recipients –
remember Harriet Tubman and Sojourner Truth, to name but a
few documented examples.

And with this mis-analysis, Ms Wallace goes on to argue that, patronisingly enough, Black women can only be liberated by asserting themselves individually. They should not join Black women's organisations, which she declares like some hysterical white middle class man might do. She criticises Black women who have got together 'because they can't find husbands', they are 'angry with their boyfriends' or because they are 'lesbians ... looking for a public forum for their sexual preference'. No, Ms Wallace, you have taken your sexual politics too far.

Black women will continue to fight against racism and male domination. To do this we have to come together because in our UNITY lies OUR STRENGTH!

What Are They?

Disruptive Units

Brixton Black Women's Group
First published in Speak Out, *no. 3, c. 1980, pp. 17–18*

At a time when the operative words in any area of public spending seem to be 'cuts, cuts and more cuts', any growth industry should be viewed with suspicion; especially when we know that the Tories are only allowing increased spending for the army and police.

In education, there will always be many swipes to eliminate what few benefits our children already receive. Over the last few years, classes and schools have been closing steadily, and teachers regularly sacked. Now, with the advent of the Thatcher government, the attacks on our schools are becoming even more blatantly mean-spirited. School transport will be cut; school meals and milk scrapped; and resources all round will be greatly reduced, i.e. teachers and teaching materials. In fact, affirmed Tory policy will force local authorities to further reduce standards and services by whatever means possible.

It is within this context – that of the Tories accelerating the process of running down our schools – that we must look at the rise of disruptive units. While small schools have been closing, these centres have been growing steadily. Call them by any name you will – support centres, sin-bins, sanctuaries, etc. – you will find a burgeoning crop of advertisements in education supplements and teachers' magazines for jobs in these centres. Certainly, for local education authorities, they are the new 'growth industry'.

Despite the fact that cuts are being implemented in most other areas of state education, more and more money is being allocated to these units. In January 1979, figures showed that the Inner London Education Authority [ILEA] had reserved £1.6 million to be spent on the extension of off-site disruptive units. There are very few figures available for local areas, but the figures for Haringey show that over 90% of children sent to disruptive units are black children.

What, exactly are these units? Who goes to them, and why? According to ILEA, they are for children who, because of 'demonstrative behaviour towards people or property or the blatant abuse of the purpose of learning, have become known as disruptive pupils'.

In order to cope with these pupils, 'special units' with 'experienced teachers' and 'smaller groups' have been set up. The students are sent for a short stay to help them 'continue their education and be prepared for life beyond'. These may sound like soothing words, indeed, but on the authorities' own admission there is no increased bad behaviour in London schools to justify such centres – rather, the reverse is true. So, why have these units mushroomed so suddenly? Who are these children who find it so difficult to settle in school, and why? Are they bored, bright pupils? Are they frustrated, slow learners? Are they pupils whose personalities clash with that of one particular teacher?

The simple answer is that we do not know, because it seems that any and all kinds of justification can be used to refer a child to a unit. It can be done on the word of one teacher, social worker or headmistress. In most cases, the parents are not involved. In fact, they are not even informed, for although some units are off-site, the pupils are still kept on the school roll. When the parents are provided with information, referral to a unit is presented as an alternative to suspension. The authorities give no clear indication of the right to appeal, but merely say that parents should be made 'fully aware' of the situation.

Few people are fully aware of what goes on in the units. From our information, the range of curriculum subjects is very narrow, because there are only a few teachers offering their specialist subject. The emphasis is on remedial work, because it is accepted

What goes on in these units?

that 'disruptive pupils' are not very bright. They are in the units for reasons other than education.

This is the really worrying thing about the units. In many, there is great emphasis on behaviour modification. This, in fact, is inevitable. The thinking is that they have been referred because of their behaviour, therefore their behaviour must be changed. Scales of reward and punishment are used based on such factors as being given teacher attention, the use of praise, awarding of points and the giving of privileges such as tea and biscuits.

Remember, this is not just the natural social relationship which develops between teacher and student, but, rather, one which is carefully worked out on a scale, matching certain behaviour with certain rewards. It is really believed that some children need to be changed before they are re-admitted to the 'normal' schools. But are they ever returned?

There are no official figures on how many pupils are accepted back, but one can imagine some schools' resistance to the boy or girl returning from a disruptive unit. Hardly welcoming! Many of those who are not accepted back end up in maladjusted or special schools. So, consequently, the one-week to one-term stay in a unit can last two to three terms and even up to seven years.

This situation must give all parents real cause for concern. We in the Black Women's Group are particularly concerned because we know how this situation can be used by racist teachers against our own children – many of whom are being placed in disruptive units. In fact, there are real parallels with the ESN (educationally sub-normal) cases of a few years ago. At that time, there were the same very real parental fears, unanswered questions and evasive official definitions. At that time, our children were being dumped unfairly in these schools because of personality clashes with teachers, biased intelligence tests, cultural non-conformity, etc. Our whole community suffered at this complete denial of education rights.

However, with publicity like that from Bernard Coard's *How the West Indian Child is Made Educationally Sub-Normal in the British School System* (1971), we, as a community, responded militantly and the authorities backed down. ESN became a dirty word. Even so, our children have quietly been receiving 'special education' in make-shift classrooms when the schools cannot be bothered to tend to the real difficulties and problems. The disruptive unit push is merely an extension of this – a make-shift attempt to evade the issue. The end result is that it is our children who suffer. When we look at the practice of the units, it is clear that they serve no other purpose than that of occupying and attempting to control those children who pose any kind of threat to the school system. For this, they are deprived of the right to a decent education and the groundings in those skills that will equip them to fight and survive in a hostile society. At a time of rising black unemployment, what can be the prospects of many of our youth when their only reference is the disruptive unit?

There are, as we see it, real problems in schools that must be faced. These relate to such areas as repressive school structures, irrelevant curriculum, racist teachers, low teacher expectation, lack of resources, overcrowded classrooms and government attacks in the form of public expenditure cuts. This is where the problems lie – not with our children.

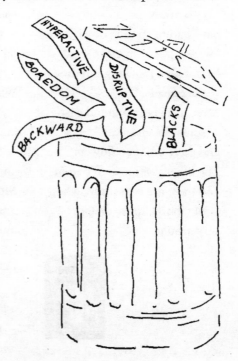

POEM

Brixton Black Women's Group
First published in Speak Out, *no. 3, c. 1980, p. 19*

PRISON VISIT

I haven't ever visited a prison
    before
and they say that's where you are
they are holding you for
    'possession of drugs'.
I've never talked non-stop for
    two hours
but I had to coming down here.
I expect it was my fear.
Its not a bad looking building on
    the outside.
Must have been a grand castle
    some time back.
and there are even flowers.
The other visitors aren't glum
and there are two sisters who
    obviously know their
way around.

What a gigantic door knocker!
The procession begins, 'careful
    mind you trip over'
there are one foot iron bars at
    the bottom of the
door. 'step up.'
I suppose this is so they can't run
    for it, they'd fall flat
on their face, and create some
    mess.
What? 'Oh, yes, his name is
    Thomas; no I don't
know his number; yes he is new.
    My name? er Jones,
and my address? OK'.
More waiting and I want to piss
    again 'do you
know if there is a toilet?
    – thanks'.
I feel sick, don't want to see him
    like that behind
a large glass window with wire
    meshing – caged
and me on the other side.

Oh God! what's he got to do
    with it? He's not on
our side anyway, he's tall and
    white with a big
moustache and a condescending
    smile, not really
interested to change anything
    (that's supposing he
could in the first place). It can't
    be behind the
wire meshing after all. Across a
    courtyard, up
three flight of cold concrete
    stairs, warders in
front – warders behind, they are
    locking us in, Its
becoming absurd almost
    theatrical.

More waiting, I'm tenth in the
    queue,
when are we going to see them,
    I'll sit on the stairs
and save my energy for later on –
    probably need it
especially if he is taking it badly.
Look at the bastard! bopping,
    smiling looking towards us

– 'Erol, you alright?' (prison
    uniform
but at least dem no beat im up).
'I'm quiet? yes its just this
    situation, you at the back
    of this table and us holding
    hands over it.'

'Errol, the point is you are here,
    you're asking me
to moralise, its not my law, I
    can't condemn you
along with them. While you're
    here I just have to
accept it, only I can see its going
    to be darned
difficult, I left the babies with
    Sylvia, she'll do it
this time, but next time I'll
    probably have to bring
them and the fare is so expensive,
    a whole four
pounds out of the little twenty
    pounds from my
cleaning job ... but we'll have to
    manage. I will
check out the solicitor, I hope
    you haven't signed any
statements. What, but the sign
    says visiting time is two hours,
    I'll look at the notice ... Yes,
    they're within their rights we
    are only really entitled to five
    minutes and the small print
    says they can refuse
that too.'

THE Brixton UPRISING

A REPORT BY THE BRIXTON BLACK WOMEN'S GROUP

Brixton Black Women's Group
First published in Spare Rib, *no. 107, June 1981, pp. 18–19*

On the weekend of April 11 and 12, events occurred in Brixton, in the South London Borough of Lambeth, which the state and the media immediately called 'a riot'. The events of this weekend were not orgies of mindless destruction – they were the result of police offensives in the area. It was a statement of resistance by the youths of Brixton to the increased pressure on the Black community by the police and the state.

> Every time they go off, my heart is in my mouth. My son, when he was 14, he went to meet his girlfriend at the bus stop. He jumped off the bus and was immediately arrested. Our experience is that, deep down, there is a fear. You expect to rely on the police, but when you can't trust them, the whole basis of the community is at risk.
>
> Black woman giving evidence to Report (see below).

Brixton suffers from chronic inner city social and economic deprivation; high unemployment, especially amongst Black youths; and a lack of recreational facilities. While this was the underlying reason for the uprising, the single issue that brought the battle to the streets was/is the racist and lawless policing practices against the Black citizens of Brixton. The uprising was a spontaneous reaction against these oppressive policing practices. The white citizens of Brixton joined in the uprising because they bore witness to this constant harassment and intimidation of their neighbours; and the white working class were themselves not immune from the brutality of the police. *The Final Report of the Working Party into Community/Police Relations in Lambeth* documents fully the grievances of the community.[1] They were told of the constant harassment by the police of members of youth clubs, both inside and outside the clubs: *'Police raided the youth club about 8pm ... Twenty to thirty police burst into the premises ... They saw a few Black youths who were part-time staff, they thought they were criminals. They burst in like commandos in Africa. They grabbed people by their hair and necks. We were helpless. The club leader and one of the part-time helpers burst into tears at the sight. The leader then approached them and said, 'Who is in charge of this group and what do you want?' They said that they were looking for somebody who cut one of them and they would not rest until they find him. They took away almost everybody from the club, in a most degrading fashion'.*

This incident is just one illustration of the attitude of the police to the youths of Brixton. These incidents cause friction in families, especially when parents, justifiably, become overprotective of their teenage children. *'The Working Party were told of Black mothers who locked up their teenage children at weekends and in the evenings for fear that they would be arrested, of mothers who rushed out and pulled their children indoors every time a police car passed. They were told of the tensions caused in the family as a result; tensions caused by constant fear of arrests for no reasons. There is no doubt that a contributory factor in family breakdowns in Lambeth is the behaviour of the police'.*

There was a time when older Black people, especially parents,

---

1 *Final Report of the Working Party into Community/Police Relations in Lambeth*, published by Public Relations Division, London Borough of Lambeth, and available from them for £4.50 (inc. p and p) at Public Relations Division, Room 19, Lambeth Town Hall, Brixton Hill, London SW2.

listened to their children's accounts of police harassment and brutality with caution. In recent years, this caution has been replaced
with bitterness as the evidence against the police has mounted.
Homes are broken into without warrants, turned upside down
and then abandoned. Young Black women are strip-searched for
any offence. Single parents are picked up with no provision made
for their children.

Tensions are injected into situations that are meant to be joyful.
One has only to look at the hysteria whipped up by member of
parliament Jill Knight against Black parties and social gather-
ings. The New Cross Massacre is but a single manifestation of
this.[2] Numerous other attacks have occurred but have not been
reported, nor given any pause for thought. The Black communities from Birmingham to Bristol, Southall, Notting Hill Gate and
Brixton do not treat these incidents with contempt, but seek to
draw lessons from them.

Attacks by the police are also attacks on the Black way of
life. They are attempts to enforce the dominant culture on Black
people. It is in our culture to gather in groups on the streets, a
culture that states that not all social interactions have to occur
within the confines of four walls. If you 'hang out' on the streets,
you are made aware that you can easily be arrested for loitering
with intent to commit a crime.

To be Black in Brixton means living under a state of siege,
which also affects the wider community. When Black people
look into the eyes of the police, they see naked arrogance, fear
and hatred.

If you are a Black woman in confrontation with the police, you
also have to contend with insinuations referring to Black sexuality.

---

2 *Editor's note:* For more on the New Cross Massacre, see Aaron
Andrews, 'Truth, Justice, and Expertise in 1980s Britain: The Cultural
Politics of the New Cross Massacre', *History Workshop Journal* 91, no. 1
(2021), 182–209. See also J. Bernard, *Surge* (London: Chatto & Windus,
2019); P. Fryer, *Staying Power: The History of Black People in Britain*
(London: Pluto, 2018 [1984]); P. Gilroy, *There Ain't No Black in the
Union Jack* (London: Routledge, 2002 [1987]); R. Ramdin, *The Making
of the Black Working Class in Britain* (London: Verso, 2017 [1987]); and
Rob Waters, *Thinking Black: Britain, 1964–1985* (Oakland: University
of California Press, 2019).

This instils within you the knowledge that the police are not there to protect, but to irritate and intimidate. This constant violence to the psyche of the Black community was the background to the further arrogance of the police in mounting their 'Swamp '81' in that crucial week.

The police believe it to be their duty to foster and manipulate a feeling of defensiveness from the community. Even the title 'Swamp '81' is an indication of the antagonistic nature of the police towards the community. The reasoning behind Swamp '81 was that the figure for crimes of violence in Lambeth is more than double the next highest figure in any other Metropolitan Police division. It has also been reported that young Blacks are overwhelmingly responsible for the rise in the crime rate. A crucial aspect has, however, been overlooked. The same top-secret police report which made these findings also recorded that only 4% of Black youths in Lambeth commit street crimes. In spite of this, the police, in their pursuit of Black criminals, put all young Blacks under intensive policing in a manner that is absent when investigating crimes committed by young whites.

In the first ten days of April 1981, 1,000 young people, mainly Black, were stopped, searched and questioned. Some 150 were arrested, and the remaining 850 were sent on their way with a deep sense of resentment.

Home Office figures indicate that, between 1976 and 1979, 'L' Division, which includes Brixton, had the highest number of arrests under the notorious 'Sus' laws than any other Metropolitan District outside the West End. 75% of those arrested were Black. Between 1975 and 1979, there were at least six Special Patrol Group operations in the Brixton area.

In October 1978, a Police Liaison Committee was established after representations from the local Lambeth Council for Community Relations. Four days later, without consultation with this committee, yet another SPG operation was launched. In February 1979, the CCRL offices themselves were raided and three Black workers arrested. In protest, the CCRL withdrew from the Police Liaison Committee. Demands for an inquiry into police community relations were taken up by Lambeth Council. The 18-month-long inquiry concluded that the police were effectively an 'army of occupation'.

Swamp '81 was the brainchild of the senior detective based in Brixton, and was carefully designed to try to combine the intensity of an SPG-style operation with the experience of a local one. No outsiders were used. Instead, 150 normally uniformed local officers, all with knowledge and experience of the sensitive Railton Road area, were put in plain clothes and deployed for the week. The inspector in charge of the operation described it as a 'resounding success'. The very next day, Saturday 11th, the uprising took place.

Since that weekend, the Black community has organised itself to ensure adequate representation for the 286 known arrested.[3] The Legal Defence Committee has been established and has drawn up a shortlist of lawyers committed to getting the best for their clients, adding their voice to the protests surrounding events such as Southall, Bristol, New Cross, and now Brixton.

As well as collecting information about people who suffered injuries at the hands of the police, the Legal Defence Committee is also investigating the provocative behaviour of the police during and after the weekend of the uprising. From this work, it

---

3   *Editor's note:* See 'Brixton Defence Campaign' (*Speak Out*, no. 4), pp. 241–2 in this collection.

emerges that those injured during the disturbances also had to face hostility from doctors and hospital staff.

Using the resources of the Black community, we've rejected attempts by the state to distort events of the weekend and to further oppress Black people in this country through the law. Why does the state now deem it necessary to have an inquiry set up under Lord Chief Justice Scarman? Five months before the uprising, our report (Final Report of the Working Party into Community/Police Relations in Lambeth, 1980) clearly stated what was coming: *'The police have got worse ... retaliation must come as this is too much'*.

SPEAK OUT

no.4   30p

Black Women's Group Brixton

EDITORIAL

BLACK FEMINISM

Brixton Black Women's Group
First published in Speak Out, *no. 4, July 1982, pp. 1–5[1]*

Feminism is the theory underlying the struggle against the systematic oppression of women based on sex. When we speak of the 'systematic oppression of women', we refer to the many factors which contribute to the oppression of women and maintain and reproduce our subordinate position. These can broadly be divided into the following categories: ideological–cultural, economic and political.

ideological–cultural oppression

Ideology is a system of values and beliefs. Within each society is a dominant ideology, which is linked to the economic and political organisation of that particular society. It acts by moulding people's consciousness so as to reproduce that particular way of life. In a highly oppressive system, such as the capitalist system in which we live, the dominant ideology attempts to make people accept exploitation, and it is successful insofar as it can make the

1   *Editor's note:* Republished in H. Kanter, S. Lefanu, S. Shah, and C. Spedding, eds, *Sweeping Statements: Writing from the Women's Liberation Movement 1981–83* (London: Women's Press, 1984).

oppressive power relations seem 'natural'. People, on the other hand, cannot be fooled by lies so easily, and there is a continual process of struggle between the dominant ideology and people's resistance to it.

Children are born male or female (determined by biology), but women and men are prepared for their different biological and social functions by the process of socialisation, which is determined by the dominant ideology. The meaning of 'woman' and 'man' in social terms is what we call gender. The female is conditioned into passivity, submission and emotional dependence, and the male into self-assertiveness, dominance and independence in the process of socialisation. As women, our consciousness is formed in the conditions of subordination and oppression. Therefore, gender, for us, means division, inequality and internalised inferiority.

The family, or, to be more precise, the ideology surrounding the family, is an important site of women's oppression. Through the family, our roles as men and women are clearly set out. We are taught how to think and *be* women and men. It is also within this concept of the family that various themes that influence our idea of gender are supposed to be fully expressed. These include such things as romantic love, feminine nurturance, maternalism and self-sacrifice for women; together with masculine protection and financial support. What this means in practice is that women are primarily responsible for all the tasks connected with housework and childcare.

A woman has to service the male, has responsibility for three categories of people – children, the sick and disabled, and the elderly – and also has to look after herself. Moreover, performing this role either excludes her from earning a living or negatively affects the terms on which she does so. Both mean she has to be financially dependent upon a man.

Therefore, within the household, there is not only a division of labour (women and men performing different tasks), but also the relationship between the woman and man is such that the woman is systematically dependent upon and unequal to the man. This ideology of the family has far-reaching effects on the position of women in all aspects of life.

economic oppression

In the present-day economic system, based as it is on wage labour, women's severe disadvantage in, if not total exclusion from, the labour market is another important area of our oppression.

In earlier periods, during the pre-capitalist feudal times, the whole household as a unit was engaged in productive labour. The development of wage labour, with the production of goods for the market rather than for use, meant that household needs had to be met by incoming wages rather than by internal production. The development of capitalism also brought with it the separation between home and workplace, which created a crisis over the daily care of children, the disabled and the elderly. This has, as we know, customarily been resolved by giving these responsibilities to women, thus cutting them off from equal participation with men in wage labour. This has been accompanied by the establishment of the privatised domestic area of 'the home' as the particular province of women, and of 'femininity' and maternalism as characteristic of women. Women have become dependent upon the male wage in capitalism, and this is accompanied by an ideology of emotional and psychological dependence.

These ideological processes are, however, not in keeping with hard economic reality, which forces most working-class women to take up employment outside the home – just to make ends meet. So, family ideology doesn't actually keep women within the home, but it does influence the nature of women's participation in employment and ensures that women do a second, unpaid job within the home.

The division of labour in present-day capitalism involves a sharp separation between male and female workers. Women are concentrated in particular industries at particular levels, and are systematically subjected to poorer pay and working conditions than men. Despite the equal pay legislation, figures for 1978 show that weekly earnings of women comprise only 64.8 per cent of those of men. Low pay is not the only thing that characterises female wage labour. Job security and wages for part-time work are greatly disadvantaged when compared to full-time work. Yet 41 per cent of all women with jobs in Britain work part-time.

Homework on piece-rate contracts (highly exploitative) is also mainly undertaken by women because of their domestic and childcare responsibilities.

Women workers are more vulnerable to redundancy in times of recession. Since 1974, redundancy among women workers has been three times higher than the rate for men. Low representation of women, in senior grades and in the 'higher professions' in general, reflects the systematic discrimination that women suffer in education and training.

In general, within a particular trade, industry or profession, women occupy jobs which are lower paid, more insecure and less likely to bring promotion than men. Furthermore, women are concentrated in certain low-paid industries. Over 60 per cent of the entire female workforce is concentrated in only ten occupations: clerical work, shop assistants, typists and secretaries, maids, cleaners, nurses, teachers, canteen assistants, shop managers, and sewing and textile workers. Looking at this list, a clear picture emerges. Most of these jobs can broadly be described as service work, the 'caring' professions and socialised forms of domestic service. In other words, the distribution of women in the employed workforce bears a striking resemblance to the division of labour in the family.

Division of labour, not only between men and women but also with regard to children and old people, probably pre-dates capitalism and is not necessarily divisive if the various tasks hold equal status. However, capitalism not only caused the takeover and strengthening of the differentiation of tasks, but divided the workforce itself into wage-earners and those dependent upon the wage of others. Capitalism did not create domestic labour, but it did create a set of social relations in which pre-existing sexual divisions were not only reproduced but solidified within the wage labour system.

It can be seen how family relations and the ideology omesticc responsibility play a large part in determining the position of women as wage labourers. As outlined earlier, responsibility for childcare forces women to be involved in the highly exploitative areas of part-time work and home. Women are channelled into categories of work such as servicing and caring, which have been established as predominantly 'feminine'. Also, the construction of a family form in which the male head of the household is supposedly responsible for the financial support of a dependent wife and children has acted against demands for equal pay and an equal right to work for women.

The fact that women happen to be the sole breadwinners in many cases, especially within the black community, still doesn't allow them to escape all the restrictions that operate within the area of women's employment. The ideology of the family also extends to family structures other than the nuclear type. For example, even in the extended family, it is the women who shoulder the responsibility for childcare and domestic work, and so get excluded from equal participation with men in wage labour.

the state and women's oppression

The state plays an important role in legitimising the various dimensions of women's oppression in this society. It actively maintains the household system, where women and children are supposedly dependent upon a male breadwinner's 'family wage'. Provisions such as the 'married man's tax allowance' and arrangements for national insurance payments are reflections of a woman's financial dependence upon a man within marriage. This same principle, extended to cohabiting couples, results in the disgusting practice of social security officials attempting to ascertain a woman's sexual relations with men with a view to depriving her of the right to benefits. Thus, the state very firmly upholds the principle of woman's dependence, in spite of the fact that the number of households fitting the stereotype of the male breadwinner/full-time dependent housewife is, at any given time, very small.

In the area of employment, the state regulates terms and conditions of employment in order to reinforce women's subordination, e.g. the banning of women from certain work (such as mining) and withholding maternity benefits from unmarried women. State provision and regulation of education clearly plays an important part in structuring the different opportunities open to women and men.

The state also creates conditions within which racism and sexism are reinforced and legitimised. For example, the Nationality Act, virginity tests and the administration of the contraceptive drug Depo-Provera are all measures that are particularly oppressive to black women. Another clear example is the recent change in the immigration law which prevents black women from bringing to Britain husbands who are foreign nationals. What this means is that, if you are a black woman, even full British citizenship does not give you the same privileges as those of either men merely settled here (who can bring their wives to settle), or EEC women who, even without British citizenship, can, under the Treaty of Rome, bring their husbands to settle in Britain. This law effectively makes us second-class citizens and constitutes yet another blatant breach of the European Convention on Human Rights, which denounces discrimination based on sex or race. Britain has been taken to the European Court of Human Rights on this issue, and the initial proceedings have found that Britain has a case to answer.

sexual harassment

In keeping with the state's oppression and subjugation of women, individual men – fathers, brothers, husbands, sons, comrades, friends and strangers – continue to exploit and humiliate women. In the family, where women are financially dependent on their men, we are treated as their property. As property, men feel that they can use and abuse women verbally and physically with impunity. We are frequently beaten, psychologically pressured and physically forced into having sex, and then often left to support the offspring of such encounters. On the streets, we are stared at, leered at, man-handled and raped at the point of a knife. Women, therefore, live a daily life of fear of violence from men, both inside and outside the home.

Our instilled fear of male violence then drives us to seek protection from other men (e.g. the police), giving them more power to control us. This control operates on two levels. First, on an individual basis, whereby women are confronted with individual police*men*, and are subjected to hostility, thinly disguised disbelief and mistrust, and an overall lack of support. One explicit example of this is police reluctance to intervene in cases of even the most brutal marital violence – respecting the privacy of 'the family' and upholding the idea that women are the property of men. In rape cases, the police are well known for subjecting the victim to an offensive and degrading inquisition in which her own sexual history is on trial.

Individual male violence becomes male social power and is legitimised by the state. This legitimised male social power and sexual aggression is used as a tool to control and intimidate women who dare to fight back. Thus, the law itself reinforces fundamental assumptions about gender division, and it is only very recently that women have been recognised as legal subjects within their own right.

The second aspect of this control has to do with the fact that the police force is an arm of the state. As such, it is another tool by which all black people are terrorised and oppressed. As black women, we are faced with the twin oppressions of implicitly condoned male violence because we are women, and explicit violence by the state because we are black.

The images that men have of our bodies are thrust upon us. We are evaluated as sex-symbols. Pornography and all types of advertising perpetuate sexist stereotypes of how we should look and behave: this is, in turn, reinforced by the mass media through films, television, newspapers and magazines. Based on the notion that women are the property of men, many women are further exploited through prostitution as a commodity to be bought and sold at will, the male pimp always hovering in the background to collect his supposed 'due'.

Sexual harassment, violence and the exploitation of women transcend class and race boundaries. Black and white men, regardless of their class position, align with each other on the basis of shared sexism. Black men, who are victimised by racism in the same way as black women, act as sexist oppressors of black women. This points to an underlying failure on their part to understand that, although sexism does transcend class barriers, it only acts in the interest of one class – the rulers. They fall for the myth of white society, which says that all black women are sexually 'loose' and treat us as such. They devalue our efforts to create a better life for ourselves, from which, as black people, we would all benefit.

As black women we are also blamed by the state for being in collusion with the black man to perpetuate our own oppression. Although this is *not* the case, we can appreciate what it means to be in a racist society where a black woman may think twice before she calls the police for violence done to her by a black man. However, as black women, our struggle is not about blaming the victim, but is a struggle against the system which has allowed men to see and treat us as mindless objects because of the fact that we are women.

black feminism and the black struggle

To be feminist, therefore, necessitates an understanding of these forces which are brought to bear to oppress us in many subtle and not always apparent ways. To be black and feminist adds a very different dimension to feminism and involves our coming to terms with the specific implications of such a position. One important consideration concerns the issue of black feminism as a cause of division within the black community.

There is a strongly held opinion that black feminism is an assault on the black family and, thus, the black community; and which further states that black women have always been sexually liberated. This argument has its foundations in slavery and is based on the so-called 'easy' life of those black women who were forced to 'service' their white masters sexually. Their condition has historically been projected as being closer to that of white women than black men. But the truth is that black women were the *most* victimised by this situation. We were raped, abused and beaten by the white masters and even by some male slaves who imitated them. We were bred like cattle. Mates were chosen; husbands and children taken away at the slave-master's command. Black women were assumed to be the sexual property of the owner, his friends, visitors and relatives. Is this what they would have us call sexual liberation???

216

The myth of matriarchy – with its image of the all-powerful black woman – has persistently plagued the black community and forms the basis for another argument against black feminism. The reasoning behind it contends that there is no need for black women to be feminists because the black woman has always wielded power in black society. Nothing could be further from the truth. Historically, the racism of the state has denied black people their right to employment, while the interaction of racism and sexism has facilitated the entry of black women into specific jobs only. This often means that the black woman is forced to assume responsibility as the breadwinner. However, the work she does is usually menial, with long hours and low pay; at the end of which she still has to care for her own family's needs. The effect of this is to create a twofold situation, calculated to produce hostilities within and thus undermine the black community; and at the same time provide a source of cheap labour for the state.

The black man, the argument goes, suffered because his position was demeaned in the eyes of the community – he was made to feel 'less of a man'. But it is the black woman who suffered most from the matriarchal myth. For not only was her labour exploited, but she had (and still has) to bear the accusations and fight against the charge that she emasculates the black man as a result of this situation. To make matters worse, some black men have seized upon this myth to blame all of their oppression on the supposedly 'domineering' black woman. We have always fought against this outrage, however, and will continue to strike out against the application of these insidious stereotypical labels to us. Furthermore, in waging the struggle, it is crucial for us to remember that the only real winners in the whole matriarchal myth/mess are the ruling classes – the state and its forces. The sooner we get rid of this issue as a bone of contention between black men and black women, the better able well be to concentrate our efforts against our common oppressor.

A further argument against black feminism says that for black women to speak out against sexist oppression causes division within the black community, because it takes time and energy away from the black struggle. We are told that the black woman should be squarely in her man's corner, but behind him. During the civil rights movement, a time when the talents and abilities of black men and women should have been jointly recognised in the struggle for black liberation, along came Stokely Carmichael declaring that the position of women in the movement should be 'prone'. Later, Eldridge Cleaver, a prominent member of the Black Panther Party, said that black women had 'pussy power'. We were expected to contribute to the movement but only in the way the black man said we could.

So black women were left in a kind of limbo – damned if we did and damned if we didn't. Our roles for the revolution were to be as coffee-makers, cooks, fundraisers and, of course, willing sexual partners, while the men conducted the important business of the struggle. We were not expected to open our mouths about the oppression we suffered as women at the hands of black men, who saw women's liberation (if they thought about it at all) strictly in terms of a minor side issue – 'a white girl's problem'. What they failed to recognise, however, was that the status of black women places us at the intersection of all forms of subjugation in society – racial oppression, sexual oppression and economic exploitation. This means that we are a natural part of many different struggles – both as black people and as women.

This brings us to another issue which we, as black women, must deal with – the question of *autonomy*. We must begin by distinguishing *autonomy* from *separatism*, as there is some confusion surrounding the two terms. An autonomous movement creates a favourable climate for understanding and evaluating the intricacies involved with the question of the liberation of a particular group; which, in turn, makes it possible to expand the whole political struggle. The black women's movement in Britain should, like those women who either belong to a women's movement or the arm of a party in Third World countries, form part of the total struggle for liberation. This is quite different from women who wish to create change for women in isolation from men. We see this evaluation of the changing position of women in post-revolutionary societies being grappled with by the women in these societies, with one striking example being Cuban women.

Black people, throughout history, have formed autonomous organisations, in the belief that it is those who are oppressed who are the best equipped to liberate themselves. No one else can do it for them. Given the nature of our oppression as black people and as women, this can be no less true for black women.

Having arrived at autonomy as a necessary option for black women raises the point of exactly what form it should take. There are two major and opposing views in the women's movement currently.

Radical feminism contends that the oppression of women is the major and primary oppression in all societies. Patriarchy is identified as a universal mode of power relationship and domination. Male domination and female subjugation, they argue, are achieved through (among other things) their construction of sexuality, masculine-feminine role models and the socialisation of children. Within this perspective, men are seen as dominant by training, and use force to maintain control of the economy, the state and a monopoly on sexual violence. Radical feminists identify patriarchy as being all-pervasive, penetrating class divisions and different societies, and as crossing cultures and historical periods. The logical outcome of identifying men as the sole enemy leads to total separation as the only solution.

The other viewpoint is *socialist feminism*, which we in the Brixton Black Women's Group hold. To us, it is clear that, while male domination goes back a long way, women's oppression today is inextricably linked with the whole system of class oppression, whereby a small group of the rich and powerful ruling class control, exploit and severely oppress the vast majority of the people, both men and women. To properly understand our situation we have to understand the roots of women's oppression both historically and cross-culturally. To achieve this, it is necessary to examine and analyse the interrelations and connections between the various factors which form the basis of women's subjugation, as discussed earlier. These areas have to be examined not in isolation, but in relation to the whole oppressive capitalist system. Likewise, the struggle for women's liberation has to be part of the concrete struggle against class oppression, for no form of liberation will be possible without the overthrow of the capitalist system.

In adopting this position, as black women we are strongly influenced by the knowledge that our countries of origin, the so-called 'Third World', having been actively underdeveloped by *colonialism* (a part of capitalism), are even now being raped and pillaged under the stranglehold of *imperialism* (yet another, and to us very relevant, aspect of capitalism). Thus, a few industrialised countries grow more and more wealthy and powerful at our expense, while our people die of starvation and our own countries fall ever deeper into dependence and poverty.

It is therefore impossible for us to consider the oppression of women separately from the international oppression by imperialism of our countries of origin and from our experience, even here in Britain, of racism, which moulds the life of our whole community. Yet we are also aware that overthrowing the whole capitalist and imperialist system does not automatically bring about an end to women's oppression. It is a specific and complex issue which needs to be addressed and dealt with directly, if it is to be dealt with effectively.

Some would argue that, given the immense task ahead of black people in liberating ourselves as a people, we should concentrate on that task first before worrying about women's liberation. But this ignores the fact that, as long as women are oppressed and this oppression continues to be ignored, we cannot take our rightful place in the overall struggle, which will, as a result, be only half as strong as it should be. Hence, in the context of the wider struggle for black, socialist liberation, it is as important to address the issue of women's oppression right from the *beginning* as it is for women involved in the struggle for our own liberation to recognise our role within the wider struggle.

It is in this context of an understanding of our oppression based on sex, race and class, and of the recognition of our struggle being part and parcel of the greater black struggle for the liberation of all our people from all forms of oppression, that black feminism is defined for us.

FEATURES

THE MYTH OF THE VICIOUS CYCLE

Brixton Black Women's Group
First published in Speak Out, *no. 4, July 1982, pp. 5–7*

I INTRODUCTION: Biological cycles

Cyclical biological changes occur in virtually all forms of life. Seasonal moultings, matings and migrations are some examples. Nocturnal animals' bodily activity is adapted so that they are active at night, whereas diurnals are active during the day; an example of marked temporal physiologic changes.

In humans, there are monthly bodily rhythms as well daily ones. Both men and women show regular fluctuations in the levels of various hormones. (This is the biological context in which to place menstruation.) Menstruation is just one type of periodic bodily activity. It is primarily a reproductive cycle, the basic changes being in the female sex organs. Menstruation is, like most bodily processes, organised by hormones. During the menstrual cycle, the female egg (ovum) ripens in the ovary (which contains a reservoir of unripe ova). At the same time, the wall of the womb (uterus), the endometrium, is being built up and developing additional supplies of blood. After about 2 weeks, the ripened ovum is released into the fallopian tube (ovulation). It then travels down the fallopian tube to the uterus, where it rests on the wall (endometrium) for a few days. If fertilisation (fusion with a male sperm) has not occurred, the ovum is shed, along with the excess blood and the endometrium. This is commonly known as menstruation and lasts for a few days, after which a new ovum starts to ripen and the cycle is repeated.

Socially and culturally, there is a lot more to menstruation than this biological outline would suggest. The menses is a uniquely female event. The menarche (first menstruation) is a crucial experience for young women, as it symbolises numerous mental and physical changes that are part of her development into a sexually mature woman.

This symbolic importance has rarely been overlooked. While only women subjectively experience menstruation, patriarchal (male-dominated) societies, religions and cultures have developed some very interesting and significant ideas and interpretations of it. Furthermore, these have affected not only how we, as women, look at ourselves, but also how we subjectively experience monthly periods.

II RELIGIOUS-HISTORICAL
(Did the Holy Virgin menstruate like Eve?)

> 'They will ask thee also concerning the courses of women, answer they are a pollution, therefore separate yourselves from women in their courses, and go not near them, until they be cleansed'.
> –Holy Koran

Islam traditionally requires the isolation of women during menstruation. They are not to come into contact with men, Holy books or objects, or to go near Holy places.

Judeo-Christianism (which includes Jews, Catholics, Protestants and all other varieties) also has a very negative view of menstruation, as is evident in that other major religious text, the Holy Bible. The 'curse', as it is still often known, was a stigma inflicted on Eve when she and Adam were evicted from the Garden of Eden, which was purportedly mainly Eve's fault. The downfall of man was supposedly caused by woman's weakness and corruption, and her flesh (of which menstruation is a visible identifier) is evil. All this despite the fact that the serpent (a male symbol) was the one who led Eve into leading Adam astray. Orthodox Jewish women are traditionally given cleansing baths after menstruation, during which prayers are said, in a ritual that allows her to once again lead a normal life, at least until the next monthly occurrence. Likewise, Rastafarianism has chosen to perpetuate this belief in the inherent corruptness of women.

Hindu people also segregate women during menstruation. The menarche is, however, celebrated as a young girl's initiation into adulthood.

The majority of prophets and religious writers, through the ages, have been male and held somewhat dubious views of the female sex. The witch-hunters of Europe represent one expression of this cultural and religious mode of thought. Menstruation has often been quoted as a sign of the sins of womankind – the curse of blood. Yet it is essential to life… The 'curse', though presumably she would be regarded as 'less cleansed'? The mystification and myths become confused and tie themselves in knots in their own contradictions; life or death – cleansing or unclean – fertility or sexuality … Sex is dirty, but babies are clean. Eve was evil, yet mother to the human race… The Holy Virgin Mary was pure and good, mother and virgin … 'Did Mary menstruate like Eve?', we ask ourselves. The confusions ricochet through the corridors of time, through the thousand re-writings of the Bible, through the thousand writings of the Koran, to infuse today's religions and even much of today's science. Where was truth distorted and lost? Where was woman's life-giving subsumed to her 'sin'?

III PRESENT-SCIENTIFIC

Today's scientists do not speak of 'curses' – they have recently gone out of fashion. The negative approach to female biology has been translated into new language, the language of disease, syndromes, symptoms and the like.

Today's menses are 'scientifically associated' with women who commit violent crimes, fail their exams, go into hospitals to harass doctors with their sick children, go mad and even lose control of an aircraft (just in case any one of us dares to think she may make a good pilot).

Today's 'experts' are saying that woman is so much at the mercy of her hormones that she cannot take her rightful place in society. Yet men do not have periods, and they commit far more crime, more violence, more successful suicides and have more road accidents (not just because there are more male drivers; proportionately as well).

'Premenstrual Tension' (PMT) and 'premenstrual syndromes' are the new jargon for this fundamental aspect of our bodies. The 'female sickness', as it is still called, is spoken of in hushed tones. The 'experts' (usually white, usually male) hook us up to tubes and wires and do radioimmunoassays (measure our hormone levels) in laboratories, and argue with each other over our female (read, faulty) hormones, our altered suprarenal activity (another hormone problem) and our 'water retention' (yet another hormone problem). All this to explain the 'sickness' that menstruation has become. A recent book published in Britain symbolises what they call 'the new approach' to female functioning … PMT: *The Unrecognised Illness – What it is; how to recognise it; and how to cure it*.[1] True to its title, the authors then go on to elaborate on 'the world's commonest illness': 'Millions of women suffer from it. It is painful, depressing, frightening and sometimes devastating'. Their bogus statistics estimate that as many as 3 in 4 of all women the world over suffer from it, 1 in 3 severely, and that it can last from 2 days to 2 weeks (half of an adult woman's time). Their 'checklist' of 'symptoms' includes 19 physical ones, 9 concentration disabilities, 13 behaviour changes and 10 mood changes to look out for, so that you, too, can detect your PMT. The implication is clear: if you monitor yourself carefully enough, all your problems – emotional, mental, psychological and physical – will be explained away as PMT, blamed on menstruation, and hence the 'inescapable fact' that woman's greatest enemy is herself – her body.

1   J. Lever, M. G. Brush and B. Haynes, *PMT: The Unrecognised Illness – Pre-Menstrual Tension: What It Is, How to Recognise It, and How to Cure It* (Collingwood, Victoria: Outback Press, 1979).

The outlook has not changed since an unknown 19th century poet wrote, 'Oh menstruating woman, thou'rt a fiend from which all nature should be closely screened...' Nor, for that matter, since 1000 BC, when Zoroaster wrote, 'A menstruous woman is the work of Uhremaun, the devil. A woman during her periodic illness is not to gaze upon the sacred fire, sit in water, behold the sun, or hold conversation with a man'.

Furthermore, a number of 'scientific' cures have been tried. In 1931, Franks reported sterilisation by X-rays to be successful for 'some' women... (survivors?). Various hormone therapies have also been tried, despite some undesirable side-effects. Hysterectomy (removal of the womb altogether, thus presumably the 'source of the evil') was also tried. Not surprisingly, Dr Green, in 1954, found that 'premenstrual symptoms *appeared for the first time*' in some women given hysterectomies.[2] 'Inexplicable!' he muttered, shaking his head and sharpening his scalpel to try again to 'cure' the female disease of being female.

So, we have had old myths, new pseudo-scientific myths and even attempts at cures for the menses. All this says basically the same thing: it is something bad, unpleasant, dirty, inconvenient, incapacitating and female. It has become the name for womanly weakness and inferiority, to be accommodated through necessity, if possible cured. If you argue or get aggressive, it is not because there is something objective to get het up about, but because you are approaching, or due, or late, or on your PERIOD. As it is a cyclical occurrence, there is, eventually, very little time when one is not on or approaching (up to two weeks before, remember) one's period. The more we watch for the symptoms, the more we will find them, and the more ashamed and angry and frustrated we will become.

Menstruation is also quite good business. 'Feminine hygiene', after all, is not a subsidised area of health, although it is essential and should be. A huge industry has developed instead, providing anti-odour vaginal sprays, anti-odour tampons (the ones that

2 *Editor's note:* This appears to be a reference to Raymond Greene, who co-authored – with Katharina Dalton – an article published in the *BMJ* in 1953 – see R. Greene and K. Dalton, 'The Premenstrual Syndrome', *British Medical Journal* 1, no. 4818 (9 May 1953), 1007–14.

recently killed a number of women through toxic shock syndrome) and 'don't-touch-your-dirty-self' applicators. Adverts for the latest, most discreet, most nobody-will-ever-know devices fill teenage girlie magazines. It is an industry that thrives on shame … not healthy, 'look-after-yourself' ads, but 'cover-the-shame', 'hide-the-stain', 'the stench', 'the filth'. It is enough to make you ill, if you haven't already recognised your 'sickness'.

Young girls are initiated into womanhood against this background, in hushed, shamed voices. Packets of sanitary towels and belts and pins are discreetly pushed towards them, or hidden in drawers with instruction booklets. Warm, sisterly advice is seldom given at this birth into womanhood. At best, it is seen as a fact of life you have no choice but to put up with.

For ourselves …

'If a woman is inconstant, good, I am faithful to ebb and flow, I fall in season and now is a time of ripening'.

We have looked at the negative way in which womanhood, as symbolised by menstruation, is denigrated, pathologised and contained. Negative myths and bogus science are the order of the day, and clearly have been as far back as we can see. What do we, as Black Women, learn from this? What are the facts behind the mysteries and taboos?

The biological facts were outlined at the beginning of this feature. The facts of how we experience this biology are also at issue. Some of us do find menstruation uncomfortable. While we may dismiss myths of curses and taboos as anti-woman propaganda, this is not to say that we must shove periods under the carpet and deny their existence. We can, however, state with certainty that it is not the crippling, incapacitating ailment some would have us believe. Nor should it be a source of shame and embarrassment.

The period pains and discomfort experienced by some women can be prevented by remedies a lot less drastic than hormone therapies and operations. Most discomfort is caused by constipation and accumulation of fluids. Both of these can be avoided by eating more fruits and vegetables, especially Vitamin B6. Exercise is also crucial – this will avoid and relieve cramps and tension. These measures apply generally, but particularly in the week or so before your period is due, so find the time to indulge yourself.

Serious spasmodic pains are extremely rare and may be associated with coming off the pill – the hormonal disruptions caused may take some time to return to normal cyclical fluctuations.

Some of the newest evidence, uncovered by the growing number of women in the field, is casting new light on menstruation. Firstly, they have found that discomfort and bad symptoms are experienced more by women who have a bad attitude towards menstruation than women in general. Therefore, women from strictly religious backgrounds, where the religion is anti-women (Orthodox Jews and Christians, for example) tend to have more PMT 'symptoms' and worse pain during menstruation. This makes sense, since women that are ashamed of their bodies and feel 'cursed' or 'unclean' are those likely to be tense and uncomfortable as they apprehensively await their period. In cultures with more positive approaches, women have been shown to have correspondingly fewer symptoms. Furthermore, these bad attitudes are transmitted from mother to daughter and on through the generations. What a heritage!

Other recent work highlights a problem with most survey research. This is that people usually fulfil the surveyors' expectations. Women knowing that the survey is looking at menstrual 'problems' will, therefore, describe all sorts of problems. All the surveys which were done 'blind' (i.e. without the women knowing what the survey was about) failed to show the periodic timing of symptoms that allowed previous researchers to dubiously conclude that they must be caused by periods.

In other words, 'PMT' cannot be found to exist unless one knows of it and wants to find it, since nearly all the 'symptoms' of it are found in all men as well as women, from time to time.

The evidence on clinical depression (depression considered by experts to merit medical treatment and confinement) is also of interest. It shows women having between 2 and 6 times as much depression as men. But this is nothing to do with biology, or periods, since it depends on her living conditions and circumstances. Clearly, putting all women's problems down to menstruation is not going to solve anything. In fact, it may do a lot of damage. It may undermine all the changes that we have been fighting for, setting back the progress of women's struggle to the eras of curses and witch-hunts and surgical incisions for those of us who complain too much about our oppression and dissatisfaction with the way things are. Oppression can take many forms and infiltrate the most apparently straightforward issues, as our discussion has shown.

For our younger sisters and daughters, a positive approach is needed. Initiation into womanhood should be celebrated and not mourned, just as we should celebrate and fight for our liberation, not just mourn our oppression.

CHILEAN WOMEN IN CLASS STRUGGLE

First published in Speak Out, *no. 4, July 1982, pp. 7–9*

The following is an article on the various struggles which Chilean women have been involved in since the CIA-backed overthrow of the Allende (Popular Unity) government in September 1973. Apart from highlighting the strength and determination of working women in the face of tremendous odds, the article reveals two important points.

The first shows how even the most liberal demands made by the women of Chile would be seen as a fundamental threat to the military regime under which the Chilean people live. In this respect, the author points out that the most basic demands made in the United Nations declaration for women's equality are denied to Chilean women, despite a formal commitment to them. This clearly shows the odds against which the working women struggle and is eloquent testimony to their strength and determination.

The second lesson is essential for socialist feminists every-where to learn. This is the need to distinguish between those women's organisations which represent and/or serve the interests of the ruling classes and those which represent the struggle of working women, and therefore contribute to the emancipation of all oppressed and exploited people. In this case, the article clearly shows that there is no relationship between the needs of the mass of Chilean women and the bourgeois women's organisa-tions espousing their ruling-class interests.

Even though it is not correct to speak of a feminist movement in Chile, a small group of women from the dominant class distinguished itself in the first decades of the century by its struggle to obtain guarantees in the exercise of civil and political rights. However, only those women who could read and write were eligible to exercise those rights. At the same time as that movement was taking place, there were women's organisations, from the working class, which were created in order to carry out their struggle against exploitation and for better living conditions.

In the early days, the emancipation of the Chilean women of the privileged classes rested upon the exploitation of the women of the people and those who migrated from the rural areas. This became evident in the '70s, when bourgeois women organised actively against the Unidad Popular regime – Allende's elected left-wing government. Several episodes demonstrated the role that right-wing women played.

1. On September 4, 1970, Allende was elected with 36.2% of the votes cast. The majority of the female electorate showed its preference for the right-wing candidates: 68.3% of the women voted for the right. Allende, on the other hand, received only 30.5% of the women's vote.

2. During the period between the election and the accession of the popular forces to government control, a group of women from the oligarchy dressed entirely in black, surrounded the presidential palace and started a funeral procession to show that they were in mourning for the death of democracy in Chile.

3. Women participated in the first mass demonstration staged by right-wing forces. This demonstration was called 'The March of the Empty Pots', which took place on December 1, 1971. This was to symbolise the right-wing's resistance to economic changes, the pots illustrating the lack of food, and, secondly, that that government was trying to erase the traditional role of women. This event constituted one of the indicators that gave Fidel Castro, then visiting Chile, cause to declare, 'During the first year, the reactionaries have learned better than the revolutionaries'.

The women's demonstrations always followed the same pattern: assembled around a central group of bourgeois women of all ages, who arrived in cars and were often accompanied by their maids, were women from the petit bourgeoisie (always in the majority), together with a lesser number of women from the shanty towns. All of these women were encircled by militia women, wearing helmets and carrying chains, who were recruited from the paramilitary faction of the extreme right-wing, known as 'Fatherland and Liberty' (Patria y Libertad), which had an active women's branch especially trained for the purpose of sedition. This group was known as 'Women's Power', a group that later came to occupy the energies of the women's front of the Unidad Popular regime in its final months.

Today, halfway through the United Nations Decade of Women (1975–1985), what is the condition of Chilean women in society? How has the military junta responded to the main objectives of the decade: Equality, Development and Peace? Evidence shows that not only has the junta totally ignored the spirit and letter of the Decade of Women, but that the daily conditions of Chilean women, especially of the working class and the poorest groups, has deteriorated. This is due to both economic/social conditions and ingrained ideological cultural factors that are prevalent, in varying degrees, amongst both the right-wing forces and the progressives on the question of women's emancipation. As a result, the Women's Section of the Trade Union Coordinating Committee organised the Third National Women's Meeting, where women delegates from all sorts of different groups, including the Mapuches (Indians), came together in order to analyse the present situation of the Chilean Trade Union Movement and the role of women in the national context; the level of unemployment amongst women and the role she has to play as wife, daughter, sister and comrade in relationship to her fellow male worker when he is unemployed.

The United Nations' objectives were to promote sexual equality, to ensure complete integration of women in the development struggle, and to recognise the important contribution of women towards friendly relations and cooperation between nations and world peace.

It was recognised that measures would be needed to change attitudes, values and deeply-rooted beliefs perpetuated by the mass media which encouraged sexism, the acceptance that women are inferior to men on biological and psychological grounds. Governments were urged to counter ideologies which allow the oppression of one sex by the other.

What, then, was the response of General Pinochet's junta? Pinochet's ideology, based around the notion of 'national security' and heavily implicit in his 1981 Constitution, encourages the view of women as being for biological reproduction only. The woman's function is therefore to serve her country, to work within the singular vision propagated by the junta, and to bring up her children as future servants of the Fatherland. In line with fascist thinking, the Chilean woman has to produce healthy, disciplined and efficient children who will mirror the system. Women must see themselves as wives, mothers or sisters of the soldiers of the Fatherland.

How equal are Chilean women? In the *official view*, Chilean women remain relegated to the domestic sphere as wife and mother, in terms of God, Fatherland, Family and Moral Perfection. The Chilean fascist junta designated, in 1981, a woman Minister for the Family. Her name is Carmen Grez. In order to understand what she represents within the ideological framework of the junta towards women, we quote her own words: 'If a woman gets married, her fundamental purpose in life is to be a mother. Therefore, I believe that the family should be educated to use natural contraceptive methods. The State should not provide contraceptive methods such as the Pill, the coil, etc.' ... 'I would not allow my 15-year-old daughter to have an abortion, under no circumstances; not even if she was *raped by a nigger*' ... 'I cannot accept abortion, as *God is the only one* who takes life away from us. I could not *justify murder*, as I believe everybody has the right to be born. *God wanted it* to be like this'. This serves to emphasise the racist/sexist nature of the junta. In Chile, the infant mortality for 1000 live births is 40.1%; 53% of school children and 44% of children under the age of 6 suffer from malnutrition. We would like to quote the Minister of Health, when he was asked in an interview about the growing number of children suffering from malnutrition: 'Those children are NOT a source of power, but a dragging weight – from a military point of view, they are useless'.

Women lose maternal rights such as paid leave and lose the right to state health benefits, and, therefore, the freedom to plan their own families; they lose the right to work training and paid employment, remaining subject to illiteracy, malnutrition and misery, for their families as well as themselves. Meanwhile, the government implements its free market economy, whose effects on the poorest are already well-known. Figures show that it is women from the poorest section of society – who often live in extreme poverty – who organise the means of survival to improve the family income, which is usually very low due to the husband's unemployment and drop in real wage levels.

After 1973, childbirth increased among women aged 20–34. These young women go to work in equal numbers, whether they have one or five children. Until 1974, women of the 36–45 age group formed the bulk of the female workforce, but they have been replaced by women of the 20–35 age group. That is, women from the poorest section have children younger and go to work younger. While middle-class and upper-class women cease work in relation to the number of children they have, working-class women work precisely because they have children and their family economy is disastrous. They are concentrated in the service sector, and their industrial importance decreases. If they are lucky enough to be employed in industry, it is usually in traditionally 'female areas' such as textiles. In both cases, women suffer lower wages than men doing the same job, and there is little chance of self-improvement due to the lack of training.

This vulnerability owes itself to ideological-cultural factors which take concrete forms when, for example, a woman carries out a 'double' working day (paid work and housework). Women, of course, are responsible for the care and welfare of their families after their day's work.

We have, therefore, an increase in young working women from the poorest sections, whose exploitation is manifested through inferior working conditions, very low wages and 'double' days, as well as the impossibility of training. In addition, their participation in labour organisations is minimal, reflecting their industrial power.

Since September 1973, repression has become central to Chilean political life. The political violence of the junta, such as torture, has a systematic ferocity, or the violence is more cunning, as in the case of 'disappeared' people. The fear generated by political repression extends right into the family, into each member. Women are repressed just as everybody is, but the methods are more sinister. In Chile, there are cases of thousands of murdered, 'disappeared' or tortured women.

Equality, Development and Peace are not only ignored in Chile, they are violated. For this and many other reasons, the military government has been repudiated by democratic countries, by the United Nations, by the Human Rights Commission, by the OAS, by all groups who work for peace in the world.

However, all is not bleak. Since 1973, Chilean women have organised to gain solidarity; to defend those in prison and those disappeared; to fight for the right to return to the homeland and for the reintroduction of civil rights such as freedom, justice and work; and for a just wage for themselves and their families. And as time progresses, these women's groups are developing and growing, succeeding in creating a popular movement whose effectiveness is now being realised.

Today, women organise themselves in order to fight against the dictatorship. For the first time in Chilean history, the working-class women are initiating all different forms of struggle; that is to say, they are playing an active role within the Resistance. As an example of this, we can refer to their participation in the dockers' strike, in which thousands of women took to the streets and confronted the repressive forces.

The war against the people was declared in 1973, with the right-wing military coup of General Pinochet. From that moment, it became the *right* of the Chilean people to fight back and get rid of their oppressors. Chilean women have come to realise that the junta has to be overthrown by force. This implies the active participation of women within their mass organisations using all types of struggle, including the military one.

REPORTS

Friends of Jamilla Campaign

Brixton Black Women's Group
First published in Speak Out, *no. 4, July 1982, pp. 9–10*

During the last few months, the Black Women's Group has been attempting to co-ordinate some support around the case of a particular sister who has been fighting to regain her youngest daughter from the care and control of a white foster mother, and out of that to form a campaign which will alert Black women to the way in which the authorities systematically try to destroy the Black family unit.

Jamilla approached some of the women in the Group for help in what had previously been a one-woman fight against the State; firstly, to live free from constant police harassment, and secondly, but more immediately, to get her daughter back.

Our first meeting with Jamilla was spent discussing the background to her plight. We learned that, in 1972, Jamilla was picked up by the police in West London, where she used to live. She resisted arrest, as she was not involved in any crime, and, as a result, she was diagnosed as mentally disturbed and was put into a mental hospital, where she was given drugs against her will. Unknown to her, her children were placed into temporary care by the social services of the borough in which she lived. Although her children were returned to her, long after her release from the hospital, they were kept under strict supervision. This supervision order gave the police, social workers and doctors licence to constantly harass Jamilla, making it impossible for her to lead a normal life.

It was due to this constant surveillance by the agencies of the State and the unwillingness of the local housing authorities to rehouse Jamilla and her children away from a vindictive husband that her children were once again taken into care; this time for the rest of their childhood lives. Her six-month-old baby was also taken away and made a Ward of Court by the social services, who then placed the child into foster care with a family whom the social services, in their judgement, considered to be a 'suitable' family. This was a couple whose own sudden marriage broke up. Although the foster mother's situation was now practically the same as Jamilla's, the social services still allowed this white woman to keep the child against the wishes of her natural mother. All attempts made by Jamilla to keep in contact with her child were denied her by the social services and the foster mother, on the pretext that Jamilla's contact with her child was 'disturbing' for the child.

Many of our experiences with the State agencies have shown us that all these agencies are inextricably linked and operate with the objective of weakening the Black family and destroying the Black community. Single Black mothers are particularly vulnerable. They are trapped by society's condemnation of them. They are prevented from earning a wage because there are so few childcare facilities, and there are *no* jobs. So, they are forced to live on social security, and punished for having to bring up their child/ren on their own. In this situation, when something goes slightly wrong, the social services jump at the opportunity to take the child/ren into care, without informing the mothers of their rights and, in many cases, against the mother's will or consent. By the time some mothers realise what is at stake, it is too late and their child/ren are gone forever.

The struggle for a mother to regain her child/ren means that both mother and child/ren are plunged into a mesh of racist bureaucracy. The child/ren's estrangement from the family is compounded by the fact that children's homes or foster parents are often isolated in rural areas, miles away from a Black community. The staff or foster parents are usually white and middle class, as are the social workers. No attention is paid to the children's cultural needs. The process of saving a child from that kind of environment is costly, both emotionally and financially.

In the case of Jamilla, this is the struggle she has been waging. She is faced with the impossible task of convincing the authorities, social services, doctors, teachers and lawyers (all of whom are natural allies) that she can provide a better alternative environment for her than that of a white middle class nuclear family, or even a tokenly mixed family.

When the campaign first started, its aim was to support Jamilla in her struggle to regain custody of her child and to provide similar support for women who were victims of this kind of State control. However, as the campaign gained momentum, what clearly emerged was the need to share within our community certain information that is only available to Black workers merely because they are employed in some of these agencies of the State.

The first task, then, was to try and reach out to the Black workers in social, health and legal services. In this respect, we have achieved a certain degree of success. Many of these workers have come together for the first time, realising how isolated they are working in such massive bureaucracies.

A further aim of the campaign is to inform women about their rights when dealing with agencies of the State, especially the social services. To do this, we are in the process of collecting information which will eventually be compiled into a campaign document, to be discussed at a one-day seminar. We will then distribute it to women in the community, whose lack of knowledge of how the system works make them one of its most vulnerable targets.

The campaign is a tribute to the strength and resistance of Jamilla, who fought at all times against her oppression, locating her personal struggle in a wider political context.

The campaign still needs the support of all those who are interested. For further information, please contact Friends of Jamilla, c/o The Black Women's Centre.

International Women's Day Celebration

Brixton Black Women's Group
First published in Speak Out, *no. 4, July 1982, pp. 10–11*

We thought we would outline some of the history to International Women's Day as background to our report on the celebrations that took place at the Black Women's Centre in March.

In 1910, the Second International Conference of Socialist Women was held. On this day, Klara Zetkin, a German revolutionary socialist and feminist who fought consistently to build a socialist women's movement, proposed that Women's Day become INTERNATIONAL WOMEN'S DAY. Women from as far as Asia came over to participate in these early conferences, and celebrations have been held in various parts of the world since. Black women were actively involved in the American women's struggles of the 1890s. In Russia, the first celebration was in 1913. In Britain, 1926 was the first major celebration – that year of intense working-class activity, illustrated by the General Strike. In 1924, Chinese women celebrated, raising slogans crucial to the situation of working women all over the Third World: 'Down with imperialism; Down with warlords; Fight for women's liberation; Equal rights for women in employment, education, wages and participation in politics; Protect child labourers and pregnant women; No child brides; No polygamy; No concubines; No prostitution' (quoted in *Spare Rib* No 104).[1]

---

1 *Editor's note:* The *Spare Rib* article – see Sue O'Sullivan, 'March 8 – INTERNATIONAL WOMEN'S DAY: Where and When It All Began ...',

Over the last 10–15 years, there has been a worldwide resurgence of feminist consciousness, and this has been accompanied by a re-emergence of International Women's Day celebrations everywhere.

For women in the Third World, this has been an integral part of their participation in the overall struggle for National Liberation and Socialism. For Black Women in Britain, International Women's Day is integral to our struggle against racism and capitalism. Thus, after a year of intensified repression and increasing racial attacks and harassment, Black Women used March 7th to remember the many struggles sisters are waging all over the world, and to give support to sisters waging similar struggles here in England.

Our coming together at the Black Women's Centre to celebrate International Women's Day was an occasion to further pledge our resolve to continue to fight to achieve changes in this society. Sisters came from all over London to join in. The atmosphere throughout the day was one of warmth and friendliness, with sisters talking, eating and relaxing with each other. This was a very rewarding and inspiring day, which served to replenish our collective energies in order that we can continue the struggle.

The day began with the showing of the film *Women in Arms*. This was our way of congratulating the Nicaraguan revolution and served to express our solidarity with the sisters' participation in their country's struggle for National Liberation. As shown in the film, the sisters are now fighting to achieve and maintain equal and active participation in national development.

The film was followed by sisters Rosemary, Jamilla, Donna and Dorett performing and reading poetry and prose. Their poetry expressed not only their individual experiences and struggles, but those of all Black Women fighting for their rights. Sister Jamilla left us with a very powerful poem expressing her bitterness and frustration toward the social services, who, having fostered out her child, now refuse to return her to her mother (see 'Friends of Jamilla Campaign').[2]

Spare Rib 104, no. 3–4 (March 1981) – itself takes this quote from Su Ping, 'The Origins of Women's Day and Its First Celebration in China', *Women of China* (March 1980).

2 *Editor's note:* See pp. 235–7 in this collection.

Sister Dorett concluded the second part of the afternoon events by reading from Alice Walker's anthology *You Can't Keep a Good Woman Down* (1971). One of the strongest stories, 'The Abortion', is based on a woman's relationship with her man and the anguish and despair she experiences when she becomes pregnant. Another child is just not what she wants. Her partner's lack of understanding and sensitivity propels her to abort the pregnancy and, eventually, the relationship.

The response and support expressed by the many sisters who passed through the BWC on Sunday 7th March reasserted that our struggle has many forms and will need many strategies for us to be successful.

Brixton
Defence
Campaign

Brixton Black Women's Group
First published in Speak Out, *no. 4, July 1982, p. 11*

The Brixton Defence Campaign (BDC) was formed following the uprisings of April 10–13th 1981.[1] It was made up of a broad cross-section of Black groups and individuals concerned to organise for the defence of the community. The Black Women's Group Brixton has played an active role in the campaign from its inception, right through to the present day. The Campaign was formed on the basis that the uprisings were a legitimate opposition to racist policing and *not* mere 'criminal acts'. BDC sought to mobilise active support for the defendants, and to publicise and campaign on the issues surrounding the uprisings.

In July, a second uprising took place in Brixton. All in all, over 600 people were arrested and charged.[2]

---

1   *Editor's note:* See 'The Brixton Uprising: A Report by The Brixton Black Women's Group', pp. 201–6 in this collection.

2   *Editor's note:* This second uprising took place in response to 176 police officers (with a further 391 in reserve) raiding eleven houses on Railton Road on 15 July 1981, ostensibly due to petrol bombs and unlawful drinking on the premises – evidence of neither of which was found. The houses raided sustained considerable damage, with windows, sinks, toilets, floorboards, furniture and televisions smashed. The Metropolitan Police paid £8,500 in compensation for structural damage, with further sums paid for damage to personal property; an internal inquiry, however, exonerated the officers involved – see J. Benyon and J. Solomos, 'The Simmering Cities: Urban Unrest during the Thatcher Years', *Parliamentary Affairs* 41, no. 3 (1988), 402–22.

The majority of the cases have now been disposed of, having been tried summarily in the magistrate's courts. Most of the charges have been public order offences such as 'threatening behaviour', 'assault on police', 'obstruction', 'possession of offensive weapon', 'insulting behaviour', etc.; but a considerable proportion, almost 40%, were looting charges. These include charges of 'theft', 'burglary' and 'handling' or 'receiving' stolen goods. There were also a few arson charges thrown in, and the occasional 'malicious wounding' and 'criminal damage', with one person more recently having a charge of 'conspiracy'. Over 65% of the April defendants were Black, with almost 50% under 25 years old, and 90% living in the Brixton area (statistics from the Legal Defence Group).

In the course of the year, the BDC has campaigned vigorously to boycott Scarman's sham inquiry (his subsequent report confirmed all our expectations of him) and publicised the political issues surrounding the uprisings through public meetings, publishing bulletins and distributing leaflets. We have also conducted active street work in the community and worked closely with the Legal Defence Group. The campaign has drawn the political links between the uprisings and resistance in the various Black communities up and down the country, and organised all-London as well as national meetings. BDC organised a day of international culture and political events, in which hundreds of people participated.

Meanwhile, the racist British state, which was shaken to its foundations by the Black resistance in the uprisings of 1981, has responded by massive reorganising and arming of the police force, making it a paramilitary one. Furthermore, Kenneth Newman has been appointed as the new boss of London's police force. with his blood-steeped history of torture and violence in Northern Ireland. The BDC is currently engaged in campaign work around the crucial and alarming developments.

REVIEWS

Brixton Black Women's Group
First published in Speak Out, *no. 4, July 1982, p. 12*

You Can't Keep a Good Woman Down: Stories and *Meridian*
by Alice Walker

Alice Walker's collection of essays and stories in her book *You Can't Keep a Good Woman Down* (1971) make for easy reading, which is good, because what she has to say to black women is best not obscured by having to wade through a mountain of rhetoric.

What comes through most in Walker is the central place she gives to the need of black women for space – space for growing, for introspection and for appreciation of what we have to offer ourselves in particular, and the black community and other Third World peoples in general. Reading the book is like getting together with a whole bunch of women friends for an afternoon and just talking, in the way that women do, about their lives – their children, loves, fears, hopes, dreams and frustrations. What emerges is a picture which is as diverse as the myriad elements which go to make up black womanhood, and one which, as a consequence, presents a more realistic and non-stereotypical view of what it is to be black and female.

Walker's book can best be characterised in terms of a celebration of self. They take as their source the rich yield of our collective experience, which has survived despite repeated and formidable attempts, historically and in the present day, to suppress it. As individuals, many of us are plagued by the residue of this systematic oppression and fall into the trap of thinking that what we are about has no importance in the real world, and therefore no place in our consciousness.

What Walker has done is to say, 'Hey, it's not a waste of time to spend some effort taking stock of who we are and where we're going' – but that, in fact, we *have* to do this if we are to survive both as women and as black people in a hostile society. In effect, she's saying we don't have to listen to what 'they' say, or accept their definition of us. It's up to us to create our own terms of reference.

Walker's characters do not allow us to shrink from our past or to be complacent about our present. They instead prod us into exploring our souls, urging acceptance and recognition of those qualities and experiences which have been good for us and the community. On the other hand, she does not gloss over those areas where we need to do more groundwork. One of her essays has to do with pornography. In it, one woman struggles to come to terms with her sexuality and, at the same time, to free herself from the confines of the racist, sexist images which proliferate in the sex magazines her husband uses for stimulation. Repulsed by their treatment of women (especially black women) she resolves to throw off these demeaning stereotypes. Their relationship undergoes irrevocable change as she works to come to an understanding of the oppression and degradation that is implicit in such images. Hers is a difficult path, which does not offer easy answers.

Walker's use of folk tales and legends in her novel *Meridian* (1976) lends to it a mystical quality. It has the feel of being steeped deep in the abundant black culture which produced, nurtured and eventually saved Meridian Hill and many other black women like her. It is an attempt to try and sort out what all the energy, sweat and blood that black women put into the civil rights movement means in terms of where we are today. Meridian is a high school drop-out in the deep South. She is also an abandoned mother who makes the decision to leave her child (in the capable hands of its paternal grandmother; and what's wrong with extended family, anyway) and joins the civil rights movement of the '60s. She eventually becomes disillusioned by the hypocrisy she finds in both the personal and the political; and, in order to save her life and her sanity, she journeys back to the people who make up the strong, weathered roots of her heritage. There, she finds sustenance and, ultimately, survival.

At this point it becomes necessary, however, to take Walker's discussion of the civil rights movement a step further. Although it is accurate to say that many black women had a 'raw deal' in terms of how they were treated by the movement (more specifically, by the males within it), this should not detract from the very real importance of the movement as such. Nor should the struggle be seen as a failure because of the frailties of individuals within it. It must be reiterated that only by coming together in such a common struggle can oppressed peoples ever hope to overthrow the ruling class, with its exploiting domination. Moreover, we must not fail to recognise that, *collectively*, ours is a political as well as personal struggle.

That notwithstanding, however, Walker's works, put simply, are a joy. For she has managed to capture on paper something of what we, as thinking, feeling, creating black women are into. She writes of our strength, our creativity, our oppression and our pain. She attacks the stereotypical image of black women with a vengeance, but her message is only partly intended for society as a whole. Primarily, it is to black women that she writes, exhorting us to never lose sight of the fact that we are growing, developing women whose consciousness will ultimately make it possible for us to have control over our lives.

REVIEW

Brixton Black Women's Group
First published in Speak Out, *no. 4, July 1982, p. 13*

The Education of the Black Child in Britain:
The Myth of Multiracial Education
by Maureen Stone

Maureen Stone's book explores the situation of Black children in the British school system today.[1] She looks at present policies being employed to remedy the situation of Black children's continual failure in the education system. She recognises that working-class education has been inferior in standards and quality throughout the history of mass education in Britain, so the problems of slum schools and educationalists' middle-class orientations are nothing new. Black children face the double-edged sword of class and racial discrimination in education.

Multiracial education is criticised for being based on the false premises of Black children having the psychological problems of 'low self-esteem', 'inferiority complexes' and 'identity problems', which have supposedly caused them to underachieve at school. She points out that Black children do not have lower self-esteem

---

1 *Editor's note*: M. Stone, *The Education of the Black Child in Britain: The Myth of Multiracial Education* (London: Fontana, 1981).

than white children, contrary to the beliefs of researchers. Some researchers have, in fact, found our children to have high self-esteem scores, but this, too, is then seen as a problem: it is a 'pathological defense' against the low self-esteem that they are convinced our children suffer from. This nicely removes the blame from the inferior education, schools, teachers and, above all, the racism that is actually responsible for the situation.

According to Stone, the using of curriculum time for steel bands and lessons in dialect, and the teacher 'relating to the kids on their level' actually worsens the situation, because they fail to affect self-esteem or school achievement. Stone further argues that these attempts are both misguided and possibly damaging, promoting neglect of the basic skills and training that education is supposed to be providing and that are necessary for survival in this society. Multiracial education is exposed as fashionable liberalism, providing professional openings for ambitious educationalists and conscience relief for white middle-class teachers, while at the same time it 'cools off' any 'unrealistic' ambitions Black children may have, reminding them that 'their place' is among steel bands and not in professional occupations in Britain.

To us, in the Black community, it has long been clear that multiracial education did not arise out of a genuine concern for the education of ourselves or our children, but as a debate to salve the guilt complexes of middle-class white educators. It was also an attempt to co-opt our struggle for Black people's history to be incorporated into the school curriculum. That this is failing is evidenced by the growing number of autonomous Black Saturday schools set up in the community. Multiracial education is not a widespread part of school curricula, nor is it part of exam syllabuses. It does not have such status.

Stone's critique is mild and sometimes more convoluted than necessary, although the basic argument is reasonable. A book that seems to have been written mainly for the purpose of educating the white educationalists, teachers and researchers that she justly criticises.

Tribute to the Bradford 12

Brixton Black Women's Group
First published in Speak Out, *no. 4, July 1982, p. 13*

The Brixton Black Women's Group salutes the victory of the brothers who became known as the Bradford 12.

We also salute those without whose hard work and courage the Bradford 12 would not have been released; that is, campaign workers, defence counsel, families and supportive friends.[1]

The victory of the Bradford 12 is a victory for the Asian community in particular and the Black community (African & Asian) in general. The acquittal of the Bradford 12 demonstrates that united action can win. Victory for one is a victory for all.

---

1 *Editor's note:* See Anandi Ramamurthy, 'The Politics of Britain's Asian Youth Movements', *Race and Class* 48, no. 2 (2006), 38–60; and Anandi Ramamurthy, 'Resisting Racism: The Bradford 12 Defence Campaign', Our Migration Story: The Making of Britain, 2016, ourmigrationstory.org.uk.

BRIXTON BLACK WOMEN'S GROUP

DRAFT AIMS AND OBJECTIVES.OCT 82.

Unpublished

The BBWG was formed in 1973 by women who had been actively involved in the Black Movement of the 1960s and 1970s. While being totally involved in struggles for the economic and social liberation of Black people, the founder members of the group also saw the necessity for the development of a politics that was antisexist.

The BBWG therefore began to organise autonomously. Central to this autonomy was the clear vision that as Black people we have solidarity and work with Black progressive organisations. We feel that our autonomy, which is distinct from separatism, creates a favourable climate for the understanding and evaluating of the complexities involved within the question of the liberation of women.

We recognise that our struggle is that of Black people and that we have an important contribution to make to the overall struggle of the working class in Britain. Black people are faced with institutionalised racism which is evident in all aspects of our lives – housing, employment, education and the law. All this is part of state policy to maintain an exploitative system for the profit of the few. This system exploits the working class, and in particular Black people. This situation forces Black people into the worst-paid jobs, poorest living conditions and limited educational opportunities. For Black women the situation is far worse, because we suffer a triple oppression, i.e. as women, as Black people and as workers. We firstly have to raise our consciousness and that of our sisters by genuine involvement in the fight against racism, sexism and class oppression and exploitation. It is only by coming together and analysing our situation as Black women in this society that we can make an effective contribution to the struggle.

The BBWG is actively involved in various community groups, such as the Brixton Defence Campaign, the Africa Liberation Committee and the Black Women's Self Health Group. Through the Organisation of Women of Asian and African Descent (OWAAD), we are able to keep in close contact with other Black women's groups and individuals. The BBWG is also actively involved in the management of the Black Women's Centre. Throughout our history, the BBWG has supported genuine liberation movements in Africa, Asia and Latin America; we also support the Irish people's struggle.

The Black Women's Movement is an important part of the movement for liberation and change in the world. In this movement, women are coming forward to take part in the struggle for personal and political emancipation.

WE AIM TO:

1. Fight against racism and sexism at all levels – social, political, institutional and individual.
2. To fight against racism and sexism in immigration policy, the legal system and the media.
3. To mobilise, organise and campaign around issues which affect us as Black women, specifically.
4. To support all those who are also engaged in the fight against international capital.
5. To hold and participate in meetings and demonstrations; to distribute literature, etc., in order to implement the aims of the Black Women's Group.

BRIXTON BLACK WOMEN'S GROUP STATEMENT IN RESPONSE TO *GRASS ROOTS* EDITORIAL (*Grass Roots* Oct–Nov. 1982).

First published in Grass Roots: Black Community News, *May–June, 1983, p. 5*

As one of the groups that has been actively involved in the formation of OWAAD (Organisation of Women of Asian and African Descent) and its subsequent development, we were shocked at the gross distortions and misunderstandings evident in your editorial (*Grass Roots*, Oct–Nov 1982, p.3, p.7).[1] As a declared black socialist feminist organisation, we also find it necessary to correct your mis-portrayal of this political position.

For a start, the aims and objectives of OWAAD, as written in the present constitution, read:

- To take up, campaign and struggle on all issues which affect black women in Britain; to oppose and struggle against all forms of sexism and discrimination against women and all forms of racism and discrimination against black people; to support those struggles of the working class which further the interests of working people, black and white, male and female.
- To support all anti-imperialist struggles and national liberation movements fighting against colonial and

---

1 *Editor's note:* Published 1978–1986, *Grass Roots: Black Community News* was the newspaper of the Black Liberation Front (BLF). Widely circulated in the 1970s, it was available in major cities across Britain. The BLF was founded in January 1971 by former members of the Black Panther Movement's North and West London branches. For more, see A.-M. Angelo, '"We All Became Black": Tony Soares, African-American Internationalists, and Anti-imperialism', in *The Other Special Relationship: Race, Rights, and Riots in Britain and the United States*, ed. R. D. Kelley and S. Tuck (New York: Palgrave Macmillan, 2015), 95–102; J. Narayan, 'British Black Power: The Anti-imperialism of Political Blackness and the Problem of Nativist Socialism', *Sociological Review* 67, no. 5 (2019), 945–67; and Rob Waters, *Thinking Black: Britain, 1964–1985* (Oakland: University of California Press, 2016).

neo-colonial domination; to support the right of nations to self-determination; to forge close links with all other anti-imperialist and anti-colonial struggles and organisations.

- To encourage the formation of and build links with black women's groups in local communities; to forge active links with existing black women's groups and all other groups and organisations which share the same broad objectives as OWAAD; to support and work with any groups which take up the issues which we see as relevant to our struggle and further the interests of black women.
- To develop a better understanding of our economic, sexual and racial exploitation and oppression through working, struggling and discussing together.

Summarising these as you did, to exclude the class perspective, is a serious distortion, especially from an organisation such as yours, which claims to have a class perspective and must therefore realise the importance of its inclusion.

With regards to OWAAD's history, we take issue with your view that the organisation's breakdown was due to groups leaving, and that they did this as a result of OWAAD's deviation from its declared aims. The actual decrease in numbers was, in fact, due to the internal problems of various member groups, as well as the actual breakup of some of them. This is part of the organisational problems of an umbrella structure and hardly a reflection on OWAAD's politics. It certainly has nothing to do with alleged movement away from them.

You then go on to say: 'by the 1982 OWAAD Conference, "Black Feminism" had become the dominant ideology within OWAAD', thereby revealing your ignorance and misunderstanding of the politics of the black women's movement as it has developed to date. OWAAD has always been a black organisation, as its name makes clear (Organisation of Women of Asian and African Descent), and it was squarely built on the foundations of socialist feminism, as its constitution and various other documents put out by it reflect. It is true that, among the wide cross-section of women attending the public annual conferences, some individuals may have expressed views that contained leanings towards radical feminism. For you to describe this as one of two distinct trends within OWAAD is quite erroneous, since it is neither distinct, defined nor clearly articulated within OWAAD. Indeed, if it was an easy task to successfully politicise and educate vast numbers of people in short periods of time against the odds we face at present, then we could in fact put revolution on the agenda for tomorrow! Unfortunately, the reality is quite different.

On a point of information, your description of radical feminists as hoping 'to gain high positions within this system' is quite wrong. What you are talking about is, in fact, bourgeois feminism. Radical feminists, along with rejecting all association with men, reject the existing system entirely and want to set up a completely separate female system. Socialist feminists, as you correctly pointed out, completely disagree with such an analysis.

Unfortunately, your understanding of socialist feminism is far from complete, which brings us to your distorted definition of the term. This is of particular importance to us in the Brixton Black Women's Group, since, as you are aware, it is our own political position. It has been developed over several years of active struggle and has been clearly documented in the editorial of our paper, *Speak Out* (issue no. 4).[2] You state that socialist feminists 'put forward the idea that all men, regardless of class, race or political consciousness uphold and support the oppression of Black women'. Within the patriarchal capitalist system in which we exist, the entire structure of society (economic, social, cultural and ideological) creates and perpetuates the oppression of women, forcing us to occupy a subordinate and secondary position in relation to men. This system of oppression does not have class or race barriers. While not all men 'uphold and support the oppression of women', all men and women do presently exist within this system which oppresses women with respect to men. It is in the interest of all those oppressed people throughout the world, and black people in particular, to recognise this oppression and work towards its overthrow as a part of the struggle for total liberation. Amongst those involved in the struggle for liberation, of course there are brothers who recognise this and

2   *Editor's note:* See pp. 209–20 in this collection.

actively fight against the evil of women's oppression. However, it is also true that the oppression of women is so deeply ingrained and pernicious that even amongst those involved in struggle, as Stokely Carmichael was at the time, backward ideas in relation to women can be maintained. Recognition of this is important to prevent ourselves falling into a sense of false security.

You go on to say of socialist feminists: 'they consider that the liberation of Black women is a concern only for Black women, and in so doing completely overlook the fundamental importance of this struggle for the liberation of Black people as a whole.' This is in direct contradiction to our actual position as stated in our editorial, which reads: 'The struggle for women's liberation has to be a part of the concrete struggle against class oppression, for no form of liberation will be possible without the overthrow of the capitalist system.' If the meaning of this was not clear to you (which would be difficult to believe), then the actions of our group, which calls itself socialist feminist, in participating within such forums as the Africa Liberation Committee and the All London Group, together with your own group (BLF) as well as others, should alone have prevented you from printing such a distortion.

Strangely enough, having misrepresented and distorted the black socialist feminist position, you go on at length in the last part of your editorial to state your own position on the liberation of black women. It turns out to be nothing more than what black socialist feminists have developed and documented. There is not a single point of contradiction between what you now say is your position and what we had already declared to be ours.

For those genuinely involved in the struggle for the liberation of black people, there is nothing to be gained in attempting to score points by unjustified attacks on others involved in the same struggle. We trust you will publish this article in its full form as a means of lessening the confusing and ultimately destructive effects of your editorial.

In Sisterhood,
Brixton Black Women's Group.
17.10.82.

SPEAK OUT

No:5 30p

DECEMBER, 1983

Black Women's Group Brixton

Editorial

ON BLACK WOMEN ORGANISING

Brixton Black Women's Group
First published in Speak Out, *no. 5, December 1983, pp. 2–7*

The demise of OWAAD has brought out the need to document our struggle before any more of our history is lost to us.[1] As an organisation, the Brixton Black Women's Group has been involved in OWAAD from its earliest stages. This is partly as a result of our own strength and internal continuity. During the ten-year history of the group we gained valuable political and community experience, which was augmented when we established the Black Women's Centre (BWC) which was to serve as the postal address for OWAAD.

It was as a direct result of the experience and continuity of the group that we felt the need, along with some other women with whom we had worked closely in previous years, to be centrally involved in the development of a national black women's organisation, one which could serve as a point of communication for black women throughout the country. Being so centrally involved in the development of OWAAD, it was inevitable that the BWG would leave its political imprint on the organisation and, therefore, we received many of the criticisms levelled against OWAAD by other organisations and individuals – male and female. Worst of all, we have been criticised by other black women's organisations for playing the dominant role that we did in OWAAD.

---

1   *Editor's note:* This editorial was republished with a small number of changes in *Feminist Review*, no. 17, July 1984, pp. 84–9.

The actual demise of OWAAD has been a painful and saddening process, because it has brought to the fore many of the contradictions – both personal and political – between black women's groups that remain to be exposed and resolved. This article is an attempt to do some of those things.

The Black Women's Movement has, to some extent, reached a critical stage with the loss of OWAAD. It is a phase in the history of black women organising that needs to be examined, As an organisation, OWAAD provided a national link between black women and serves, here, as a means of analysing some of the problems that we face when organising locally and nationally.

Growth of OWAAD

In February 1978, African women who were becoming active in the African Students' Union (UK) launched the Organisation of Women of Asian and African Descent (OWAAD). These origins do not reveal the far-reaching implications of its birth and development. It was not the first or the only black women's organisation. In other areas, African women, such as ZANU Women's League, were forming separate caucuses to their national liberation organisations. Black women resident or born in England were beginning to meet in study groups; still others had begun self-help groups, like the Manchester Black Women's Co-op; others were spearheading the 'Stop Sus' campaigns. OWAAD performed a different function. It presented, as a possibility, a chance for black women from all over England to meet with each other, share ideas and give help and support to what each were doing.

The guiding forces behind the first OWAAD meeting were women who had already been active in the few local groups there were. In the earliest months, African women students from Ghana, Ethiopia and Eritrea, for example, were prominent in the discussions about how best to organise a network federation of black women. After a short while, women activists from the indigenous black community became involved, and the proposal for a national black women's conference was developed. As the organisation of the conference progressed, it soon became clear that the main thrust of the conference was to be the position of black women in Britain.

Few of us expected the 250 women who turned up at the first conference. We in BWG had made informal links with other women organising, but did not imagine there were so many ready and eager to begin to organise and articulate around the specific oppression of black women. The conference discussed a wide range of issues around health, education, the law and immigration, as we saw these to affect us. The women who came were greatly inspired and went away to form black women's groups in their own communities in places like Hackney, east London, west London, Southall and others around the country.

With this growth, we realised the need for a newsletter to ensure links were maintained with women who were intensifying their activities in their communities. There were many important issues and campaigns that had to be fought. The newsletter *FOWAAD!* was launched to ensure that women from OWAAD knew what other women were doing, and could be called upon to give practical support. An example of this was the protest over the use of virginity tests at ports of entry. As soon as we were alerted to the use of this offensive practice on Asian women, OWAAD organised a sit-in protest and picket at Heathrow Airport.[2] This later culminated in a demonstration in central London, against state harassment, organised by women from AWAZ (Asian Women's Movement) and Brixton Black Women's Group.

In other cases, women from OWAAD gave support to women on strike (e.g. Futters); to women involved in education battles against sin-bins and expulsions; to women fighting the SUS laws; and to those facing deportation. OWAAD had all the energy and vibrancy that the Black Movement needed at that time.

---

2   *Editor's note:* The sit-in protest and picket at Heathrow Airport took place in July 1979. It was organised by AWAZ and the Brixton Black Women's Group, working together as part of OWAAD. For more on AWAZ, see 'Black Women Together: The Need for a United and Autonomous National Black Women's Organisation', pp. 135–44 in this collection; see also Amrit Wilson, 'Charting South Asian Women's Struggles against Gender-Based Violence', in *Violence against Women in South Asian Communities: Issues for Policy and Practice*, ed. R. K. Thiara and A. K. Gill (London: Jessica Kingsley, 2010), pp. 55–79.

By the end of the second conference of 1980, the organisation, which was becoming very large, had developed a structure which we had hoped would facilitate the widest participation by both groups and individuals. Committees responsible for the co-ordination of the different aspects of OWAAD's work were set up. These were the newsletter committee, the calendar and diary committee, the media committee, and so on; each was then accountable to a large collective co-ordinating group, which was the final decision-making body. Ostensibly, there were no appointed leaders or spokeswomen.

Because the organisation was made up of groups, campaigns and individuals, leadership was exercised according to the demands of each situation. Between the second and third conferences, some contradictions started to surface. Some were structural – the umbrella structure proving unwieldy; others were centred around black women's sexuality; whilst still others dealt with the complexities of putting the political principles of Afro-Asian unity into practice.

By the third conference, these cracks in OWAAD presented themselves visibly as major rifts. Meanwhile, the internal contradictions of some local groups led to their demise. Moreover, the third conference, held in 1981, coincided with the uprisings in black communities nationwide. Consequently, much energy, time and organisation was devoted to the co-ordination of legal and political defence campaigns. The urgency of the situation reinforced the drift away from involvement in women's groups.

At the conference itself, the major points of friction were over sexuality and the general line of organisation. Both of these were political questions which it was impossible to discuss properly, let alone resolve, without any agreed political framework to guide the debate, and any necessary re-organisation. The impact of the breakdown of political consensus was particularly acute at this time. Consequently, OWAAD, as an organising body, was left with virtually nothing for the year. Attempts were made to draw the organisation together and to reconstitute the co-ordinating committee with the few groups and individuals that continued to attend meetings. The result was the fourth conference, in 1982, which was inevitably a debacle. Few of the older founder members were left. Moreover, the theme of this conference – 'Black Feminism' – brought angry criticism from newer members, who did not understand the history behind the theme, and/or were 'hostile to feminism', and therefore saw its choice as a retrogressive step.

The failure both to discuss the differences and develop a way forward for OWAAD was illustrative of our inability to explain the historical trajectory of OWAAD, and to integrate a feminist analysis into our practice whilst retaining socialism as our major foundation stone.

Since then, several attempts have been made to revive OWAAD, but the organisation is, in fact, now dead.

Contradictions

The demise of OWAAD is very important because it exemplifies in specific terms, the general difficulties that black women face when organising. In its very early history, an issue which appeared to us as relatively small became crucially important, since it highlighted the way in which concrete political situations affect the specific kind of analysis developed by a group. The issue at hand was that of Afro-Caribbean and African unity. This became important in itself because, whilst we all recognised such unity as an objective reality, we were unprepared to deal with the kinds of differences between us which resulted from our concrete experiences.

At one level, such differences of approach revolved around the form of struggle we could wage. There were sisters from the African continent who were involved in liberation struggles there, which they wanted us to focus on. On the other hand, those of us from the indigenous black community saw the need to integrate these issues into our overall work. We were also concerned to keep a focus on black political struggle in Britain and the Americas. How could we all come under one banner? How could our primary fight against racism and sexism be reconciled with our African sisters' fight?

Differences over emphasis raised analytical questions such as the place of Black Consciousness in situations outside Europe, the Americas and apartheid states. What we were beginning to

learn very quickly was that the concept 'black' had very different meanings for those of us living in white-dominated societies
and regions compared to those of us from societies which were
ostensibly independent. Whilst all of us were dominated by imperialism, the manifestations of this domination were obviously
very different in the two types of situations. In our attempt to
develop a political analysis and practice which recognised the
anti-imperialist base of all our struggles, we had failed to take
account of the subjective impact of specific situations and their
practical implications. Thus, the fact that our aims and objectives
were all-embracing might have avoided, rather than confronted,
the problem.

Paradoxically, it was [from] the recognition that we had to be
more specific on our platform [–] coupled with the involvement
of even more local women, [which] led to our concentrating
on black women's lives in Britain [–] that a second, but related,
contradiction emerged.

In focusing on Britain, it became clear that an organisation of
African and Afro-Caribbean sisters could not take up the issue of
racism without responding to the questions being raised by Asian
sisters. The aims and objectives were seemingly contradictory,
even when applied to the British situation. In one sense, we were
all-embracing, but in another, more practical way, we had not
widened our base consciously to include all of those who could
and should be involved.

It was not until the winter of 1978 that OWAAD became the
Organisation of Women of Asian and African Descent. Perhaps
it was because the issue of Afro-Asian unity had not been there
from the beginning that it was problematic. More fundamentally,
perhaps, it was problematic because our political line, whilst
basically correct, was still unable to fully realise itself in our
practice. Just as our practical focus had led to the de facto exclusion of African sisters, so, too, was our line to prove unable to
adequately deal with cultural differences within the indigenous
black community. There seemed to be a fear that recognising such
differences between us would lead to a breakdown or denial of the
objective unity which contemporary British racism and historical
colonialism imposed on us. Thus, when some sisters raised the

cultural aspects, differences between us were seen by others as divisive.

Consequently, the unwitting exclusivity of OWAAD's focus, which resulted from the numerical strength of Caribbean sisters in the organisation, became symbolic of our inability to grasp the fact that recognition of cultural differences can be a political strength which helps us to transcend the divisions which our colonial and neo-colonial masters (and mistresses) and their agents attempt to foist on us.

Sexuality

Another issue that played a major part in exposing our differences was that of sexuality – the questions of our relationships with men, with other women and society at large. From the first conference there had been questions asked about the absence of a debate on sexuality. We who had been founder members of OWAAD attempted to defend ourselves, and thereby deflect the criticism, by showing how we had attempted to widen the definition of black women's sexuality by relating it to the way in which imperialism structured women's lives.

Our argument was that imperialist relations structured and determined not only our role in production – in factory and field – but that these relations also determined the emotional, sexual and psychological aspects of black women's lives. Consequently, we could only understand our sexuality in terms of the interplay between, on the one hand, class and race relations, and, on the other, those relations between men and women. It was inevitable, therefore, that the specificity of our social, psychological and emotional dependence on men would lead to a different kind of feminism from that of white, European women. The struggle for a new and self-defined sexuality was therefore part of the anti-imperialist struggle, since such self-definition, centred around the nexus of relations of production and relations of gender, involved a challenge to both our traditional cultures and cultural imperialism.

The potentially explosive issue of sexuality was now taken

out of the realm of sexual activity or sexual preference, and into the wider and more 'politically respectable' terrain of gender relations.

This was, however, a double-edged sword. On the one hand, many of us felt (and still feel) that this was a positive development for two reasons. Firstly, we felt that we had begun to place gender relations and women's oppression onto the political agenda of black organisations. This was certainly a progressive step, since, as feminists, we knew that revolutionary analysis and practice had to address itself to the fact of women's oppression and, particularly, to the structures and processes which reproduced the conditions of that oppression. Secondly, we also felt that a full understanding of women's sexuality could only be gained in relation to, and as an aspect of, the total complex of social relations of class, race and sex. Such an approach could keep us from falling into the trap of making sexual orientation the basis of organising, or the basis of divisions between us. On the other hand, however, this approach served as a guise *not* to discuss the construction of sexual orientation (rather than sexuality) at all. We thereby rendered sexual preference to the realm of the 'private', even though our argument was that *all* aspects of life were social. There was, therefore, an inconsistency in our approach.

The fact of the matter was that we were unsure how to deal with an issue that, more than anything else, showed the weaknesses which became exposed when oppressed women try to organise around both the 'traditional' areas of struggle and those issues specific to our oppression as a sex. Stated bluntly, we became the unwitting victims of our own and our communities' 'homophobia'.

It was felt that sexual activity, as it came to the fore, was too sensitive to be discussed publicly. The question was constantly posed as to how could we 'waste time' discussing lesbianism, heterosexuality and bisexuality when there were so many more pressing issues. It was, besides, a weapon the brother could use against us, as supposedly illustrative of our lack of seriousness. Political men who had witnessed the disintegration of the black movement and felt threatened by a vibrant black women's movement could, and did, use it against us. Perhaps the favourite and most effective line of attack against black women organising has been, and still is, that we are all 'frustrated lesbians'. And black ones, at that! A charge which was effective in the sense of undermining our sense of legitimacy, since it nurtured either our own belief that such issues were irrelevant, or our lack of confidence in raising these issues at a political level. Moreover, the irony in this situation was that it was supremely illustrative of the dependence on men, which we argued was a part of women's sexuality and oppression.[3]

Another popular way of undermining black women organising consisted of accusations about 'dominant, middle-class bourgeois women', who are isolated from the 'woman on the streets'. We succumbed and continue to succumb to the fraudulent and divisive analysis that 'women on the streets' could not discuss, articulate and somehow begin to fight their oppression. The argument goes that, because we are organised, we are no longer 'typical' of black women; and, therefore, the campaigns and issues we take up are misguided. These kinds of attacks seriously undermined the early unity of OWAAD.

At a practical level, events such as the uprisings had an enormous effect on many women. Black women took a leading role in some defence campaigns. Women were arrested and involved on the streets; many had fathers, brothers and lovers who were arrested, while others had to contend with their homes being broken into and destroyed in the aftermath. Despite this, the input of women – as women – somehow became marginalised. Part of the reason for this was that when women became involved in defence campaigns, we could not devote the time to our own women's groups, and many felt they shouldn't. Consequently, the strength we gained from our women's groups did not play the major role it should have done. Why was this and what input should we have made?

What these developments pointed to was some uncertainty about what we were struggling for – or, more correctly, what our priorities were. Overt feminism, i.e., raising the question of

---

3 *Editor's note:* See also 'Rise and Fall of OWAAD' in V. Mason-John and A. Khambatta, *Lesbians Talk: Making Black Waves* (London: Scarlet Press, 1993), pp. 12–13.

women's specific oppression, seemed sometimes inconsequential, eclipsed by the larger black struggle. These ideas went back to the heyday of the black movement, when it was felt that women's issues or 'the woman question' was a secondary matter that could divide the struggle.

One other difficulty that OWAAD highlighted was the internal weakness in our organisations and groups. Many of us had rejected the male idea of leadership through the totem pole. The backward ideas that had existed in the black movement was that leaders were singularly the baddest, the toughest towards their own comrades, and that leadership was the prize after a cockfight. What could we put in its place that was less destructive and individualistic?

OWAAD provided the alternative of co-operative organisation without positions of leadership to be fought over. Working through committees provided women in OWAAD with the supportive ground to develop their political consciousness. However, it left too much space for dissension – for political shifts from the anti-imperialist base. It was open for any small group to attempt to take over the organisation and try to move it in a different direction.

The problems highlighted here seem large. It might cause some to wonder how OWAAD lasted so long, and how black women are still able to organise. It is clearly because the problems of women organising are not insurmountable, and we still need to form strong organisations. We should, however, learn some lessons from the demise of OWAAD.

Lessons

The first of these involves the need to develop political unity without minimising the differences between us as black women, whether these be of a cultural or tactical nature. Such differences have come about as a result of the different colonising influences we have experienced. These need not and should not continue to be viewed in a negative way, but rather accepted and made use of, so long as there is no major difference in ideological perspective.

The oppression we have suffered (and continue to suffer) as black women, whether in Britain, the Americas or Africa, serves to keep us divided, but this oppression must also be the objective basis of our unity. We must learn to appreciate our different cultures, understand our different experiences and distinguish between these differences and objective political differences. It is from this perspective that we can then attack the various forms of oppression which divide us. Only in this way can we facilitate our continued growth as black women and thus be in a better position to react against the source and substance of our oppression in a strong, informed and concerted fashion.

Another important lesson to be learned from OWAAD's demise must be the acceptance that we must continue to stress the importance of keeping the question of gender relationships on centre stage. This will inevitably involve an understanding of the relationship between sexuality and women's oppression; but the traditional resistance amongst the black community to such an examination must not prevent us from publicly declaring the need to look at the construction of sexuality, and [from] publicly support[ing] lesbian women.

Similarly, our focus on gender relations is the only way in which we can ensure that the question of black women's oppression is not relegated to a secondary level of political consideration. As black socialist feminists, it is incumbent upon us to point out that women's oppression is inextricably bound up with the issues of race and class; and that it is right and necessary to tackle all three simultaneously, and with equal determination.

However, having declared the inextricable links between sex, race and class, we have the responsibility to carry through the political arguments with regard to feminism. This means that the thrust of our work will have two strands. On the one hand, we will continue to organise autonomously and address the issues we face as black women. On the other, we must bring a feminist perspective to the work of our comrades in mixed, progressive black organisations. In this way, we will be raising the consciousness of the black community within the context of the totality of black socialist politics.

The Brixton Black Women's Centre is at 41 Stockwell Green, SW9. The BWC aims to give help and support to black women in the community. We do this by: providing a welfare rights information and referral service; participating in a health group; providing meeting facilities; holding open days on themes reflecting black women's lives and struggles; having a small but growing library; running children's projects at Easter and summer holidays. In the near future we intend to develop a craft centre; a girls' project; a film group; regular women's socials; and relaxation sessions. If you have any ideas and/or want to participate come and join us. For further information, phone 01-274-9220.

The Police and Criminal Evidence Bill — a Briefing

Southall Campaign Against the Police Bill
Published in Speak Out, *no. 5, December 1983, pp. 8–10*

In order to sell the Police Bill to the public, the Home Office has disguised the whole exercise in a cloud of other proposals. So, there is a White Paper on an independent prosecution service for England and Wales; procedural guidance on the tape-recording of police interviews with suspects, in addition to a reference to it in the Bill – a White Paper on police complaints and disciplinary procedures; and draft codes of practice for police detention, treatment, questioning, identification, searching of premises and seizure of evidence.[1]

The independent prosecution service is supposed to promote consistency and fairness and reduce the number of cases pursued despite lack of sufficient evidence. The proposal is to give the function to the Director of Public Prosecutions with staff under him – but this is only likely to conspire against local police accountability. Anyway, there is nothing whatsoever on the whole idea in the Bill. So, when might we get it? We don't know. Similarly, the new provisions for tape-recording of police interviews is purely discretionary – the procedural guidance refers only to field trials, and similar experiments in Scotland have failed because of attempts by the police to sabotage and circumvent requirements.

The other provisions in the Bill are likely to result in a dramatically increased reliance by the police on extracting confessions from suspects, and this makes tape-recording even more necessary, but it will make an impact only if accompanied by a provision

---

1 *Editor's note*: The Police and Criminal Evidence Bill discussed was passed as an act in 1984. For more, see Louise Christian, *Policing by Coercion: The Police and Criminal Evidence Bill* (London: Greater London Council, Police Committee Support Unit, 1983).

excluding all other oral evidence from the police station. In any case, even the cursory 'commitment' to tape-recording does not tell us when it is likely to be translated into practice.

The other red herring is the idea of an independent 'supervisory' role in the shift of investigation of complaints against the police. This tinkering with the complaints against themselves [comes] despite strong representation against this from the Law Society and the Police Federation.

But all of these proposals are merely concessions. The actual extensions of police powers are buttressed by a new mischievous concept with reference to which several of them are supposed to be restricted, i.e. 'serious arrestable offence', which has been defined to include offences which in all other contexts would be considered minor. Such offence become 'serious' if their commission has led or is likely to lead to one out of a list of possible consequences:

- serious harm to 'the security of the state or public order'.
- serious interference with the 'administration of justice' or 'investigation of offences'.
- death or serious injury to anybody.

- substantial financial loss or gain to anybody.

This extended definition will embrace public order offences such as threatening behaviour or obstruction together with scheduled offences such as murder, rape and kidnapping. The significance is enormous: virtually anyone who the police finds 'odd' could be detained without charge for up to four days for the purpose of extracting a 'confession' – or search warrants for 'evidence' could allow the police to enter virtually any premises they like!

The catalogue of new powers includes:

1. STOP AND SEARCH: a new power of forcible stop and search for stolen goods, offensive weapons and equipment for stealing will be established throughout the country. The basis for this power is supposed to be 'reasonable suspicion', and, as such, it is a return to the old 'sus' law. But now, for the first time, the police will be given the power to use 'reasonable force if necessary' in carrying out a stop and search or detaining a person for that purpose.

2. ROAD BLOCKS: an effectively random new police power to set up road blocks for seven days, renewable indefinitely. They can

be set up merely by reference to the 'pattern of crime' in an area, i.e. anywhere at any time. Any protest, demonstration, picket or gathering could be the target of these siege tactics.

Searches

3. SEARCHES FOR EVIDENCE: the consolidation and extension of powers under the various existing acts will include a new power to enter and search premises, whether the occupants are suspected of any crimes or not. It amounts to a license to fishing expeditions for 'evidence'. All kinds of speculative information may qualify as admissible in court, even though it may be totally unrelated to the original purpose of the search. Warrants for the searches are supposed to be authorised by magistrates, but they need only be satisfied that a 'serious arrestable offence' has been committed.

4. ACCESS TO CONFIDENTIAL INFORMATION: the above carte blanche power to enter premises on 'fishing raids' also gives the police access to confidential information on the application of a warrant from a circuit judge – such an application could even be made ex parte without informing the person whose premises are to be searched. Specific exemptions include:

a) solicitors' files
b) medical records
c) other personal records held by priests, counsellors, etc.
d) personal records held by social workers, other voluntary agencies, and other journalistic material.

However, there is no attempt to provide a legal definition either of journalism or of social work – and the implication remains that such activities will be subjected to wholly unacceptable regulations of the state.

5. ARREST: a new power to arrest and detain persons suspected of minor offences (such as littering or parking), if one of the following applies:

a) the police believe you have given a false name and address;
b) the police believe service of a summons is impractical or inappropriate;
c) the police think you are obstructing the highway;
d) the police think you are causing an affront to public decency;
e) the police think you might damage persons or property.

On closer inspection, these powers turn out to be outrageous. Homeless people or those with temporary addresses are going to find it virtually impossible to satisfy a police officer on the street of a 'reliable' address. The condition regarding 'an affront to public decency' is tantamount to a license to random police harassment of anyone who they think looks 'odd': gay people will be especially vulnerable.

Detention

6. DETENTION: the power to detain without charge for up to ninety-six hours in order to obtain evidence by questioning, or to secure or preserve evidence, in the case of a 'serious arrestable offence'. Access to a lawyer could also be delayed for up to thirty-six hours. This power is a direct attack on the traditional 'right to silence', since it legitimises the incarceration and interrogation of people simply in order to extract confessions. Moreover, it is a license to police harassment of the kind of people thought likely to be responsible for offences according to the current and dangerous pseudo-sociological stereotypes held by the police, i.e. blacks, gays, leftists, etc.

7. TREATMENT IN CUSTODY: new powers to:

a) allow random and forcible strip searches to be carried out by police officers;

b) carry out intimate body searches of vaginas and anuses of suspects – condemned by the British Medical Association;

c) forcibly take fingerprint and body samples from detained suspects, including children aged ten or more – condemned by the Law Society as tantamount to legalised assault.

According to misleading Home Office statements, the power to intimate body searches is supposed to be used only for articles which could cause physical injury, and not for investigative purposes. But as there is little if any means to enforce such a restriction, the very real fear remains that this power will be used to intimidate and could be tantamount to legalised rape by police officers.

To reiterate, the whole point of this new Bill and its provisions seems to be the promise of virtually unlimited power for the police to assert their authority on our streets through random harassment, arrest, detention and general coercion of the public. While we are concerned about the abuse already prevalent of existing powers, the Bill simply legitimises such abuse to make it lawful! We pay a third of a billion pounds to the police force every year, so why shouldn't we have control over it? There is no turning back from the demand for democratic accountability of the police force to the ordinary people who they are supposed to serve.

The NATIONAL CAMPAIGN AGAINST THE POLICE BILL has called a NATIONAL DEMON-STRATION on SATURDAY 21 JANUARY – assemble at Brock-well Park to march to Trafalgar Square.

Thanks to SOUTHALL CAM-PAIGN AGAINST THE POLICE BILL for allowing us to reprint this summary of the Bill.

For more details, contact the Campaign at:
50 Rectory Road
London, N16
01-249 8334.

Namibia Women's Day

December, 1982

Bience Gawanas
Published in Speak Out, *no. 5, December 1983, pp. 10–12*

*The following piece was delivered by Comrade Bience Gawanas
at the Namibian Women's Day celebration held in Birmingham.
B.W.G. sisters went along to participate in the celebration, which
was well attended. Many of the Namibians who were present were
either presently in this country as students and/or were political refugees from the brutal apartheid colonisation of Namibia
by South Africa. It was a day to remember; between speakers,
there was discussion, punctuated throughout with revolutionary singing. We join Bience Gawanas in saying: LONG LIVE
THE INTERNATIONAL SOLIDARITY BETWEEN BLACK
WOMEN!*

Today, 23 years ago, a day was marked in the history of the
Namibian people as a whole and the Namibian women in particular. We are celebrating and commemorating this day at the
same time because, while we think of those who lost their lives,
we also sing our praises for their historic deeds. I could not have
been able to stand in front of you today and address you if it
was not for the contribution made by our people on the 10th
December 1959. Namibian history is a long history which can
be traced back to the 19th century; unfortunately, traces which
speak only about the deeds of men. But our names came to be
synonymous with this history when the 10th December came.
Before explaining the essence of this day, I would like to give you
a brief description of why and how the event came about.

South Africa's policy has always been one of divide and rule,
thus the allocation of land to each ethnic group in Namibia, which
embraces the whole homeland; or Bantustan Policy. Blacks were
driven into desolated lands and only a few were given the privi-
lege to live in an urban area. These people occupied an area very

near to the white city, Windhoek. Their houses were made of zinc, carton boxes and only a few were made of bricks. However, the Namibian people adapted themselves to live in extreme poverty and for years this place became a shelter to them. These people were allowed to live there just because their labour was immediately needed in the white households and industry. A people living in poverty, degraded to second-class citizens and living an insecure life, for they could be evicted to 'homelands' anytime, if it so pleases the white authorities. [They] could not live as such for ages, and our people's patience had run down. Overwhelmed by the fear of uprising near precious white homes, the racists intended to move our people to a new apartheid-built township called Katutura, which is located about seven kilometres from the city centre. The site was identical matchbox-like houses lined up in rows, where not even basic facilities – i.e. running water, sanitation and lights – were available at that time. Of course, nobody could accept that, and the people refused to be moved. They showed their disapproval through demonstrations which took the form of protests and boycotts of public transport, theatres and beer halls. as well as demands to see the administrator.

As the Africans demonstrated, the South African combined police and army, who have no sense of human dignity, opened fire and killed eleven and wounded about fifty-four. The demonstrators, who were mostly women, fought back and what was a peaceful demonstration turned into a fight between armed and unarmed. The Windhoek shootings – Namibia's Sharpeville – transformed the perspectives of liberation for Namibia, because shortly after that SWAPO was given birth. Here, I need to mention the name of a Namibian hero whose deed and life has given our women's struggle a forward thrust. Though fatally wounded, Rosa Kakurikadi set alight a police car and then died. She and the many other women who took part in this demonstration laid a foundation for all the Namibian women struggling today for liberation.

It is true that in Namibia, just as elsewhere, patriarchal attitudes and traditions date back to pre-colonial times. Among the attitudes that colonialism has intensified and re-enforced are traditional notions about woman's work and man's work. Women are the ones working in the fields, fetching water, grinding grain into flour, preparing meals and looking after children without rest. And this was aggravated because colonialism reduced the participation of men in cultivation by recruiting them as cheap labourers in the industries, mining, fishing, etc. Since women in rural areas are not allowed to live with their husbands, they assume complete responsibility of the family in the absence of their husbands.

Children grow up without knowing their own fathers. These patterns are carrying on, so that the girl, when she is big enough, has to assist her and the boy has to follow the footsteps of his father, with the result that illiteracy runs high, especially amongst Namibian women.

Discrimination against women in employment in Namibia is marked by the fact that they are not regarded as workers and are thus excluded from any bargaining process. Furthermore, few jobs are open to women outside domestic service, and those who find work as wage-earners have to tolerate the worst pay and conditions of all. Professional jobs are limited to nursing and teaching, which in themselves extend the roles of women as home-makers, but even then are obtained only by a few. For working women, life is made more miserable because they have to leave their children unattended while they are going to take care of the children of their 'missies'. This is because no provision is made for nurseries, and mothers are not always sure whether their children attend school because there is no compulsory education for Blacks. Under South Africa's colonialism, there is no area of her life which the Black woman can call her own – discrimination by sex, race and class combine in a system of exploitation, and oppression degrades her to a useless being. The Windhoek shooting made the women realise that they have a great part to play in the struggle. After the formation of SWAPO, and especially 1970 and onwards, women started to take an active part in organising meetings and rallies. SWAPO Youth League meetings were now not only attended by men but by women as well, and South African prisons started to be filled by women. Men started to rethink the prejudices they had of women, not because we asked them to recognise us as equals but through our same suffering and sacrifices. When, in 1974, thousands of Namibians left the country to join the People's Liberation Army of Namibia (PLAN), the majority of them were women. Today, we find women at every level of our movement structure.

SWAPO's aim or wish has always been to lift up the standard of the Namibian women so that they can become full participants in the struggle for liberation. Therefore, the SWAPO Women's Council was called into being in 1969 and given the immense task of mobilising the Namibian women. Women are suffering daily under SA's brutal rule. Rauna Nambinga and Anna Naujonjua were victimised because they refused to provide the South African authorities with information about SWAPO. They were arrested in 1975, tortured, tried and sentenced to six and seven years in prison, respectively. In the Cassinga massacre, women defended the camp until their last drop of blood. One such woman shot down an enemy plane and then sacrificed her life on the same spot. Ida Jimmy, who was seven months pregnant at the time of her imprisonment, was sentenced to seven years in prison last October for having addressed a SWAPO public meeting. Gertrude Katanga, deputy secretary of SWC inside Namibia, was also detained without trial for one year. These are but just a few Namibian women to note for their bravery and determination.

SWC's task was not only to mobilise women politically, but to tackle the problem of illiteracy and do away with all the myths attached to womanhood. It was not an easy task, taking into account the cultural and educational background of the Namibian women, but despite all these hardships good results are already showing. There are about 32,000 women refugees in settlements in Angola and Zambia, and it's here where the embryo of the New Namibia is taking form. Problems of health, literacy and social welfare are being tackled on a collective basis. While the regime in Namibia provides no adequate health services, education facilities and training of personnel in respective fields, men and women now have access to all these facilities. The SWAPO Education Department and the SWAPO Women's Council are running literacy campaigns amongst Namibian refugees. Schooling is provided for young people and adults – a radical alternative to the degrading education of the SA regime. Apart from the lack of resources, there is the constant danger of SA raids into Angola and Zambia, where untold damage to life, property and livestock is caused not only to the Namibian but also to the local population. During SA's attack on Cassinga, many people were captured and reports had it that they are being tortured, and some people, amongst them women, have been completely deformed.

Despite the above-mentioned facts, the Namibian people are not deterred by the brutal acts of the SA regime. Our motto still remains: UNTIL FINAL VICTORY. We, the women of Namibia, will continue to fight alongside our male comrades till victory is achieved.

Today we think of the Sharpeville massacre, of the women of El Salvador, Chile, Guatemala and many, many more who have sacrificed their lives and who are still placing their lives on the altar of freedom, human dignity and peace, and I call upon all of you to observe a minute of silence to remind ourselves that they have not died in vain. That when liberation comes, they will be remembered as the torchbearers of our struggles.

Given this opportunity, allow me to express our solidarity with the oppressed women the world over. Let us fight not against men but alongside them to achieve our ultimate goals. The women's struggle is not an isolated struggle but that of emancipation. President Samora Machel once said: 'Liberation without the emancipation of women is no liberation at all'. The struggle does not end until all peoples are seen as equal. Therefore, I appeal to all of you to contribute the least [sic] each one can, be it morally, materially or otherwise to the well-being of all humankind.

Our slogan remains:

WOMEN ALL OVER THE WORLD – UNITE!
EVERYTHING FOR THE STRUGGLE – ALL FOR VICTORY!
INDEPENDENCE OR DEATH – WE SHALL WIN!
LONG LIVE THE SOLIDARITY AMONGST STRUGGLING WOMEN THE WORLD OVER!

Thank you.
Bience Gawanas

STRIP SEARCHES IN ARMAGH JAIL

London Armagh Co-ordinating Committee
Published in Speak Out, *no. 5, December 1983, pp. 13–14*

The following account is from the London Armagh Co-ordinating Committee and tells of the horrific conditions facing women in Armagh Women's Prison and the degrading practice of strip searches, which is carried out there.

The present situation in Armagh jail is very tense, with petty restrictions, harassment and the strip searches of the 27 to 30 sentenced and remanded women republican prisoners continuing.

The withdrawal of privileges – letters, parcels and visits – and the victimisation of particular women is continuing. At least one recently sentenced woman has been strip-searched scores of times.

Prison officers watch the women constantly, and the 'on report' trips to Governor Murtagh have become a daily routine. Punishments range from one day total lock-up to 10 days' solitary confinement, and loss of privileges for up to a month. The situation has deteriorated and tensions have increased to such a degree that the treatment meted out to the women republican prisoners is now worse than at the height of the dirty protest.

The systematic practice of naked inspection of women's bodies every time they leave the prison began on November 9, 1982. The strip search includes internal probing in front of both men and women prison officers. A refusal to be strip-searched resulted in one woman being sentenced by Governor Murtagh to five days' lock-up in her cell. Refusal to be strip-searched, by a woman being held on remand awaiting trial, has resulted in her being dragged out of the cubicle by about 11 prison officers and being

Mural from Falls Road, Belfast.

thrown onto the floor. By struggling and kicking she resisted their attempts to remove her clothing. Two of the male officers twisted her arms behind her back. One sat on her legs and another female sat on her stomach. The rest dragged her clothes off and when this was done, they stood around her smiling, as she lay naked and shivering on the floor.

Secretary of State James Prior, answering a question in the House of Commons on strip searches, insisted that the search is 'a brief visual one, carried out by a woman officer, and with no contact with the prison officer'. If a prisoner is menstruating, he said, a woman hospital officer was in attendance during the search.

This is a complete distortion of the facts. Republican women prisoners in Armagh have pointed out that 'Not one, but a minimum of 10 prison officers are present to carry out a strip search. In the presence of these prison officers assigned to the "duty", a frontal and back inspection of her naked body is carried out. This, in itself, takes at least 15 minutes, during which the woman remains completely naked and is often subjected to vulgar remarks about her body'.

In their statement, the women have indicated that 'strip searching is, in fact, a totally humiliating, embarrassing and indecent experience for the prisoner'.

The women have requested that, while menstruating, they retain their pants and sanitary towels. At least one woman has been forced to the floor and this request ignored.

'The remaining prison officers then proceed to remove the pants and soiled sanitary towels. Furthermore, no hospital trained officers were present.'

On one occasion when two members of the Board of Visitors were present, a sheet was thrown over a woman once she had been forcibly stripped. The two visitors, one with an English accent, told the women republican prisoners individually that if they were injured during strip searches they had only themselves to blame. Thus, the supposedly independent body to which prisoners can appeal against practices taking place in the prison is in collusion with Governor Murtagh, the British government and prison authorities.

The present regime in the prison seems determined to break the resistance of the women republican prisoners – and the strip searches are a central part of this. They are, according to the Governor, <u>not</u> being carried out for 'security reasons'. He has also recently separated the women into individual cells because he claims that two women to a cell would encourage lesbianism. It is reported that the Governor recently introduced a uniform to be worn during strip searches – a little skirt and top – which apparently the woman may wear as an alternative to standing naked. The inspection of their naked bodies could then be carried out by a prison officer lifting up the skirt and top and inspecting the woman's naked body.

Petty harassment of the women has also increased, with punishments meted out for:

- switching the TV channel without permission in the association cell;
- for sitting on a windowsill on the wing;
- for washing and ironing clothes outside the prescribed time.

With the ending of the dirty protest, the women began to do work. The work allotted is making prison uniforms and doing the laundry of male prisoners in Crumlin Road Prison in Belfast. The women have been refused permission to make children's toys. Educational facilities, promised when the dirty protest was ended, have still not been provided, months later.

The strip searches, the punishments and the separation into separate cells has led to increased tension in the prison. The prison authorities seem determined to provoke the women back onto the dirty protest. Such is the anger in the six counties against the strip searches that Cardinal O'Fiagh has been forced to call for them to be completely stopped.

The relevance of the strip searches to Britain is highlighted by the recent incident in Brixton in which the police forced a young black man to remove his trousers and pants in the street. Similar incidents have gone unreported. The new Police and Criminal Evidence Bill gives the police the power to strip search (including doing internal inspections) whenever they like.

LONDON ARMAGH CO-ORDINATING COMMITTEE

PECKHAM BLACK WOMEN'S GROUP

Peckham Black Women's Group
Published in Speak Out, *no. 5, December 1983, p. 15*

The Peckham Black Women's Group started meeting in October 1981. After attending the OWAAD Conference, a few of us from within that area decided that it would be good to start our own group after listening and seeing what groups there were already.

Most of our time – especially recently – has been taken up with grant applications to various committees, attending local meetings to try and establish ourselves within the community, and to see what the Borough of Southwark, as a whole, is doing in the areas of race relations, women's issues, etc.

We are in the process of negotiating for premises. We are going via the Southwark Women's Committee for this, and, as the GLC Women's Committee recommends that every borough should have at least one women's centre, we stand a pretty good chance, although we are facing a number of difficulties now.

We have a temporary meeting space and one part-time worker, and have GLC funding for additional workers. We are presently advertising for another three.

At present, we are meeting twice weekly – Thursdays at 6.00 p.m. and Sundays at 4.00 at St. Giles Hall, Benhill Road, London S.E.5. We have run a ten-week self-defence course, as part of which five members of our group went to Holland to a ten-day self-defence conference.

We have also run various other courses. So far, we have had the South London Immigration and Nationality Group in to talk to us about the implications of the

Nationality Bill, and we hope to be able to set up a system whereby we can help women to fill in application forms for citizenship, etc. We have also arranged for other speakers from relevant groups to talk to us, and have taken part in various women's events. We have regular discussion groups and should resume our study group shortly, when we get over the administrative load.

Obviously, as the group is still fairly new and we get new people coming often, we have different ideas politically and otherwise. We have to adapt to a certain extent, to try and encompass many views.

There are differences between women in the group, which makes it difficult at times; but most, if not all, groups will have this hurdle to overcome.

We strongly encourage and would like to see as many black women's groups as possible.

We can be contacted by post at:

PECKHAM BLACK WOMEN'S GROUP
c/o 130 Evelyn Street
London S.E.8.
or ring:
Pat – 639-3976 after 6.30
Sharon – 274-8685

WOMEN AND EL SALVADOR

El Salvador Women's Committee
Published in Speak Out, *no. 5, December 1983, p. 16*

The Women and El Salvador Group has produced some materials for sale/hire which might be of use to solidarity groups or women's groups who are interested in support work for the women in struggle in El Salvador. The cost of making these materials available has been met entirely by our women's group and, therefore, we would appreciate it if you could pay for them in advance, to help us avoid cash problems.

Our group is presently involved in the following:

1. A campaign of fund-raising to support a health project being organised by the Association of Salvadorean Women (AMES) to provide basic health care for children in the controlled zones of El Salvador.
2. The reproduction of information about Salvadorean women in struggle, particularly about AMES and its work and aims inside the country, in the controlled zones and in the refugee areas.
3. A petition campaign for the release of four Salvadorean women political prisoners.
4. Arranging speakers for women's meetings on the struggle in El Salvador and in support of Salvadorean women.
5. Participation in conferences, meetings, etc., within the women's movement in Britain, to further the cause of international solidarity with Salvadorean women.

To help us financially, we have materials available for your use.
Please send your order and cheque made payable to:

El Salvador Women's Committee
c/o CARILA
29 Islington Park Street
London N1

THE CRIMINAL
INVASION OF GRENADA

Brixton Black Women's Group
Published in Speak Out, *no. 5, December 1983, p. 16*

On the 25th October 1983, the U.S.A. invaded the sovereign state of Grenada, ostensibly to end the threat to lives, to restore order and to return the island to 'democratic rule'. We in the Brixton Black Women's Group join with others throughout the world to condemn this deliberate transgression of international law. The American invasion of Grenada is an outright act of military aggression, determined to crush the revolutionary process which began in Grenada in March 1979. We unequivocally condemn this act of international terrorism and demand that all foreign invading forces be withdrawn from Grenadian soil.

As progressive people, we were shocked and saddened at the internal dispute within the New Jewel Movement which led to the tragic killing of Prime Minister Maurice Bishop, his ministers Unison Whiteman, Norris Bains and Jacqueline Creft, and many other unnamed Grenadians by the military forces on October 19th. We are grieved that an internal dispute should end in the loss of so many lives, and we bitterly condemn those killings.

This sad and tragic loss, however, must not be allowed to kill the revolutionary process. We must take our lead from the heroic and courageous struggles waged by the people of Grenada against the American and Caribbean invading forces. We also salute the noble people of Cuba who rallied to the aid of Grenada.

The continued struggle of the Grenadians acts as a symbol

to imperialist America and its lackeys – Adams, Seaga, Charles, Osbourne, Cato and Simmonds – that the people of Grenada are not going to allow their country to become anyone's 'back yard', and that from Grenada the seeds of revolutionary hope have been sown within the Caribbean as a whole, which not even military invasion can crush.

WE SALUTE THE COURAGEOUS STRUGGLES OF THE GRENADIAN PEOPLE.
<u>FORWARD EVER … BACKWARD NEVER!</u>

TRIBUTE TO SYLVIA OME ERIKE 1953 – 1983

Organisation of Women of Asian and African Descent
Published in Speak Out, *no. 5, December 1983, pp. 17–18*

All of us are grieving deeply at the loss of our dear sister, Sylvia. And although she would have wanted us to see it in context with the many other untimely and unnecessary deaths with occur daily throughout the world, how can anyone who knew and loved her not feel sorrow and a deep sense of loss at the knowledge that she's gone?

I doubt that Sylvia realised just how many people she touched in her short life. The news of her death has gone through our community like a shock-wave, and those of us who knew her through her political activities know that we have lost a sister, a comrade, a friend who can never be replaced.

What a woman she was! The image of Sylvia at the first Black Women's Conference in 1979, delivering her paper on 'Black Women and the State' – so nervous and yet so powerful – is engraved in our memories forever. She was a sister who felt the injustices of this world so deeply that she gave everything she had to the struggle – her tremendous energy, her sharp, intelligent mind, her heart and her soul were dedicated to the cause of black people.

Many of us got to know Sylvia early in 1979, when our first attempts to organise black women were drawing together sisters from all over Britain. Having completed her degree at Lancaster, she had just spent two years at Manchester doing her M.A. She threw herself into the work of preparing for our first conference and her outstanding ability to analyse and articulate our collective experience made a lasting impression on us all. Sylvia's upbringing and her first-hand experience of racism had given her an insight into our lives which touched something deep in all of us. Her warmth, her intensity, her beauty and her humility made it impossible for anyone who knew her not to love and respect her.

Throughout 1980 and 1981, Sylvia worked on the Co-ordinating Committee of OWAAD (Organisation of Women of Asian and African Descent) and devoted herself to the task of organising with other black women around the issues which concerned us then. Although she was, by this time, enrolled at the London School of Economics and writing her PhD thesis, she still found the time to write prolifically about our struggles and played an active part in a variety of black community and women's groups around London. It was Sylvia who helped organise and run our day school for black women on Afro-Asian unity, understanding as she did the destructive nature of cultural nationalism in our community. It was Sylvia who jumped to her feet on numerous occasions, defying anyone present to make light of the day-to-day realities of racism and sexism. She was always amongst the first to volunteer when there was work to be done – an article to be drafted or an issue to be discussed – and many of us will remember her in particular for her readiness to offer support and

encouragement at times when we were feeling confused, under pressure or just in need of a friend. Despite the ongoing pain of her mother's illness and eventual death, she managed to maintain a level of political activity which has taught us all a great deal about strength and sisterhood. Despite her own vulnerability, she supported us – through our births and our deaths, our joys and our sorrows, our successes and our failures – Sylvia was there, right beside us, giving it all she'd got. Let no-one lament that her life was wasted! Sylvia died at a time when many of her plans and ambitions were on the point of being realised. Her lecturing and research work into racism and sexism at Thames Polytechnic enabled her to combine her outstanding capacity to write with her obvious charisma as a teacher, and anyone who ever heard Sylvia speak, either in a classroom or a conference hall, will know how she shone in these roles. Her thesis on black women in Britain was on the verge of completion and she had intended to use the information she had compiled as the basis for an evening course at Hackney College this autumn. She was also making a determined effort to confront and come to terms with the pain and frustration of her own life, which had caused her for some time to seek to drown her sorrows. Her longing to establish her African roots had led her to plan a trip to Nigeria this December – and how we wish for her sake that she could have made it. No, Sylvia did not waste her time here; nor did she intend to leave us all right now, when so much was ahead of her.

Those of us who knew Sylvia know that she loved life. She celebrated every positive aspect of black womanhood to the full. Her passionate love of music and her insistence on her right to be exactly who and what she was are among her many attributes which bear witness to this fact. Picture Sylvia now – Sylvia laughing; Sylvia dancing; Sylvia doing the sounds; Sylvia weeping; Sylvia shaking her fist, indignant and angry at the injustice of oppression. We will remember you, sister, not as you are now, lying there in peace at last, but as you were then, <u>a revolutionary black woman right down the line!</u>

From your sisters in OWAAD
August 1st, 1983

REVIEW

Brixton Black Women's Group
Published in Speak Out, *no. 5, December 1983, pp. 18–19*

The Color Purple
by Alice Walker
The Women's Press

Alice Walker won the 1983 Pulitzer Prize for this novel. She was the first Black Woman to win the literature prize. The awarding of this prize to a Black Woman, [writing] about Black Women, primarily for other Black Women is an achievement in itself. This prize is awarded to the best novel dealing with an aspect of 'American life' ...

This is without doubt the best novel I have read in years. It touched me on so many levels, and after staying up all night to read it I found myself just crying. This is a beautiful and at times tragic (life) story.

The style of writing is in the form of letters by Celie to 'God'; then to her sister, Nettie; and finally to the stars, trees, sky peoples and everything. It encourages you to lose yourself in the reality of this life story. To be honest, I find it difficult to express all the emotions that were aroused in me – anger, frustration, despair, respect, hope, love, dignity and just plain happiness are just a few.

It's not like a 'story', because you instinctively feel the truth of it. Even now, I have to remind myself that this is (in a sense) a product of another Black Woman's imagination. But, like most 'stories', you know it is derived from 'Every Black Woman', bringing together the essence of those times.

In trying to create a Black Feminist critical analysis, our sisters have suggested searching for how both sexism, racism and Black and female identification occur. Also, for the use of a specific Black female language, lesbian/women-identified (as being central, pivotal and positive) relationships, self-definition and the discovery of the limitations of Black Women's prescribed role.

Within *The Color Purple*, all these aspects are explored. Black identity, in the harsh segregated world of the South, is a prerequisite for survival, in the sense of having to know your place – or not, as in the case of Celie's friend Sofia and her Amazonian sisters. Their experience was a combination of 'pore black woman' and the retribution for daring to bring any pride to these aspects of their lives. Sexual and radical politics account for the rape of Celie by the man she knew as her father, her sister Nettie having to leave, losing her children and her marriage to a man she does not love or enjoy sexually. These combine to restrict her growth in all dimensions. 'Life' is narrowed to day-to-day existence and the acceptance of her 'fate'.

Discovery of this narrowness and self-definition comes through the letters of Nettie from Africa, which show that she is not alone in her experiences. Also, through the love and friendship of the other Black Women in her community, she is allowed the freedom to express herself.

This is one book expressing the many aspects of Black Women's experiences. For me, it was a re-declaration of my belief in 'God' –

When I found out ... God was white and a man, I lost interest ... I believe ... God is inside you and inside everybody else ... God ain't a he or a she ... it ain't something you can look at apart from anything else, including yourself.

It also declared the Black Lesbian experience, in the fullest sense of that word: Women giving strength and support to each other, Black Women as women-identified. Shug Avery, a Blues singer and 'bad-talking Woman' who is never too 'shamefaced to put singing and dancing and fucking together' is saying out loud that we are (among other things) sexual beings. For me, too, presenting the love between Shug and Celie in the way it was – 'natural' and 'healthy', unproblematic to their growth as individuals – was good to see. There was no agonizing over this 'other' love, it just was. Through their love, they realize self-discovery and self-determination, rather than self-loss and sacrifice.

As a Black Lesbian who has searched for <u>any</u> written acknowledgement of my life, this 'made' the novel for me, although at times I did wonder what had happened to the much-expressed homophobia (hatred and fear of homosexuals) of the Black Community. An unanswered question, for me, was how Nettie and family would react to Celie and Shug. Nevertheless, presenting the relationship in such a way was an inspiration, even encouragement, 'to be'.

I was prompted by sisters in the BWG to read the book. After I read it, I had the sensation of having been somewhere, stood on the outside and watched these goings-on. This isn't a story, it's a life experience that is Black Female, Woman-identified and Lesbian.

At the end of the novel, Alice Walker thanks everybody for coming, signing herself author and medium: 'Believe it'.

Thank you, Alice Walker

REVIEW

Brixton Black Women's Group
Published in Speak Out, *no. 5, December 1983, p. 20*

Women, Race and Class
by Angela Davis
The Women's Press

It is to be hoped that Angela Davis' *Women, Race and Class* will serve as an important guidepost for feminist thought.[1] It not only provides a reasoned, compelling perspective about the division between black and white feminists, but is also a well-researched, scholarly work which gives a much-needed grounding to the black and white feminist movements. Her thesis – that both sexism and racism are deeply rooted in class oppression – lays the blame squarely where it belongs, in the lap of capitalism.

Davis argues for more commitment to the struggle against sexist and racist oppression, but from the basis of a more realistically accurate historical perspective; one which would necessitate an understanding of the fact that black people, women and other oppressed groups are all manipulated for the sake of the survival of the capitalist patriarchy.

Although the book is loosely tied together chronologically, it is more like a series of essays. Her analysis of the early women's rights movements in the United States (both black and white) documents the racism which was always just below the surface in the white women's movement. In a noteworthy chapter entitled 'Rape, Racism and the Myth of the Black Rapist', she challenges

---

1   *Editor's note:* Published by the Women's Press in 1982, *Women, Race and Class* was republished by Penguin Modern Classics in 2019.

the racism inherent in the conclusions of white feminist anti-rape campaigners. Most notable of these is Susan Brownmiller, of whom Davis says:

> Her failure to alert white women about the urgency of combining
> a fierce challenge to racism with the necessary battle against sexism
> is an important plus for the forces of racism today.

Davis examines the impact of industrialism on black and white women workers, the plight of black women under slavery, and also the position of middle-class white women and the inconsistencies and contradictions raised by the abolitionist/suffragist movements.

Her discussion of the racism inherent in the birth control campaign was particularly compelling and should provide food for thought for those who criticise black women for lack of involvement in those movements. The early Abortion Rights Campaigns, she says:

> failed to provide a voice for women who wanted the right to legal
> abortions while deploring the social conditions that prohibited
> them from bearing more children.

Davis covers a lot of ground with this book, and it is not just a book for black and white women, but for all those who bear the brunt of oppression in the name of capitalist expansion and profit. Throughout, she pays tribute to those courageous black women – Ida B. Wells, Claudia Jones, Frances E. W. Harper and many others – who fought against incredible odds, most often without the aid of their white sisters, for the survival of black people and the recognition of the rights of black women in particular.

REVIEW

Brixton Black Women's Group
Published in Speak Out, *no. 5, December 1983, pp. 21–3*

Ain't I a Woman: Black Women and Feminism
by bell hooks

bell hooks' intention in writing this book was to document the impact of sexism on the social status of black women. By providing concrete evidence, she sought to refute the anti-feminist argument which claims that black women are not the victims of sexist oppression and are not in need of liberation. The tool used to refute this anti-feminist argument lies in black women's experiences of racism and sexism, and, according to hooks, can only be understood through the politics of feminism. As such, bell hooks presents a history of black women's participation in American society during and after slavery – a participation which has been and is conditioned by patriarchal ideology, the racism of white America and the sexism of black men. From the 19th century suffrage movement to the contemporary Women's Liberation Movement, women's organisations are shown to be submerged in their own racism, which prevents them from having any real meaning to black and other Third World women.

sexism & slavery

The first chapter deals with the impact of sexism on black women during slavery, and shows how white slave owners imposed European values on their slaves.

Enslaved black people accepted patriarchal definitions of male-female sex roles. They believed, as did their white owners, that woman's role entailed remaining in the domestic household, rearing children, and obeying the will of the husbands.[1]

The structural contradictions thrown up by these models were further complicated by the notion of 'womanhood'; role definitions became even more contorted with racist sociological theories of 'demasculinisation/emasculation' of the black man by black women.

The writer takes up the emasculation theory in more depth in Chapter Two. Here, she evaluates the impact of literature, science, sociology and the media in perpetuating the negative image of black women. Racism and sexism act to neutralise any potential political alliances black [women] might make. The vicious use of sexism, as specifically related to the supposed looseness of black women, is examined at great length.

By perpetuating the myth that all black women were incapable of fidelity and sexually loose, whites hoped to so devalue them (black women) so that no white man would marry a black woman.[2]

Not only is the black woman told she is emasculating her man, her character is presented as ranging from sexually loose to the passive 'mammy image'[3] – acknowledging her inferiority to white people but loving them. This chapter draws on many racist/sexist ideas prevalent in American society about the black woman. Unfortunately, it does not present a counter-argument, nor indicate positive strategies. After offering such persuasive evidence to support her argument about the systematic devaluation of black womanhood, hooks leaves her reader wondering what black women have been doing through the centuries to fight for their emancipation. In fact, despite her account of black women's involvement in both the abolitionist and suffragist movements,

---

1 *Editor's note:* bell hooks, *Ain't I a Woman: Black Women and Feminism* (London: Pluto, 1981), p. 47.
2 *Editor's note:* Ibid., p. 61.
3 *Editor's note:* Ibid., p. 84.

one is left with the distinct feeling that black women were the only group who failed to respond politically to their own oppression.

Chapter Three, 'The Imperialism of Patriarchy', while identifying the impact of patriarchal ideology, also stresses the unity which exists between black and white men – the agreement on the oppression of women through sexism. However, the main concentration in this chapter is on the sexism of black men, which is traced from the 19th century to the present day.

misogyny

Black men have been sexist throughout their history in America, but in contemporary times that sexism has taken the form of outright misogyny – undisguised woman-hating.[4]

With the support of 'sociological' evidence which says that black men must prove themselves – and seeing that violence is an expression of male strength – men are violent towards women to keep them subjugated, and this is acceptable to modern society. In this chapter, it is made evident that while black men are struggling to achieve an end to racial oppression, they cannot gain their 'manhood' at the expense of black women.

Black female/male relationships (like all male/female relationships in American society) are tyrannized by the imperialism of patriarchy which makes oppression of women a cultural necessity.[5]

bell hooks pulls this together and makes the connection between white patriarchs and black men's sexist behaviour, which for many years has been excused and unchallenged, or interpreted as resulting from black men's experience under slavery. Her exposé of black men's oppression of black women is welcome and overdue. The problem is that she attempts to reveal the extent of black women's suffering under slavery – racial and sexual – by denying that black men also suffered sexual humiliation and degradation.

---

4 *Editor's note:* Ibid., p. 102.
5 *Editor's note:* Ibid., p. 117.

> Racist exploitation of black women as workers ... was not as de-humanizing and demoralizing as the sexual exploitation. The sexism of colonial white male patriarchs spared black male slaves the humiliation of homosexual rape and other forms of sexual assault. While institutionalized sexism was a social system that protected black male sexuality, it (socially) legitimized sexual exploitation of black females.[6]

What form of protection and status was enshrined in the history of lynching!

Chapter Four examines the historical tensions between black women and white women's movements. hooks shows how racism acts to successfully stop white women from identifying their struggles as one with black women, as the absence of true feminism. This historical tension is as prevalent in the contemporary women's movement. Racism is seen as the obstacle to 'true Sisterhood'.[7] White women need to recognise and confront racism and the question of how they are going to incorporate black women and their experiences into the women's movement in a meaningful way.

> Relationships between white and black women were charged by tensions and conflicts in the early part of the 20th century. The women's rights movement had not drawn black and white women close together. Instead, it exposed the fact that white women were not willing to relinquish their support of white supremacy to support the interests of all women.[8]

The women's movement as it is now constituted is viewed as a negative place for black women to be because it does not reflect the race and class nature of black and Third World women's experiences. White feminism has served to make people aware of sexism, but has gone no way in eliminating sexist oppression. The feminist ideology is the tool to unite all women, but racism must be removed as an obstacle to this realisation.

---

6   *Editor's note:* Ibid., p. 24.
7   *Editor's note:* Ibid., p. 149.
8   *Editor's note:* Ibid., p. 136.

The final chapter of this book fails to deliver the expected final focus. While it re-emphasises some important points and rightly locates black women's historical contribution to the struggle for black liberation, it does not outline contemporary involvement and struggles – a disappointing final chapter after what started as a stimulating and historical analysis of black women's contributions. bell hooks fails to take her definition of feminism and use it to analyse the life of black women. She seems to see feminism as a vanguard for the liberation of all oppressed peoples. This point is too sweeping, since it conveys to the reader that the philosophy of feminism is a panacea for all types of oppression. To some extent, this is at odds with the socialist world view of political struggle.

I would have liked some more in-depth analysis, especially in the vital last chapters in which hooks discusses radicalism and feminism, and black women and feminism. Still, a book which I recommend for black women and, as another critic noted, '… not only for women, but for unenlightened men, too'.

REVIEW

Brixton Black Women's Group
Published in Speak Out, *no. 5, December 1983, pp. 23–5*

*All the Women Are White, All the Blacks Are Men, but Some of Us Are
Brave: Black Women's Studies*
Edited by Akasha (Gloria T.) Hull, Patricia Bell-Scott
and Barbara Smith

This book is not intended as a reader, rather, it is meant to provide
examples of research and 'teaching' about Black women, and
seems to be aimed primarily at those involved in education.
Nevertheless, I found it valuable and diverse reading.

Black Women's Studies, as an independent discipline, began
to emerge in the late 1970s. The book is made up of syllabi,
reading lists and articles on various topics. The three editors –
two of whom hold posts at universities, as well as being active in
the movement – are dedicated to the need for a Black Feminist
perspective within this area. This is an ambitious attempt to
repair the damage and draw together the pieces of Black women's
stunted existence.

The book is divided into sections, each dealing with an aspect
of Black Women's Studies/lives in America. Our sisters' efforts
to define a feminism, by, for and about Black women's experience includes Michele Wallace's 'Search for Sisterhood',[1] coming

---

1 *Editor's note:* M. Wallace, 'A Black Feminist's Search for Sisterhood',
in *All the Women Are White, All the Blacks Are Men, but Some of Us
Are Brave: Black Women's Studies*, ed. A. Hull, P. B. Scott, and B. Smith
(New York: Feminist Press, 1982), pp. 5–12.

through the Black Consciousness Movement with the realisation
that Stokely was serious when he'd said her 'position in the movement was "prone"', and 'understand that the countless speeches
that all began "the Black man ..." did not include' her.² Meeting
together since 1974, the Combahee Collective also outline their
attempts to develop an integrated analysis.³

The articles on racism include writing from both Black and
white women, giving meaning to the heading of 'Roadblocks and
Bridges'.⁴ Alice Walker and Barbara Smith are among the contributors. Ways of tackling racism through consciousness-raising
are included, the emphasis on recognising our own 'roadblocks'
to putting up 'bridges' – or being receptive to them.

'Black Women and the Social Sciences' was especially interesting and enlightening to me, as a student of the subject.⁵ Racist
(and sexist) assumptions going unchecked for 'Black women' as
an area of study means that a great area of our lives is ignored
or misinterpreted. Unfortunately, Black women social scientists may work within these assumptions or 'problems', and so
continue to misrepresent our experiences. A realistic redefining
of Black women's identity, sensitive to racism and sexism, is
called for.

health

New considerations were offered to me in the section on health
– physically, mentally and spiritually.⁶ Exploring these areas can
lead us to discover not only how we can be broken, but how we
can strengthen and survive. Beverly Smith offers us references
(which, unfortunately, like many of the others, are difficult, to say

---

2 *Editor's note:* Ibid., p. 6.

3 *Editor's note:* Combahee River Collective, 'A Black Feminist Statement', in ibid., pp. 13–22.

4 *Editor's note:* 'Section Two – Roadblocks and Bridges: Confronting
Racism', in ibid., pp.35–58.

5 *Editor's note:* 'Section Three – Dispelling the Myths: Black Women
and the Social Sciences', in ibid., pp. 59–100.

6 *Editor's note:* 'Section Four – Creative Survival: Preserving Body,
Mind, and Spirit', in ibid., pp. 101–54.

the least, to follow up in Britain) dealing with such areas as mental health, sexuality, violence against Black women, etc.[7] It is pointed out that the references are not without their shortcomings, as none are written from an integrated Black Feminist analysis. Constance Carroll deals with the stress that Black women in higher education face, with the effort to achieve and maintain their position in an environment where to be Black and female means one has to constantly prove one's worth to white women as well as men.[8]

Avenues of expression and relief accessible to Black women have been music and religion. With both of these, we are shown how Black women, through decades, have used these as mental and spiritual power houses. By teaching and learning about the literature of Black women, it was shown how one could trace out the patterns of our survival using our Black Feminist perspective – recognising our lesbian writers, drawing from their intensified experience to corrode the constraints of male-defined womanhood, [and] at the same time supporting (and urging the re-discovery) of women who do and have recorded their – our – experience. Zora Neal Hurston – who was an independent, woman-identified, Black, female artist and social scientist – and Alice Dunbar Nelson deserve to be acknowledged not only for their sakes, but for our own.[9] The book acts as an introduction to these women and encouraged me not only to read their work but to think of Black women here who have struggled and are struggling to do the same.

Section six is made up of an amazing and thought-provoking group of bibliographies and bibliographic essays, no doubt painstakingly compiled in an attempt to retrieve the lives and work of Black women in America – performers, composers,

---

7 *Editor's note*: B. Smith, 'Black Women's Health: Notes for a Course', in ibid., pp. 103–14.

8 *Editor's note*: C. M. Carroll, 'Three's a Crowd: The Dilemma of the Black Woman in Higher Education', in ibid., pp. 115–28.

9 *Editor's note*: L. Bethel, '"This Infinity of Conscious Pain": Zora Neale Hurston and the Black Female Literary Tradition', in ibid., pp. 176–88; A. Hull, 'Researching Alice Dunbar-Nelson: A Personal and Literary Perspective', in ibid., pp. 189–95.

playwrights, poets and writers.[10] The final section gives us an idea of how concepts put forward by the contributors have materialised within actual college and university general and literature course syllabi.

For me, the book touched on many areas of my life, made me re-examine these and see in them a new value. It also made me consider the struggles of my own Black Women's Group to form an ongoing practical analysis, and that thankfully we are not the first (and definitely not the last) to attempt this.

Hopefully, these kinds of 'studies' of our history will, in fact, not only be open to the very few of us who (in spite of the system) make it to the more conventional seats of learning. Some of the contributors, thankfully, talk of taking these studies into the community, through what I imagine would be the equivalent of our Adult Education Institute and as shorter courses at community and women's centres. (This history belongs to all of us.)

Racism consciousness-raising – or what we call racism awareness – is very popular at the moment, especially with some employers. Although on an individual level it might make a person appreciate how it can feel to be a victim of racism, this is only at a personal level. As we come to realise, racism is not just about personal attitudes – it can also affect us on an institutional and social level. Racism CR can be misleading in this respect.

'All the women are white, all the Blacks are men...'. This phrase sums up the aspect of Black women's history ... 'But some of us are brave' revealed to me our rightful place among the achievements and struggles of women and Black people. Reading the whole book revitalised my sense of purpose and offered new directions for my struggles. The conscious inclusion

---

10 *Editor's note:* 'Section Six – Bibliographies and Bibliographic Essays', in ibid., pp. 219–334.

by most contributors of heterosexism – along with the other
three 'isms' (racism, sexism and classism) – I found comfort-
ing, and supported my hopes of the same for my British-based
sisters.[11]

---

11 'Heterosexism': The belief that heterosexuality is better, more
'natural' or 'normal' (both words no feminist should use without extreme
caution) than homosexuality. Like sexism and racism, it ranges from the
overt and violent ('queer-bashing'; believing homosexual sex should be
illegal) to the subtle (asking lesbians, but never oneself, 'how you get that
way'; thinking that some lesbians and gay men are too 'blatant', even
though displays of heterosexual sex are all around us). All of us, gay or
straight, have taken in very negative images of homosexuals – lesbians as
failed men, or failed women who couldn't get a man; gay men as counter-
feit women, frivolous and bitchy. But just describing the prejudices shows
how much heterosexism and sexism are intertwined. While lesbians suffer
discrimination and harassment, all women are kept in line; but heterosexual women must take care that they don't buy their 'respectability'
at the price of anti-lesbianism. 'A to Z of Feminism' – courtesy of *Spare
Rib*. *Editor's note:* see Robyn, 'A to Z of Feminism: AmaZing Pull Out,
Part 1', *Spare Rib*, no. 136 (November 1983), 27–31.

POEM

Kadifa
Published in Speak Out, *no. 5, December 1983, p. 26*

If I could turn back the hands of
   time
I would have been there
to cushion her fall...
She was an inspiration to all
of us that knew her fine mind
Though there were times
when things were rough
She was always angry
when things were tough
for black women and people
She would probably laugh
to see us now
commiserating her death
She may have wished
that we would see
that we should all be
more sisterly ...
'Ome' was her African name
and she was proud
of her blackness
and she was glad

to be a woman
loving woman
and fighting for the rights
of all oppressed people.
She lived her life
in ups and downs
and those she touched
upon the way
will ever forget
her passion for change
in this foul society

If I could turn back the hands of
   time
I would have been there
to cushion her fall ...
Sylvia!
Why did you have to leave us all
   so soon?

Kadifa
25.7.83

FROM THE INSIDE LOOKING IN: A REAPPRAISAL OF HEART OF THE RACE

Sisters in Study
First published in Charting the Journey: Writings by Black and
Third World Women, *edited by Shabnam Grewal, Jackie Kay,
Liliane Landor, Gail Lewis, and Pratibha Parmar.
London: Sheba Feminist Publishers, 1988, pp. 91–6*

To review anything – a play, book, film or piece of music – is a
tricky situation at best. To issue forth a subjective opinion, among
a host of others, offers few rewards. Yet, those of us who continue
to do it do so with the somewhat precarious consolation that we
might possibly change a mind or two, or at the very least, steer
the reader along a path towards alternative or different lines of
thinking.

The intent of this review leans more towards the latter position.
We seek to pass comment on the recent book, *Heart of the Race*,
a history of Black women's lives in Britain (and a book which is
very close to our hearts) not because the authors got it wrong, but
because we feel that as one of the groups of women with which
the book deals, there needs to be an assessment of it, given our
frames of reference.[1]

---

1 *Editor's note:* First published by Virago in 1985, *The Heart of*

One reason why it is difficult to write about *Heart of the Race*, has to do with the close involvement that many of us had in the early stages of the book's preparation, and the fact that for one reason or another we were unable to write it ourselves in a more active way. Thus, it is with the benefit of hindsight that we write about it now.

First and foremost, however, must come praise for a remarkable achievement by the authors in beginning to document the history of Black women in this country. It was a project that had to be undertaken before any more of our history is lost to us and future generations. Without Beverley Bryan's, Stella Dadzie's and Suzanne Scafe's perseverance and efforts, this precious setting down of our history may indeed have been lost or misappropriated.

As it happens, this is the book's strength. It is an excellent reader; and is without parallel insofar as relating the history of one segment of Black British women. *Heart of the Race* fills a void that needed filling; detailing as it does the day-to-day struggles and triumphs of a generation of Black women in a hostile society.

> For those of us who have been brought up in isolation from our communities, without the security and instinctive support that comes from having other Black people around, the experience of cultural isolation can be equally confusing ... The reality of racism in Britain has debunked the idea that we can escape this feeling of alienation and 'otherness' for all but a few. Whether born or bred here, our experiences at the hands of employers, police, teachers, and white society at large have forced us to acknowledge that we are something other than 'British', sharpening our collective awareness of our differences.[2]

The political understanding which the authors bring in analysing the situation of Black people in Britain, in particular, is exemplary. However, due to the book's somewhat limited frame of reference

---

the Race: Black Women's Lives in Britain was republished by Verso in 2018.

2 *Editor's note: The Heart of the Race*, pp. 228–9 (in both the 1985 and 2018 editions).

regarding Black women, it has failed to pursue events which were, and still are, of major importance in the history of Black women organising in Britain.

We take note of the authors' proviso that their aim was to 'tell it as *we* know it, placing our story within its history at the heart of our race, and using our own voices and lives to document the day-to-day struggles of Afro-Caribbean women in Britain over the past forty years'.[3] However, we feel this statement does not justify or account properly for the omission of the significant numbers of Asian women from the Caribbean, who also contributed to the history of Black women in Britain.

The experience of those of us who were involved in the Brixton Black Women's Group was that Asian women from the Caribbean were significantly involved in Black people's struggles, not only in Britain but in their home countries as well. Asians have been in the Caribbean for generations, having been brought as indentured servants who could eventually work off their bondage and buy land. Some went back to India, but many stayed. The 1981 Census for Trinidad, for example, recorded a 42 per cent Indo-Caribbean population.

The book's failure to acknowledge their contribution, in even a nominal way, contributes to the schism which exists between people of African and Asian descent. It is an omission which cannot go unchallenged if we are engaged, as we purport to be, in a progressive struggle for the benefit of *all* Black people.

This leads onto another point which the book fails to take up adequately – the dynamics which accompanied the debates in the Black women's movement around Afro-Asian unity. The Organisation of Women of Asian and African Descent (OWAAD) was the forum for Black women for much of the debate around this difficult issue in the latter part of the 1970s and early 1980s.

Yet, in the book's discussion of the OWAAD years, no mention is made of this very important issue. It does acknowledge that OWAAD 'could no longer project itself as a united front', and that this fact contributed to its demise.[4] But the reasons for

3   *Editor's note*: Ibid., p. 2 (in both the 1985 and 2018 editions).
4   *Editor's note*: Ibid., p. 177 (in both the 1985 and 2018 editions).

this are limited to differences of opinion between feminists and non-feminists in the organisation. While this was the case to some extent, by far the over-riding reasons for OWAAD's departure centred around its failure to bridge the differences between the different hues – both literally and in the political sense – of the Black women within it.

To an extent, we have still been unable to entirely move beyond these differences (though progress is being made). This could explain why the authors decided against trying to tackle the issue head on. But, as this critique is about injecting new thoughts, it can be argued that this fact presented all the more reason why the subject should have been dealt with more effectively.

Failure to respond to it, however, does not make the problem go away. On the contrary, it needs to be aired and analysed and worked through so that those who come after can gain and build upon our experiences. The discussions which went on around this issue within the Brixton Black Women's Group and OWAAD were real and relevant. They raised significant issues with which we are still grappling.

The discussions centred around the contradictions between, on the one hand, reconciling the seemingly conflicting aims of women from established Black communities in Britain with those of women living here but involved in liberation struggles in Africa[; on the other hand,] there was the need to be accountable to different groups of women from Asian backgrounds and cultures who had yet another set of perspectives and mores. In its very early years, OWAAD had been the Organisation of Women of Africa and African Descent. It was launched in 1978 by a group of African women active in the African Students' Union, and soon attracted activist women from the establish Black communities. It became clear, however, that an organisation made up of African and Afro-Caribbean women could not take up the issue of racism without responding to the questions being raised by Asian women.

The inability to handle the ambiguities in the objectives and the inter-relations between the varied groups of women contributed greatly to OWAAD's eventual departure. Many people were fearful that recognising and acknowledging the differences between us would cause a breakdown or a denial of the objective unity which contemporary British racism and historical colonialism imposes on us. Thus, differences between us became daggers of division.

Another major rift within OWAAD, which *Heart of the Race* fails to take up, occurred around the issue of sexuality – the questions of our relationships with men, with other women and society at large. Specifically, the issue of lesbianism divided us.

By and large, the Black communities' traditional homophobic attitudes remain staunch. Because of this, some Black women saw the issue of Black lesbianism as a tool which could be used to denounce others of us within our communities; running counter to this was a body of opinion which came to regard discussions on sexuality as an irrelevant pursuit, ill-suited to the forums of 'ideas' and 'struggle'. The fact of the matter is, however, that we ourselves were unsure how to deal with an issue that, more than anything else, showed the weaknesses that become exposed when oppressed women try to organise around both the 'traditional' areas of struggle and those issues specific to our oppression as women.

Black lesbians, however, with the help of others, forced the issue within OWAAD. They refused to accept the consignment to second-class status that Black lesbians had been made to endure. They rightly argued that the homophobia of the Black communities in general, and many Black sisters in particular, had to be exposed and dealt with in a progressive manner; and, furthermore, that the whole issue of sexuality, of necessity, had to become part of the Black political agenda. This was the only acceptable set of circumstances which could enable Black lesbians to be part of their communities on their terms – with no apologies. Despite the fact that there were no lesbians involved in the writing of *Heart of the Race*, the *issues* they represent should have been addressed. After all, that is what our discussions were about; that is, the need for the *whole* of the Black community to take on board the considerations raised by the fact that lesbians exist as part of the community.

The reverberations, from these two debates, in particular, are still making themselves felt within the Black women's movement in Britain. Both instances represent a continuing and pivotal part of our struggle. In the process, we are all getting a bit wiser and thus better able to manage our own survival as Black women, and ultimately, that of our communities.

> Even centuries of slavery, oppression and sexual abuse, of attacks on our culture and on our right to be, have not succeeded in breaking Black women's spirit of resistance. Instead of distancing us from the African heritage which sustained us, the thousands of miles we have travelled and the oceans we have crossed have simply strengthened our collective sense of self-worth.[5]

Our final criticism of *Heart of the Race* rests mainly on the mechanics of the book. In particular, we regret the authors' decision not to put names to the women they quote. We believe this is important for two reasons. To have identified the women whose experiences are re-lived would have given the text more life and would have also helped to legitimise these experiences in a more visible way, both for the women themselves as well as in relation to their communities.

Too much of our history is consigned to anonymity, which makes it all the more desirable that we humanise our past, whenever possible, by bringing alive the names and faces of those who went before us. It is a collective history on which the book is based, and the cause might have been better served had this fact received more prominence.

Notwithstanding these criticisms, however, the writers who wrote *Heart of the Race* are due our unreserved gratitude for getting a piece of Black women's history down on paper. But perhaps it was too much to expect that it could all be said in one place. Nor, in retrospect, should we want or expect it to be. We have many voices.

It is the first of what promises to be a watershed of history – taking on the lives and struggle of Black women in this country. It remains for others among us to carry on where *Heart of the Race* left off.

---

5 *Editor's note*: Ibid., p. 239 (in both the 1985 and 2018 editions).

BRIXTON BLACK WOMEN'S CENTRE: ORGANISING ON CHILD SEXUAL ABUSE

Marlene T. Bogle
First published in Feminist Review, *no. 28, 'Family Secrets: Child Sexual Abuse' (Spring 1988), pp. 132–5*

The Black movement on racial oppression and exploitation in Britain was born out of the fact that no one but ourselves can fight for our liberation. But, just as we have to fight against imperialism and one of its tenets, racism, so as women we have to fight against sexism and male chauvinism, which is part of our oppression as Black women.

Over the years, experience has shown us that if we are to play a part in determining our own destiny, as women and as subjugated people, we have to raise our own level of consciousness and lead our own campaigns. It was with this awareness that the first Black women's group was formed in Brixton in 1973, to organise around the specific issues affecting us. These issues were never discussed, much less taken up, by the already existing organisations in the area.

The lack of resources in the Black community made it necessary for us to meet in each others' homes for the first two years after the group was formed, as we had no other suitable place to do so. In 1975 we found a meeting place and were able to meet more regularly and to attract more women to the group.[1] In the course of meeting and discussing some of the difficulties that were being faced by us and many other Black women in the community, a member of the group raised the issue of lone mothers and how, as a women's group, we could support these mothers who were often isolated in their homes with their children. As a result of this discussion a group was started in October 1976, aimed at bringing together unsupported mothers, both Black and white, and particularly the young and inexperienced, who were isolated in the home. Its function was to encourage these mothers to learn to work together in a stimulating and creative setting where their children would also be cared for. This stimulation enabled several of the women to return to college and some to part-time work.

Whilst some of the women in the Black Women's Group worked with the craft group, others were active in other community groups and organisations in the area. We chose to work in this way as it was impossible to initiate any long-term projects, owing to the lack of a permanent base.

As Black women organising, we realised that we needed a permanent base inside the community, where we could continue to develop our ideas and provide facilities for women and children to meet on a regular basis. We worked for funding and, in July 1979, we appointed two workers. The major task of one worker was to find suitable premises to be used as a centre; the other continued the work with the women in the community. It took a long time to find suitable premises, but the Black Women's Centre was officially opened in September 1980.

The aim of the centre is to provide and establish a permanent base where Black women in the community can seek support, help and encouragement in coping with specific problems which they may face in terms of isolation, poverty, racism, sexism and class oppression. Although the emphasis is on Black women, no woman who wished to seek advice would be excluded.

We have developed a bank of information which is made

---

1 *Editor's note:* It is likely that Bogle is referring here to Sabarr Books, at 121 Railton Road. See footnote 7 in 'Memories of Olive: A Very Strong and Fearless Black Sister' (pp. 177–8 in this collection).

available to all those who use the centre. Other areas of development are a craft workshop, a crèche for mothers who use the facilities, and a library and resource centre specialising in women's literature and Black history. We also run an information and advice service on such matters as health care and legal and welfare rights for women. Through regular meetings, seminars, discussions, films and study groups, women who use the centre are developing our political awareness, enabling us to understand our particular position as Black women in this society, and to guide our practice in our struggle for change.

My work around child sexual abuse started in 1985. Two women who knew of the centre asked to use the space to start a Black survivors' group. They advertised the meetings, and fifteen women attended. They had had enough of the racism and stereotypical images that were portrayed again and again at predominantly white, middle-class incest survivors' groups.

Unfortunately, the group folded after some six months, leaving only three women to carry on this very important work. I concentrate on one-to-one counselling. This is mostly with women who now feel ready to talk about their abuse and abusers.

The majority of women who contact me have seen our telephone number on leaflets and other publications; some are directly referred through other women's centres or other voluntary organisations in London. There are also referrals from YTS [Youth Training] schemes and social services in Lambeth, which seem to be lacking in social workers with the necessary experience in sexual abuse cases.

We feel that statutory bodies use us at their convenience and when it suits them. They refer to us cases which they cannot manage, and they come to us for advice on specific cases, but they do not open themselves to the criticism, advice and help we could offer them to develop a more appropriate service to Black children and adult incest survivors. We see ourselves as women who have the experience and expertise to make a valuable contribution to policy and practice within statutory organisations, as well as working alongside them. This would not usurp their power. This state of affairs leaves us feeling exploited and taken for granted.

Our help is desperately needed and we cannot give up on the women and young people coming to us for help, but the centre receives no extra funding for this important work. The work, therefore, has to be done outside of and sometimes during my normal working hours (as in the case of telephone counselling). There is also the additional strain of being responsible for and bearing the whole burden of counselling and advising often vulnerable women without the backup of an organisation which is ultimately responsible.

The majority of women who contact the centre were abused during childhood, so there is no need to inform social services or obtain police involvement. More recently, children and young people have been referred to us for counselling but social workers deal with the statutory side. This has alleviated a lot of anxiety, because our past history of relations with the police has left its mark on the Black community. Black women, in trying to protect their own children, face racism from the police which can compound the abuse already suffered by the children. Black mothers do not want to put their children through this, yet they wish to get justice for their children. They find themselves in a cleft stick, wondering whether to go for police involvement or not. Social services are often not sympathetic to the quandary that mothers and children feel on this question.

The Black Women's Centre has had to organise around child sexual abuse because, although sexual abuse has been an issue in the context of the women's liberation movement, it has for a long time been portrayed and dealt with as a 'white' problem. Books that have been written on the subject have ignored and excluded any experiences of what it means to be a Black survivor. All the myths, stereotypes and racism that surround child sexual abuse have portrayed incest as problematic only for white women and children. Black women did not have a place in this because of the racism inherent in explanations of child sexual abuse. Incest has been seen and believed to be the norm within the Black culture and way of life. This is not true.

Black women and children do *not* expect to be sexually abused as a normal part of life. To dismiss this myth, one has to be factual and say that child sexual abuse does not know race, class and creed. It is an international issue and affects us all. What has to be understood is that what it means to have been abused is different for each incest survivor, dependent on their other experiences. Black women survivors have the experience of racism as a factor in the meaning for them. It was recognition of this which started the work on sexual violence of the Black Women's Centre.

Marlene Bogle is centre co-ordinator at Brixton Black Women's Centre. This article is a modified version of a paper given at a conference in April 1987: 'Child Sexual Abuse: Towards a Feminist Professional Practice'.

Talking personal Talking political

Gail Lewis, Melba Wilson and Olive Gallimore
in conversation with Agnes Quashie
First published in Trouble & Strife *19, Summer 1990, pp. 44–52*

Agnes Quashie talks with Gail Lewis, Melba Wilson and Olive Gallimore of the Brixton Black Women's Group about its activities, strengths and weaknesses, the contradictions of funding and the complex relationship Black women had and have to the women's liberation movement. This interview with Olive Gallimore, Gail Lewis and Melba Wilson is a discussion about their individual reflections/perceptions of the Brixton Black Women's Group and is not to be taken as the final word of the collective as a whole.

Agnes Quashie: Shall we begin with a history of how the group started?

Gail Lewis: Basically, it was a mixed group that started in 1974; women from *Race Today* and women from Sabarr bookshop who were working in mixed organisations and trying to form a women's study group. The aim was to get a space for themselves to look at the questions of colonialism and the nature of capitalist society, African history and these sorts of things. The object, then, was probably to locate themselves as women but not particularly as feminists.

The context of Brixton at the time is important, because it was when there was a very big local surge of political activity in a number of fields. There was, for example, a very active South London Women's Charter group that was a predominantly white women's organisation, but very much focused around questions of working-class women's relationship to work/

employment. Some of the early Brixton Black Women's Group (BWG) women felt that was a women's organisation that they could have at least some sympathy with, because it seemed to be related to questions of class, whereas much of the Women's Liberation Movement was organising in consciousness-raising (CR) groups and was deemed to be not really to do with them – certainly not to do with working-class women, as it was thought to be a 'petit bourgeois' diversion, if you like.

Something else that women were involved in, at that time, was the whole move in Brixton and other parts of the country on the question of housing and the demand for empty houses to be given over to local people to be renovated. At that time, a squatters' movement was developing, and one of our sisters, who is dead now, a woman called Olive Morris, was involved in that and in setting up the study group. This was important, that we saw ourselves as an organic part of local community-based political struggle. She was also involved in trying to set up Sabarr, which was the Black bookshop, because that was a time when we, as Black people, were particularly vocal, both in Britain and in the US, in expressing the need for the learning and writing our own history, literature being central, particularly resistance literature.

This also related to the whole question about imperialism politics, where literature was seen as a part of the resistance struggle; you know, the decolonisation of the mind and all that. Olive, in fact, got the Sabarr bookshop, the original one we had at the end of Railton Road, by going out as a part of the collective and claiming the building. In fact, when the council was going to evict them, she went up onto the roof and said 'I won't come down until you let us have the building'. So, what I'm saying is that the history of the group started as a study group, out of two locally-based Black organisations, but saw itself very much as part of a community-based organisation, campaigning on a number of issues.

AQ: How and why did each of you become involved?

Melba Wilson: I came to this country in 1977 from California, where I was involved with consciousness-raising type women's groups, and I had done a lot of things in terms of Black politics and community politics. However, when I came here, I was looking for more of a consciousness-raising group. Also, I was looking to get connected to the Black community. I am married to a white British person, and so I was cut off from the Black community, so in that sense the group was a sort of mainstay, a grounding.

CR was one of my main thrusts in the group, and I kept on pushing that; that the personal is the political. But, ultimately, the group became for me a political education, because even though I had done a lot of work in the States, it was in the narrowly defined strictures of Black politics, and basically it was all aimed at getting a piece of the pie, the American pie. BWG broadened my whole perspective in making me more aware of what Black people outside of the States were doing, and what Black people were doing outside of Britain, and, in a sense, it opened my eyes to the world.

Olive Gallimore: What was talked about little then was that women came out of different educational experiences or abilities or political understandings of their situations, but there was the need to move beyond that. I was brought up in west London, I was a 'single parent' living in Vauxhall. I got to know other women, single women, women who were less articulate than the other women who were in BWG, and I suppose in that sense I was part of this group of women who came in, but I wasn't intimidated by that, because there was some purpose behind it in sharing and moving beyond our current situation. Lots of things were happening at a community level, and people were organising around education, quite specifically. What was missing, at that time, was a clear political or feminist analysis of what was taking place and to find a way of using that to absorb as many women as there were. I think later on that created conflicts, and it was quite an important political lesson for everyone involved.

GL: BWG was not the first women's organisation that I had been involved in. As a teenager, I had been involved in things like the Soledad Brothers Support Campaign here,[1] and, briefly, in

1 *Editor's note:* See George Jackson, *Soledad Brother: The Prison*

something called the Black Liberation Front, when it first split off from the Black Panthers.[2] I developed what I considered to be a Black consciousness, I had always thought of myself as some kind of a socialist as well, and during that period, before the late '60s, I met one of the women who had been involved in setting up the study group and was introduced to a number of Black political events, really, rather than a whole active network. Then I went away for a while, because prior to that I had thought that feminism had nothing to do with Black women and working-class women of any 'race'. Then I started to read a few things and thought that maybe there is something in this, and then got involved, in 1975, in the National Abortion Campaign, as the lone Black woman in the area where I was living.

I wanted a Black women's group but was terrified, because by this time I had also come out as a lesbian. I heard about a group that met every Sunday and I thought about it for a long time and then thought 'No, I can't possibly go to a Black women's group, because I'm a dyke', and then one day I just took courage and went.

I joined the group because I felt not only did I want to be involved in a Black women's group, but I wanted to be in a Black women's group that defined itself as socialist and anti-imperialist. There had to be some form of continuity for me in terms of my previous political development.

Letters of George Jackson (Chicago: Lawrence Hill, 1994 [1970]); and Angela Y. Davis, ed., *If They Come in the Morning…: Voices of Resistance* (London: Verso, 2016 [1971]).

2   *Editor's note:* For more on the British Black Panthers, see A. M. Angelo, 'The Black Panthers in London, 1967–1972: A Diasporic Struggle Navigates the Black Atlantic', *Radical History Review* 103 (2009), 17–35; R. E. Bunce and P. Field, 'Obi B. Egbuna, C. L. R. James and the Birth of Black Power in Britain: Black Radicalism in Britain 1967–72', *Twentieth Century British History* 22, no. 3 (2011), 391–414; R. D. Kelley and S. Tuck, eds, *The Other Special Relationship: Race, Rights, and Riots in Britain and the United States* (New York: Palgrave Macmillan, 2015); J. Narayan, 'British Black Power: The Anti-imperialism of Political Blackness and the Problem of Nativist Socialism', *Sociological Review* 67, no. 5 (2019), 945–67; and Rob Waters, *Thinking Black: Britain, 1964–1985* (Oakland: University of California Press, 2019).

OG: For me, the influence came out of the Black Panther, Angela Davis era; you know, the 'most wanted woman in the United States' and that kind of thing, and because as a single parent I had been working on those issues and, like Gail, wanted to belong, I got involved. What I wasn't clear about at that time was feminism, so to speak, it wasn't something close to me.

AQ: How were you run, was it collectively? Did you have funding?

GL: At that time, we would have rejected funding. Our demand was that there are empty houses; we have a right to them as Black folks, we're going to take them.

The study group used to meet in people's houses, and by the time we joined in 1978 we used to meet in Sabarr bookshop, in the room at the back. Clearly, that was not satisfactory, but it was a necessary step, because when we eventually came to discuss whether we should set up a centre there were many long and important discussions about whether an organisation like ours – one that was supposed to be revolutionary, supposed to be about change and centrally supposed to be critical of the state in the way in which it controls all Black people and working-class people – how could we take money from the state?

AQ: What did the organisation consider were its aims and objectives? Did it have a particular kind of politics; any particular labels by which to identify the people who were involved?

GL: We were a collective, but at the same time we had, like all other collectives, different individual women there. We had different forms of knowledge, we came from different kinds of political histories and political understandings, but there wasn't one leadership position. On the contrary, actually, that manifested itself more in organisations such as the Organisation of Women of Asian and African Descent (OWAAD) than in BWG or in any of the local Black women's organisations that we developed links with.

OG: I think that individuals were struggling to identify themselves, and the community also saw us in a particular way. It was not until later that we sat down and decided who we were and wrote a position paper. It was not an overnight thing that you suddenly had one uniform concept of who we were.

There was a lot of individuality within BWG. This is why the identity of the group involved at times a very deep and painful debating, to get those different focuses on the agenda.

MW: I suppose we were all already political women, which is what made us come to BWG in the first place. We were all a certain type of Black woman, and while we saw ourselves as being very much a part of our community, that did present problems in terms of Black community politics, male/female Black community politics. However, in terms of the workings of the group, the coming together around a political basis was what provided the impetus and is what I think got us over a lot of those contradictions – even though we may not have dealt sufficiently with them at the time. For instance, the heterosexual/lesbian divide, which is still hanging up the Black women's movement to this very day, as I am sure you are aware.

At the same time, I do think that we did try and deal with these issues, but it was after some prodding. When Gail got up in a meeting and came out to us, it precipitated a whole load of discussion, heartache and soul-searching, which was good in terms of the group having to face its own weaknesses.

GL: The group, for most of the years that I was involved, was a heterosexual women's group. I can remember saying to myself, 'I have to tell these women that I am a lesbian'. I was living with a white woman at the time and I felt this enormous split in my life, in terms of living as a lesbian and with a white woman then, yet being involved in anti-racist and Black women's liberation politics. But I did not necessarily want to go into a discussion about it, because I felt alone. I knew that some other women in the group were lesbians, and for one woman in particular it was hidden from the rest of the women in the group for a long time. Granted, there may have been some discussion about lesbianism and what it meant, but, in the late '70s/early '80s, lesbianism was not seen as a political issue; it was seen as something you did privately and was therefore your own business. We really managed to hang ourselves up with that, because like every other Black organisation at that time, we had a notion of the Black community as traditional, as homogeneous and as unable to deal with difference.

After we got the Black women's centre in 1979/80, a Black lesbian group was formed. I was not a member of that, but they asked at some point it they could meet at our centre, and there was one hell of a furore amongst women from BWG, saying things like, 'We can't possibly have lesbians meeting in our centre, what would the community say? – they'll know', and all this kind of stuff. By that time, though, there were enough other women, and not only the lesbian women in BWG but heterosexual women as well, who were saying, 'This is crap, are they not our sisters?' So the lesbian group met in the centre, but if you talked to any of the women who were involved in that, they never felt as if the centre could be claimed as their own; they always felt hostility.[3]

There are also other questions about other identities and political positions. Some women may not have said that they were socialists as individuals, but the group always said it was socialist.

MW: It wasn't only the lesbian issue that was not adequately dealt with. For instance, I am in an inter-racial relationship, and I had great angst about wanting to come out in that way and not feeling that I could. In the end, I did pluck up courage and said it and one of my enduring memories is just how many other women in the group were in inter-racial relationships also, and we just did not know it. We were all afraid to come out in that way, which is why my thrust was always the personal becoming the political, because there was that sense that we could not talk about stuff that happened outside in our other lives. It was like having a split personality, but, in a way, I felt a bit of a fraud, being in an inter-racial relationship, coming to a Black women's group and not being able to discuss that whole other aspect of myself. This is why I pushed for the consciousness-raising aspect of the group. Not to the exclusion of the active political campaigning work that we also did and which was the main

---

3   *Editor's note:* For other accounts of this incident, see V. Mason-John and A. Khambatta, *Lesbians Talk: Making Black Waves* (London: Scarlet Press, 1993), p. 13; and Julia Sudbury, *'Other Kinds of Dreams': Black Women's Organisations and the Politics of Transformation* (London: Routledge, 1998), p. 241.

thrust of the group, but I also thought that other strand was important. So, we had these two strands working within the group for very much of its active period. However, I do believe that we began to deal with it in as straightforward a way as we could at the time, given our frame of reference. You have to remember that we were seen as an anachronism within the Black community; we were taking time away from the valuable Black struggle, talking about women's politics, women's rights and so on, and that was seen as a white women's issue, diverting our energies away from the Black struggle. There were all these things going on at the same time, which we were just trying to work through on a daily basis.

GL: I was probably one of the most vocal women in the group, and I can remember saying, 'I don't want a CR group'. I mean, there was an Irish war going on, there was Palestine, there was Southern Africa, there was class struggle in Britain, and we had a wealth of information and something to offer. So, I wanted to foreground all that stuff.

MW: I don't think it got in the way of our work. It was left hanging, but it was left hanging while we got on with the business of fighting the SUS laws and fighting the virginity testing at Heathrow Airport, and doing a lot of really good work.[4] I mean, we did have an agenda, and in those Sunday meetings when we met from three o'clock until six/seven, the things that were on those agendas were about the SUS laws, about how we could organise as a community to stop young Black boys being stopped and hassled by the police. We organised around health, fighting against Depo-Provera injections, and all that kind of stuff.

---

4 *Editor's note:* In July 1979, as part of the Organisation of Women of Asian and African Descent (OWAAD), AWAZ and the Brixton Black Women's Group organised a sit-in and picket at Heathrow Airport in protest of the 'virginity testing' many Asian women were subjected to by immigration officials on arrival to the UK. See 'Editorial: On Black Women Organising', pp. 257–67 in this collection; see also Amrit Wilson, 'Charting South Asian Women's Struggles against Gender-Based Violence', in *Violence against Women in South Asian Communities: Issues for Policy and Practice*, ed. R. K. Thiara and A. K. Gill (London: Jessica Kingsley, 2010), pp. 55–79.

OG: There was also the issue of whether or not the group ought to accept partnership money (funding). As I remember it, the discussion was quite fierce and went on for weeks. In the end, it was agreed that we would, but Olive (Morris) also insisted that she be statemented as saying she did not want to be a part of this, based on a political analysis of the state getting involved in the lives of Black people and buying them off.

GL: The cost was that we lost individuals. Women would come for a short period of time and then feel that the set-up wasn't for them. This was usually for different reasons. Sometimes they would say, 'I am not a socialist'; some of them were more separatist; for some, it was not a feminist enough type of group. But I think the key thing here is that it was contradictory. It was contradictory in the sense that I was the only out lesbian for quite a while, but I was also one of the people who was arguing against talking personal, that this was a political organisation and not necessarily a friendship organisation.

AQ: How did you see BWG's relationship to predominantly white feminist organisations; about the idea of women being in sisterhood, Black as well as white women? Did you have close links with other women's groups that had a predominantly white involvement? Lastly, what do you think about white women who are involved in politics and struggles pertaining to Black women? How do you see these things fusing together, or don't they?

GL: Let's start with the 'easiest' one about what other women's organisations we were connected to. We were connected to many, and we also worked alongside many, and we were actively involved in other Black women's groups that started. We were very much involved in setting up OWAAD. We were connected to other women's organisations fighting around anti-imperialism: to SWAPO Women, Zanu Women and with women from Ethiopia, Eritrea; with Black American women's organisations, with Irish women's organisations. To some extent, we were also involved with women organising around Palestine and anti-Zionism. We also mixed with many other organisations, like the Depo-Provera campaign, for example. We also had links with, but a different type of relationship with, other white women's organisations that did not have a specific anti-imperialist focus, like reproductive rights. It was a much more tense relationship with such organisations, but we weren't necessarily fighting against each other.

What is problematic is, because there is scanty documentation about our work and aims, both Black and white women have picked up a very wrong picture of the politics of Brixton Black Women's Group; saying things like we were completely against free and safe abortion on demand on the NHS, for example. We always supported the demand for a woman's right to free and safe abortion, but we also said that abortion was not the sole issue. I mean, from our own experiences, from what we knew to be happening to Black women in this country, and from a kind of picture of the world.

MW: With regard to the second part of your question, I think BWG set itself up to be an autonomous Black organisation, and I think that was partly because some BWG members had been involved with white women's organisations/movement and had come away feeling very disillusioned by the racism that they found within them; as well as the refusal generally to accept that there were issues that concerned Black women, or that Black women were involved with, that meant that we operated within a mixed (female/male) context within our communities and that we did not see ourselves as separate from our communities in their entirety. We consciously organised as a Black women's organisation because we wanted to address those things. I suppose that it was a reaction to the racism in the white women's movement, as well, and it was also a reaction to the sexism of Black men, so in that sense we were a consciously Black and female organisation.

GL: I don't think that we had a principle by which we responded to white women feminist organisations or white women socialists, or whatever. What guided us, despite the fact that some women felt extremely suspicious of white women's organisations, even when they were organisations like Women Against Imperialism, for example, was saying that we come from a position of Black socialist feminism; our central concerns are the anti-racist/Black Liberation struggle, the anti-imperialist struggle and the struggle against capitalism. Therefore, we decided that we would work with, we would make alliances with people, as and when we could see that they were also fighting for those things. We acknowledged that alliances are not a matter of principle, alliances have to be strategic.

AQ: Was it difficult to negotiate all those different identities, i.e. at one and the same time being a Black women's organisation, a community-based organisation, and negotiating that with wider women's issues – as you say making alliances – and also at the same time acknowledging the racism that can come from those alliances and dealing with them? Was it difficult to negotiate all those things and come out with something that you felt was positive?

OG: It was a minefield. Rather than use the white women's group terms 'in sisterhood with' we would say 'in solidarity with'. This is because we were still working out the racism, or at least forcing them to look at that. Again, in terms of this concept of 'in sisterhood', although I did not have any formal contact with white women's groups, I think very warmly of individual white women who contributed very significantly to my understanding of what was going on. At the time, I did not see how valuable it was to me. However, now I can see that it has been extremely important in shaping and giving me hope.

GL: But I think the way we negotiated it, and negotiated is exactly the right word, was because of the way we operated. We would have our Sunday meetings and then we would go off to do things that we had been collectively delegated to do. The strength of that is that you could always argue with other organisations that you were representing BWG. BWG grew in terms of how much respect it had; it was recognised in terms of socialist feminist networks at the activist level. There was a great deal of strength in that, because you knew if there was a problem you could always go back to the group to get some feedback and work out how to proceed.

In many ways, the most fraught sorts of negotiations that we had to deal with were with the men involved in the Brixton Defence Campaign. After the 1981 uprising – we had close links with the organisations in Toxteth by now – the women from BWG and the women and men from the Brixton Defence Campaign joined and went to Liverpool. We still had to make it known that we had something to say; that we were not just the providers of space – they used to meet in our centre – and the people who did the typing. We still had to fight to be heard. I remember there was a big row on the coach on the way back from Liverpool, between the women and the men, and that created quite a big rift between us. Some of the sharpest contradictions that arose arose in relation to Black men, rather than in relation to white women.

OG: Although it did not affect me directly in my confrontation with some of those men, I know that some very strong sisters were physically quite shaken by that experience. Where there were differences between the women in those different groups, we could argue quite forcefully about them, but there still remained a great deal of respect amongst us. However, that sort of respect was missing in our disagreements with the men, and they were often quite dismissive of us in very derogatory terms, and they did not want to look at why they were behaving in those particular ways.

AQ: I am conscious of what I am going to ask next, because at times I get slightly wary of the motives behind questions that are constantly asked about the relationships between Black women and Black men. However, having made my qualification, why do you think your relationships with white women were less problematic than with Black men?

OG: Black men, those so-called political men, saw Black feminism as divisive, in the sense that it was splitting the movement, and those of us who had a long and continuing relationship with Black men weren't communicating with them on that political level. With white women, that is the basis on which a lot of relationships have been formed. But the immediate problems between the Black man and the Black woman were not analysed in that way; communication was about personal things – the way you treat me, the personal not being the political – and I don't think that the Black men had grasped that. Also, they themselves were struggling through nationalist politics and had become quite entrenched in their own sexism and domination of women. It was only a privileged few of those men who were able to come out and look at all these things in a political context, but even they did not really want to spend a great deal of time looking at those issues we were raising, because it struck at the very foundation of their own existence. They would have to undo a lot of things to get it right, but they were not prepared to do that.

GL: We were working with them, we were part of the Brixton Defence Campaign, we were meeting on our territory and some of those guys felt extremely threatened. I mean, we did have political time for some of them, but others were just jokers; separatist, chauvinist people that we did not have much in common with politically, over and above Black nationalist politics. Even those that we did have political time for felt threatened. I remember we had this Hindi poster with a woman holding a machete-type thing, and some of those guys would come into the meetings saying that they really couldn't handle the poster. They would say things like, 'I don't know how to be with you anymore, just talking to you individually'. I can also remember being asked, 'Do you think that Black feminism is becoming so strong now that all Black women are going to become lesbians?' There was also some disagreement as to how these tensions could be rationalised. Some of the men and a few of the women would say it was all about personal relationships and others of us argued that it was about politics.

OG: These problems show where we were at that time, and I think we have made tremendous strides since then, with still a long way to go, and we are very hopeful because I don't think that we are in a position to cut off any form of voice, because we are all oppressed in one way or another. However, being oppressed does not mean at the same time you cannot oppress others. That was always another issue: was it possible for us to oppress each other within the group? As you can imagine, some of us said 'yes' and others said 'no', but I do think that at times we did intimidate one another.

MW: Not intentionally.

OG: I believe that we can turn oppression on each other: I can oppress you at one time, and you can oppress me on another. Whether it is intentional or not, the effects linger on.

AQ: So, do you think the conflicts that came out of all that were productive, even though it was a hard and painful struggle?

OG: In the main.

GL: I agree, but with costs, because we lost some good women. I mean, there was so much going on, there was friendships breaking down.

OG: It was too much to handle.

AG: How did the group change, in terms of its earlier days, to that point at which the group as a collective 'dissolved' itself?

GL: We began to document our history. By then, we had come to some agreement that documentation was quite important. Before, we would just write position papers which we discussed, because this was a way to encompass the division of interest amongst us, a way to share information. If you look in the earlier newsletters, nothing was given an individual person's name, besides the poetry and contributions that came from other organisations. Later, it became the case that you could write individual pieces in *Speak Out*, for example.

Another move that we made was to become very definitely and very statedly socialist feminists, actually saying we were a socialist feminist organisation.

OG: We also started moving towards taking up lesbian feminist struggles, for example. But going back to what Gail said about the organisation losing many good women, we have to acknowledge that some of those women left because they did not agree with the direction in which they thought the group was going. Some of those that left wanted to become engaged purely in practice, and they thought that BWG was becoming an elitist organisation by, say, sitting down and writing 'position papers' on these areas.

MW: There was also some recognition of the personal as well, towards the end. And, in fact, when we finally closed BWG, one of the things that came out of it was a group called 'Sisters in Study'. This group not only dealt with study but with our personal interaction with each other, and this was now an equal part of our agenda.

334

GL: We also moved from the earlier days where we were about creating a space in which women could meet together, for whatever purposes, to being a Black women's organisation which foregrounded gender relations as being the object of political change.

OG: Even the day and time that we met was an empowering factor in our lives. I mean, we met on Sunday afternoons between two and whenever, and that was generally a time of day when people stayed at home.

MW: In fact, that was quite liberating for many of us, because to get that space was not easy for some BWG women; you know, to leave the cooking and all the rest of it.

GL: I suppose the puzzle is, with all that going for it, why did it end?

MW: Many of the issues changed, for a start. Many of the issues that we were involved with – Depo-Provera, SUS, disruptive units – in a sense, had been won. At the same time, while we were looking for a new focus, younger women were coming into BWG. I think we began to feel a bit like old fogeys, and some of us who had been involved in that ten-year period of high activity felt as if we had given as much as we could at that point, and that perhaps it was time to make room for the younger women coming along with new ideas.

GL: But they couldn't hold the group together, either. I think, to a certain extent, we had won some of the battles, but there still remained other issues. For example, policing as an issue is still there. I think a split appeared in the group between women who had been involved in the organisation for a long time and who had come to formulate a 'shared' perspective, and between women coming from outside who did not share that perspective and many of whom would not define themselves as socialist. There were some who did not see the campaigning issues as being the same ones as we would have.

OG: Also, some people were just physically exhausted.

MW: We were just tired. I mean, it is hard to get across the level of intensity during that period. It required a lot from all of us, in addition to the rest of our lives – you know, working and living, and families and children, and that kind of thing.

OG: There was also the effect of losing certain sisters at that stage in the group; the death of Olive, the death of Sylvia and others was quite a devastating experience as well.

GL: The other thing that happened was the grants strategy; you know, we became a bloody management committee with workers – we became employers. We stopped doing the things that we used to do, like standing on street corners selling papers – or more usually giving them away. We weren't knocking on doors anymore. All we had to do by then was to give out a few leaflets through the council premises. At first, we didn't; at first, we would go out and encourage women, but we weren't doing that anymore; instead, we just put it through the internal Lambeth mailing. We had become bloody managers, and this is what happens so often. You know, to get funding you have to meet certain criteria; to meet those criteria you have to adopt certain structures, and to a great extent the structures dictate the relationships.

OG: Also, those who hold the purse strings know that we have certain unmet needs and goals, and it's like a carrot dangling. I think the obvious thing is that we had not thought it all through, you know; what it meant to acquire those things through those means.

MW: I think we did think them through, but we thought that we could overcome them.

OG: And we might have done, could have done, if we had tried even harder still.

GL: Maybe, if we were still the same group, but obviously we weren't anymore. You see, the membership changed and was fluid by this time. Also, things might have worked out if we were centred around a particular project, like Southall Black Sisters, who organise around the whole question of women and violence and everything that stems from that.[5] We were more amorphous. We were also victim of not only the internal dynamics of BWG, but also the fracturing of Black political

---

5 *Editor's note:* See southallblacksisters.org.uk; and R. Gupta, ed., *From Homebreakers to Jailbreakers: Southall Black Sisters* (London: Zed, 2003).

activity; the fracturing, if not the demise of women's liberation political activity; and the general political environment.

OG: With all its imperfections, if we were to do it again I would still be a member of BWG. But, you know, I take the African saying that there are no mistakes in life but only lessons to be learnt, and I know that my life has certainly been enriched by that experience.

GL: Oh yes, I totally agree.

MW: Definitely, and in that sense it has not finished, because all those people who went through BWG in those early years remain committed to its principles, to its ideals, and conduct their lives in that way. Of course, we carry it through in different ways: for example, I am a freelance journalist, so whatever I do, whatever I am involved in is informed by those years. Olive is an educational social worker and acts accordingly in the work that she does. Gail lectures in trade unionism at a polytechnic and her work is also informed by her years in BWG. So, in that sense, BWG lives.

AFTERWORD

Beverley Bryan, Stella Dadzie, Liz Fajemisin, Sindamani Bridglal, Takumba Ria Lawal, Gail Lewis, Amina Mama, Monica Morris, Suzanne Scafe and Jocelyn Wolfe in conversation with Jade Bentil

On the beginnings of the Brixton Black Women's Group

Jade: Thank you so much for coming together today! I'm really excited that the collected writings of the BBWG are going to be out in the public domain for the first time, particularly for younger people, scholars, readers and activists. I'm looking forward to this conversation so that we can delve more into the group's history and activism.

I wanted to begin by asking those of you who were founding members of the BBWG about how the group came to be. What was the impetus to begin organising collectively and what did that look like?

Beverley: I think I'm the only one here from the early days, so I'll begin. I'm trying to remember the year – you know this thing about memory!

I'll start off by talking about 1973. I'll start by saying how I came to be part of the group. I was in the Black Panther Movement, which by that time was known as the Black Workers' Movement. I'd been in that organisation since about 1970. I had just come to Brixton, and I was teaching at a primary school in Brixton. I joined the organisation after Olive [Morris] – I joined some months after her. I was in that organisation for about three years and that's when it started to disintegrate. I don't want to go into all the reasons why that happened, but at the very end when that organisation broke up, one of the most important things that happened was that the people who were like the senior people in that organisation also controlled the property that we used to meet in, and they wanted us out, so we didn't have anywhere to meet. One development that was also evolving at that time was that we had a women's caucus in the Black Workers' Movement, and in that caucus there was Olive, Pat Gordon and Liz Obi as well, I think.

So, as the BWM broke up, a number of people, including some brothers, said we wanted to continue meeting. The women in that organisation also wanted to continue meeting, and we had to find somewhere to meet. I think at that time, a number of people in that organisation were living on Railton Road and just off Railton Road. Farrukh [Dhondy] was living somewhere on Railton Road, and Olive certainly was too. I know that Monica Dawkins was living on Malvern Road, so we were able to meet at each other's houses. I was also saying to Suzanne [Scafe] recently, this was also a time when there were a lot of empty houses on Railton Road. They weren't derelict but they certainly hadn't been occupied for a long time, and the council wasn't doing anything about them – there was a lot of homelessness. So that was the beginning of the squatting movement. Olive and Liz Obi were *very* involved in that – but in fact, Olive, I would say, was the leader of that movement. You know, Olive was fearless! If a house was empty and we needed somewhere to meet, she'd just break off the lock and we'd go in!

We'd meet at different places and a group of us continued to meet after the Black Workers' Movement disintegrated. As I said, we'd started a women's group while we were in the Panthers, so there was still some kind of cohesion that we could work together – the same issues that we'd been campaigning around were still there and were still relevant and really important. Issues to do with police brutality, to do with education, to do with what were then called 'sin bins', to do with the curriculum and the lack of Black teachers – these were still important issues at the time, so we still wanted to continue meeting. I think it was around about '74 that Olive squatted the corner house, 121 Railton Road. I'm pretty sure that Farrukh lived in that building. It was quite an old building and we spent quite a few months cleaning it up and getting everything connected. We had to renovate it because we wanted to make it into a bookshop.

We wanted to have a Black bookshop in the community because, remember, there was nothing! We had a study group in the Panthers, but the books were hard to get hold of. We had a Saturday school and we had hardly any books for children, so it was important that we had somewhere where we could get access to the books we needed. Ira, who had been part of the Black Workers' Movement, was also involved in bookselling and that was one of the things he wanted to do as well. The women in the group also wanted somewhere to meet – we wanted to meet as a group of women and we wanted to continue with the studying we'd been doing as well. There was a change in texts, but we still wanted to meet and understand our condition – what was happening to Black people around the world in a more comprehensive way.

Jade: You've just mentioned the change in texts from when you were gathering in the Panthers to when you were gathering autonomously. Can you talk a bit about that change in texts?

Beverley: We read texts like *The Origin of the Family, Private Property and the State* by Engels. I found that really useful and it wasn't something we would've read in the Panthers. Two others I remember reading were from America: *Our Bodies, Ourselves* by Boston Women's Health Book Collective and another text about Black women's lives, about how Black women survived in America, *From Sundown to Sunup*.[1] It was about the kind of life that slave women made.

We were using a Marxist analysis to understand our situation

---

1   *Editor's note:* Originally published in 1884, Friedrich Engels's *The Origin of the Family, Private Property and the State* was republished by Verso in 2021; *Our Bodies, Ourselves* was published by Simon & Schuster in 1973; *From Sundown to Sunup: The Making of the Black Community*, by George P. Rawick, was published in 1972.

while also recognising that there were issues related to women, related to patriarchy, that we needed to understand in a much more fundamental way.

Gail: I joined BWG after I reconnected with Gerlin [Bean]. I first met Gerlin a long time before, when Gerlin was doing work in the Harrow Road area, which is where I grew up. I had bumped into her again when I went to university at the LSE [London School of Economics and Political Science], and she was there as well. I wanted a Marxist, feminist organisation to join, and she said, 'Come to the Brixton group'. I think that was about 1977, that kind of time.

I came especially because of the Marxism in the feminism – it was socialist feminism, but it was *Marxist* socialist feminism, and anti-colonial. I remember reading Engels. I remember reading *Our Bodies, Ourselves* and the Combahee River Collective statement![2] I think we got an early version of that! I know that before we met Barbara Smith we had that statement.[3] The Combahee statement was written in the context of being socialist feminists in the States, and really trying to think about class alongside gender, alongside race and racism and importantly, feminism, which is what we wanted, too.

The other thing I remember is the pamphlets that came from

---

2 *Editor's note:* Named after Harriet Tubman's 1863 guerrilla action which freed 750 enslaved people in South Carolina, the Combahee River Collective was a Black feminist organisation active between 1974 and 1980. Their 'A Black Feminist Statement', collectively written in 1977, is widely regarded as a landmark document in the history of contemporary Black feminism. See K. Y. Taylor, ed., *How We Get Free: Black Feminism and the Combahee River Collective* (Chicago: Haymarket Books, 2017).

3 *Editor's note:* Born on 16 November 1946, Barbara Smith was a founding member of the Combahee River Collective. She has edited, among several landmark books, *All the Women Are White, All the Blacks Are Men, But Some of Us Are Brave: Black Women's Studies* (1982), a review of which was published in *Speak Out*, no. 5 (pp. 302–6 in this collection). For more on Barbara Smith, see the collection of her essays: Barbara Smith, *The Truth That Never Hurts: Writings on Race, Gender, and Freedom* (New Brunswick, NJ: Rutgers University Press, 2000 [1988]); and A. Jones, V. Eubanks, and B. Smith, eds, *Ain't Gonna Let Nobody Turn Me Around: Forty Years of Movement Building with Barbara Smith* (New York: State University of New York Press, 2014).

the women's sections of the Southern African struggle. We used to read those and try and make links. Those pamphlets and leaflets were educational tools for us. I was very excited by the idea that we could read Marx alongside reading the sisters of the ANC [African National Congress].

Beverley: I think we should underscore that anti-imperialism was central from the very beginning! I'd been in the Panthers, and Gerlin was also involved in the Black Unity and Freedom Party [BUFP]. She would've brought that anti-imperialist element as well. We didn't necessarily call it 'feminism' at the time but our 'woman talk' was about Marxism and anti-imperialism. The first issue – *the first issue* – of *Speak Out* states that 'in Africa and everywhere, women are fighting to build a new society and unite against racism and sexism to defeat capitalism'.

Jade: Thank you so much for sharing how you both came to the BBWG. Could I ask Monica, Jocelyn, Suzanne, Liz, Sindamani, Takumba and Amina to also share how they came to be part of the BBWG, and the political histories and understandings they arrived from when they became part of the group?

Monica: I had lived in inner-city Manchester prior to going to university in Lancaster. I came down from Lancaster in 1977 having heard about the Black Women's Group, because in Manchester there was some amount of organising happening in the local area. BUFP were there, and I had links with them, but actually, I have to admit that I was a church girl! Going to university, I got into feminism good and proper. I was into thinking about Black liberation from an internationalist perspective – I remember having people like Walter Rodney come to speak to our African-Caribbean group.[4] It gave me an appetite for politics of that kind and a strong sense of being a feminist. When I heard about the Black Women's Group, I was determined that I was going to find them the minute I got to London, which is what I did!

---

4 *Editor's note:* For more, see Walter Rodney's *The Groundings with My Brothers* (first published by Bogle-L'Ouverture in 1969 and republished by Verso in 2019) and *How Europe Underdeveloped Africa* (first published by Bogle-L'Ouverture in 1972 and republished by Verso in 2018).

What Gail and Beverley have been saying resonates with me in terms of the base of our ideology. The anti-colonialist base. The African liberation, Black women's base and lenses. Wanting self-determination was at the base of how we were and what we went on to do.

Jocelyn: I had come from Trinidad where I'd been involved in organising. Those were the days of Eric Williams, when he'd returned home to start the People's National Movement.[5] He got all the women involved and all the young people involved. Everyone referred to the women's involvement in a very derogatory way as the 'fat arse brigade' that followed Eric around. What it did do, though, was say to the women, 'You've got a voice'. For instance, in those days, my mother never voted and never even thought she'd vote. It got us all organised.

So, I was in this organising phase and, as a youth, I was out there delivering stuff, signing up people for elections. And then I came to England. I opted to go and live in Wiltshire, and I worked in a hospital there. There were three of us – three people of colour. You really stood out!

I did my time of three and half years in Wiltshire and thought, 'I've got to find some company; I've got to find a group of women!' I ended moving to London and living in Camberwell. I was working at Maudsley Hospital. Someone said to me, 'You should come to Camberwell Consciousness-Raising Group.' It was lovely! It was women, together. At that time, there was the Earlham Street Squat with the women's liberation movement. I was down there working with the team, and I was enjoying myself! I was off on demonstrations; I was part of everything that was going on in terms of equal pay and sexual discrimination.

In '75, there was a demonstration for equal pay and I got

5 *Editor's note:* Eric Williams (1911–1981) was a pioneering historian and politician born in Port of Spain, Trinidad and Tobago. He became Trinidad and Tobago's first prime minister. For more, see T. L. Shields, ed., *The Legacy of Eric Williams: Into the Postcolonial Moment* (Jackson: University Press of Mississippi, 2015); see also his groundbreaking book *Capitalism and Slavery*, first published in 1944 and republished by Penguin in 2022.

arrested. We had gone into the police station to ask about some people who'd tied themselves to the railings. I was singled out, taken round the back and thrown in a cell. It was pretty horrible and I'm still reliving it to this day. I realised I was the only Black person in that group. Although I can't say I experienced much overt racism on a personal level in my daily life at that time, I was beginning more and more to see the wider picture. Although I got a lot of support, I think it was after that experience that I realised I needed something else, and it just so happened that I went to a conference and bumped into Gerlin. She saw me from across the room, came to find me and we started chatting. She said, 'You've got to come to the Black Women's Group.' I was so excited to go, because I just hadn't had the experience of going to a women's group of Black women.

I can't remember if the first meeting I went to was in Sabarr or at another house on Railton Road, but I remember turning up there and just being high on the excitement of being in a room full of Black women! It might sound silly because by that time I'd been in London for three years, but I'd just never been in that kind of environment! I lived in the staff hostel, and we were a mixed group; in the women's group I'd been going to before, I was usually on my own as the only Black woman. It was a completely new experience! Learning that everyone had come from all sorts of backgrounds, not just physical and cultural backgrounds, but in terms of education and personal experiences, it was just ... I used to go home on a high just from being there! For me, it set me off on a new path.

I remember – it was probably you, Bev – people explaining things to me. I had been involved with the abortion movement that was going on and I remember having a discussion at a BWG meeting where I learned that, in fact, for Black women, getting access to an abortion wasn't a problem. I spoke to someone at King's College who said if you were a Black woman and you came in for an abortion, you got it straight away! That was all new to me. In those beginning days, I started looking at things from a new perspective. Those are my first memories of being part of the group and I still smile when I think back, remembering everyone's faces, the people who spoke a lot (mentioning no names!) and the people who would challenge you. It was great.

Suzanne: So I came much later; I came in September 1980. I do remember exactly when because I left university in '76, probably the same year as Monica, and, in early '77, I went to teach in Jamaica. I was there for nearly four years. It was an amazing time for me. It sort of made me, actually. I was working in a very progressive school where we had a very egalitarian relationship with the students. It was very progressive culturally – the curriculum was very African-centred. The school itself was very much in dialogue with African liberation struggles.

I was also involved in teaching adult literacy while I was in Jamaica. I joined the Committee of Women for Progress [CWP], which was the more left-wing arm of the PNP [People's National Party] Women's Movement, and they were loosely affiliated with the Workers' Party of Jamaica, which was led by Trevor Munroe.[6] The CWP was very hierarchical; there was a co-ordinating committee of four women, they sat at the front and gave their reports and so on. Nobody really noticed you as an individual, but when you were asked to do something, you did it. Nevertheless, I was really fired up! I was totally committed. Being in the Caribbean, in Jamaica, in that period was just transformative for me! Being involved in anti-colonial, anti-imperialist, liberation struggles was central to our lives at that time! I really believed in the things we were struggling for – things around welfare, education, international solidarity, building relations with Cuba, and so on. Some of the women would do exchange visits to Cuba and went as Brigadistas. We got a lot of pamphlets and readings from Cuba.

When I came to London, I needed a job. I saw a job advertised to work with this young women's project. It happened to be located next to the Black Women's Centre (BWC). The people who interviewed me were Gerlin, Beverley and Rita Fray – Rita was the project manager. So I first met Gerlin because

6 *Editor's note:* See Trevor Munroe, *The Politics of Constitutional Decolonization: Jamaica, 1944–1962* (Kingston, Jamaica: Institute of Social and Economic Research, University of the West Indies, 1972).

she interviewed me for the job! I started working next door to the BWC, with young women in Stockwell Green, in September 1980. One evening I went to the BWC, and there wasn't a sign or anything, but I saw Sinda working there, and she asked me to come and help – so that's how I went to my first meeting at the Black Women's Group. Having been in this politburo-type organisation, I just felt I could speak!

Beverley: You felt heard!

Suzanne: I felt valued, more than anything! In the environment that I was used to there was a lot of suspicion because there were a lot of CIA infiltrators at that time, and they came in via a particular route, usually via education and teaching literacy. Some of them were extremely destructive and they ruined the futures of people I knew. So that's why there was some suspicion around me. When I came back to London and started attending BWG meetings, I felt welcomed with open arms.

Sindamani: After university, I went back to Guyana, I went back to try and figure out my mother, who baffled me. Our family is political in a local activist way and were very much a part of the 1950s post-colonial struggles sweeping the former colonies across the globe. The split between Forbes Burnham and Cheddi Jagan informed my parent's decision to leave Guyana along with the need for new opportunities for themselves and their children.[7]

When I returned to Guyana (I had left when I was seven), I went to a street meeting in Georgetown where Walter Rodney was speaking, and it wasn't very long before I became a founder member of the Working People's Alliance. While a member of the WPA, I met Maurice Bishop – he came to Guyana and we had meetings together with other members of the New Jewel Movement.[8] I certainly felt that the progressive forces in the

---

7   *Editor's note:* For more on the split, see Moe Taylor, 'Walter Rodney, Forbes Burnham, and the Specter of Pseudo-socialism, *Canadian Journal of Latin American and Caribbean Studies* 45, no. 2 (2020), 193–211.

8   *Editor's note:* See Maurice Bishop, 'Revolution in Grenada: An Interview with Maurice Bishop', *Black Scholar* 11, no. 3 (1980), 50–8; see also Fitzroy Ambursley and Winston James, 'Maurice Bishop and the Jewel Revolution in Grenada', *New Left Review* I, no. 142 (1983), 91–6.

Caribbean were making headway. It was a very fast-paced time which, sadly, ended tragically.

The Caribbean sisters were very much trying to formulate a Caribbean feminist perspective alongside new progressive ways of making inroads into working women's lives and the lives of all the peoples of the Caribbean, and I think that is what Suzanne is alluding to. There was a lot of political turbulence and violence in Guyana during this time, 1978/79. WPA activists were chased with staves with long nails and beaten and shot at by the anti-progressive forces aligned with the then prime minister, Forbes Burnham. Burnham resisted the coming together of the African and Indian populations, who saw themselves as citizens of Guyana rather than different races with a Guyanese passport.

In between all of this, the women in the WPA had feminist discussions, and that old chestnut about which should come first, the struggle or women's rights, arose. Things got very dangerous; Andaiye (who later became international secretary of the WPA and a prominent Caribbean feminist, thinker and writer) and I were chloroformed in her flat in Georgetown.[9]

I returned to London quite burnt out and lived with my sister Kamini in north London. I think it was one of her friends who suggested I speak to Gerlin Bean, who became a mentor, helping me to find my way back, especially after the assassination of Rodney. The BWC provided a space for meetings and discussions, and the BWG got behind the Walter Rodney campaign. During this time, Andaiye visited the BWC. My sister was going out with a Turkish guy, Haluk, who was at Lancaster with Sylvia Erike, whom I had met at the BWG, so there were many connections between BWG members and

9 *Editor's note:* Andaiye (1942–2019) was a Guyanese social, political and gender rights activist. She was an early member of the executive of the Working People's Alliance (WPA) in Guyana, as well as a founding member of the women's development organisation Red Thread in 1986. Andaiye was also an executive member of the Caribbean Association for Feminist Research and Action (CAFRA). For more, see Alissa Trotz, ed., *The Point Is to Change the World: Selected Writings of Andaiye* (London: Pluto, 2020).

other progressives at the time, and this informed *Speak Out*. Monica Morris was also a big part of the post-Rodney times at the BWG/BWC as I recall, and she met Andaiye.

I think Suzanne and I brought the 'hot breeze' of the 1970s Caribbean movements into our BWG discussions. I was thrilled to find her and the BWG as we were all trying to find a way to fuse our anti-imperialist, post-colonial, post-1950s-influenced thoughts with the emergent feminism of the 1960s and 1970s, and then the craziness of Thatcher's Britain – then trying to put it all down in words for *Speak Out*. I must say it was exhausting being a woman in the 1970s and 1980s.

Liz: From my perspective, I came to know about the BWC through Beverley. At the time, I was involved in further education and studying childcare. At that time, when you did that level of education, you also had to do O-Level English, and that's how I came to know Beverley, because she was our English tutor. Beverley was our English teacher, and it was a real pleasure because she challenged students in ways that I'd never really seen before. Also, what I resonated with is that I'd had quite a troubled experience of education – I wasn't an 'A' student, I'd been excluded from school, and I'd had quite a traumatic end to my education as my dad had had a stroke. I was really what would now be called a 'young carer', so to work as a nursery nurse and go to college was quite an achievement!

Around that time, I was also politically active, and that was mainly from the messages I'd received growing up. I grew up in a household where working-class values were important – my mum was Irish, and I grew up in a household where the IRA [Irish Republican Army] and the Irish struggle were very prevalent in terms of some of the messages I received. I'd actually come to be politically active and, I don't know how, but I ended up joining the Socialist Workers' Party. Somebody probably just grabbed me and sold me a newspaper and, before I knew it, I was going to these political meetings, I was going on coaches and I was reading *The Communist Manifesto*. I think for me, having left school, it felt like I was getting my first positive experience of education. I was living in Lewisham at a time when the NF [National Front] were active and I can

remember coming out when they marched outside my house.
I knew people who had died in the New Cross Massacre, so
that was probably my first experience of being active in the
Black community; I remember going to the meetings in New
Cross and going on the march.[10]

I think I was also starting to think about feminism. I was
working in an area where childcare was a big issue in terms of
women being able to go to work. I also remember a lot of my
involvement revolved around me eventually living on Railton
Road. I remember I was housed in one of those derelict flats
that Bev was talking about, and I was housed by Ujima, which
was a Black housing association. I used to get *TimeOut* and
I'd look and see what meetings were happening and I was just
really getting involved. I was working in children's day care and
there were a lot of Black children at a time when there was a
lot of social services involvement in the lives of Black children
and Black families. I remember then being exposed to the
conversations at the Black Women's Centre and the literature.

I was also reading *Spare Rib* and I went to a few OWAAD
conferences, and I think what it did is add a dimension from a
Black woman's perspective, like some of the issues that existed
in the Black community between Black men and Black women.
I also remember volunteering at the Ahfiwe Saturday school.[11]

10 *Editor's note:* For more on the New Cross Massacre, see Aaron
Andrews, 'Truth, Justice, and Expertise in 1980s Britain: The Cultural
Politics of the New Cross Massacre', *History Workshop Journal* 91, no. 1
(2021), 182–209. See also J. Bernard, *Surge* (London: Chatto & Windus,
2019); P. Fryer, *Staying Power: The History of Black People in Britain*
(London: Pluto, 2018 [1984]); P. Gilroy, *There Ain't No Black in the
Union Jack* (London: Routledge, 2002 [1987]); R. Ramdin, *The Making
of the Black Working Class in Britain* (London: Verso, 2017 [1987]); and
Rob Waters, *Thinking Black: Britain, 1964–1985* (Oakland: University
of California Press, 2019).

11 *Editor's note:* The Ahfiwe ('All for We') supplementary school was
established by Ansel Wong in 1974. It was based at 1 Gresham Road,
Brixton, and had strong links with the Abeng Centre (the location of the
first OWAAD conference) at 7 Gresham Road. For more, see Rob Waters,
'Student Politics, Teaching Politics, Black Politics: An Interview with Ansel
Wong', *Race and Class* 58, no. 1 (2016), 17–33. A photo of the cover of
issue 2 of *AHFIWE: Journal of the Ahfiwe School and Abeng* – in the Ansel

Bev used to get me involved in all sorts of things, one of which was the Brixton Community Crèche – which I think was one of the first crèches that was specifically designed for students who had children, so that they could continue their further education.

One of the positive things I remember is that I ended up becoming friends with Beverley's younger sister and Monica's younger sister. We were like the young women who were around these really academic women, and we'd be at the meetings and we might come for part of it and we probably had our own way of processing the information, but it was always in the context of the Black struggle.

Takumba: My background is that I am Irish-Nigerian. I was born in 1952 and brought up in Ladbroke Grove/Notting Hill Gate. I was working class and, as a child, I was in and out of care. I remember the 1958 riots on the street, and my mum protecting me and my Dad by hiding us under the bed.

I knew the Black Panthers and other activists who went to the Mangrove because my aunt's boyfriend was a good friend of Frank [Critchlow].[12] My friends and I went there to hang

---

Wong collection at the Black Cultural Archives – can be seen online as part of a collaboration between the Black Cultural Archives and Google Arts & Culture: artsandculture.google.com.

12   *Editor's note:* The Mangrove Restaurant, owned by Frank Critchlow, was located at 8 All Saints Road in Notting Hill. After opening in 1969, it became known as a hub for the area's West Indian community, including political organisers; it was also the target of sustained police harassment. Following a 1970 demonstration protesting this harassment, Barbara Beese, Rupert Glasgow Boyce, Frank Critchlow, Rhodan Gordon, Darcus Howe, Anthony Carlisle Innis, Altheia Jones-Lecointe, Rothwell (Roddy) Kentish and Godfrey Millet were prosecuted, in a three-month trial at the Old Bailey in late 1971, on thirty-one charges (including incitement to riot, numerous counts of bodily harm to police officers, and possession of offensive weapons). This group, which became known as the 'Mangrove Nine', included members of the Black Panther Movement (and, later, of the *Race Today* collective). The arrest, trial and acquittal of the Mangrove Nine, on the principal charge of incitement to riot, have come to be regarded as landmark events in twentieth-century British political history, and a pioneering moment in official recognition of institutionalised racism within the Metropolitan Police. For more,

out, but we were not part of what we saw as the 'big people' – the intellectuals. I went on the demonstrations but didn't take part in the political discussions. I felt very much a part of the Black activist working-class community in the Grove.

I became aware of women's liberation through various women at the Gateways, and my political activism started there – although I always had a strong identity as a Black woman.[13] But you could count the Black sisters on your hand in women's liberation at that time. It was a middle-class movement until the white working-class women from out of London started joining. In '78/'79, I trained as a carpenter. The only woman apart from those learning cookery at the training centre – the first Black woman to train as carpenter. I was the first woman to work as a carpenter on a building site, with 120 men and one woman cook.

By the time I joined BWG, there were about twenty-two of us. I used to be dizzy with excitement Sunday morning to late afternoon! I was an activist helping shape events: marching on demos, speaking at schools, centres and workshops, pushing our views through mountains of campaigning and standing on street corners everywhere. It felt like every city and town was writing to us for help and explanation. The Depo-Provera campaign was a big thing. I went to health centres where women who might be being offered the injection were – I talked to them and the health centre workers. I handed out the leaflets and was on the ground supporting women.

Amina: I studied in Scotland at the University of St Andrews. It was so isolating; I think in the four years there, I met one other

---

see J. Procter, 'Mangrove Trials', in *Companion to Contemporary Black British Culture*, ed. A. Donnell (London: Routledge, 2006), pp. 264–5; A. M. Angelo, 'The Black Panthers in London, 1967–1972: A Diasporic Struggle Navigates the Black Atlantic, *Radical History Review* 103 (2009), 17–35; R. E. Bunce and P. Field, 'Mangrove Nine: The Court Challenge against Police Racism in Notting Hill', *Guardian*, 29 November 2010; and Waters, *Thinking Black*.

13 *Editor's note:* For more on the Gateways Club, see Jill Gardiner's (2003) *From the Closet to the Screen: Women at the Gateways Club, 1945–1985*; and the 2022 documentary *Gateways Grind*, directed by Jacquie Lawrence.

Nigerian woman. I was a medical student in that very white environment. I came to London from Scotland all by myself – in fact, it was my second visit to London. The draw of London was very strong after four years at St Andrews!

I did my master's thesis on Rastafarianism when I first got to London. I chose that topic so I could be on the streets and hang out at Rasta cafés, so I got to see what the Black British community was like. I eventually found myself living at number 2 Acre Lane in Brixton. I tried to join a women's group – I read *Spare Rib* and looked one up. I found one, went along to a meeting, and a very pregnant Jewish woman asked me why I hadn't gone to the Black Women's Group. I said 'Oh is there one? Really? Where?' She said she didn't know, but after that, I went to look for it myself and found it. She was right! I wasn't focused on race at that age; I was aware, but I wasn't hugely conscious.

I went along and found the newly opened Black Women's Centre. This is probably around 1980. I benefited enormously from joining the group. I was in BWG for political-intellectual work. I remember Gerlin as being the elder of the group. She was clearly a Marxist feminist and she'd read so much! She was very influential! I also remember that I made friends with women in ELBWO [East London Black Women's Organisation]. I was also friends with Stella [Dadzie] up in Camden. We all had our different trajectories into the group, and I had links with different groups throughout London. I was kind of a bit of a transient, but I didn't know that at the time.

On *Speak Out*

Jade: I wanted to begin to think about the *Speak Out* newsletter and all the things that grew out of it. How did the idea for *Speak Out* come about and, once you came up with the idea to start the newsletter, how was it produced among the group?
Beverley: I'm not sure I can remember completely how we started off, but I have to say, Jade, that no self-respecting organisational group could go on for very long without a newsletter!

You had to have a newsletter where you shared your ideas!
All that reading we'd been doing! We always had an editorial,
so that people would have an idea of where we were coming
from. The newsletter was a way to clarify our ideas and set
out our ideas into the wider world. In selling it, you also got
involved in discussions with people. It was a way in which
you brought people into the group. In terms of the content, it
would always cover the campaigns we were involved in, the
issues we were most concerned about, the stuff that was making
the news that we felt we had to take a position on. Each piece
was usually written by the person who had the most interest
or was most involved in a specific area. I think some of the
articles were shared. I don't think we all read all of the articles,
but we all decided together what was going to be in. We didn't
put it all together – the professional in the group for that was
Pat Adams. She was a professional typesetter, so she did that
work. So, the newsletter was something we had to do because
it was part of the work of the group. After we stopped moving
around and we settled at the bookshop, then we started writing
the newsletter. The first issue came out … I don't know if you
remember, Gail, when the first issue came out?

Gail: Didn't it come out after we'd squatted the centre?

Beverley: No, I think it was before! I think Olive was involved
in the first issue.

Gail: Yes, she was!

Beverley: I think we should repeat some of the names of the
people who were involved: Sylvia Erike, Gerlin Bean, Olive
Morris, Sinda Bridglal, Clover [Graham], Lindiwe Tsele, Olive
Gallimore, Judith Lockhart, Joan Morris, Dorothea Smartt.[14]

Gail: Clover was really important on the legal stuff, wasn't she?

Beverley: Yes!

Suzanne: There was also Claudette Williams.[15]

---

14 *Editor's note:* Dorothea Smartt discusses her time in the BBWG
in SuAndi, D. Smartt, and C. Leeming, 'Women, Black Arts, and Brixton
in the 1980s: A Conversation', *Contemporary Women's Writing* 11,
no. 2 (2017), 137–48. For more on Clover Graham, see the obituary at
theguardian.com.

15 *Editor's note:* Claudette Williams writes about the political context

Beverley: Yes, Claudette! There was also Marlene Bogle.

Jocelyn: Not all of them have left us. Some are not well, but they're still here.

Beverley: Yes, exactly. I think it's important that we mention them. People like Sylvia Erike.

Suzanne: Caroline Redfern.

Gail: Pat Agana.

Suzanne: I don't think she was in the group, I think she was often at the centre?

Gail: I think she was in and out.

Beverley: Yes, I think she was in and out. We had this core of people who really held the group together, but we also had people who came in and played a part.

Gail: What was also important is that some of the women who came in and out of BWG were also connected to other groups. Through that, we were part of a network.

Suzanne: Annette [Blair] was like that, because she was in BUFP – that was her primary organisation – but she visited the Group and the centre quite a lot.

Amina: I was primarily involved in *Speak Out* and I've been involved in publishing Black feminists ever since! *Speak Out* was one of my first babies! My main ally and collaborator in editing and producing newsletters, bulletins and posters was Pat Adams. She had graphic design skills, so she taught me how to do paste-ups and cuts. I started doing editing work and we put it together. I remember it was primarily she and I who put the journal together and printed it – I did a lot of the graphics, for example. She and I did all the logos for the Brixton Defence Campaign.

Monica: We didn't only write *Speak Out*. There were times when we'd go and give presentations at conferences. We'd do presentations at events for International Women's Day. I remember that process; it was really rigorous. We'd sit and talk together at length. Somebody would take notes and go off and write it up and bring it back, so that the group could look at it again

of this period in 'We Are a Natural Part of Many Different Struggles: Black Women Organizing', in *Inside Babylon: The Caribbean Diaspora in Britain,* ed. W. James and C. Harris (London: Verso, 1993), 153–63.

and make changes to it. I think a lot of what went into *Speak Out* was done with that kind of rigour. We went through that process until it represented us all, our thinking, and we were satisfied with it.

Jocelyn: We wanted to be known as a collective. It probably has its disadvantages today, looking back at it, but at the time it was important.

Gail: Frankly, Jocelyn, sometimes I think that in terms of being in a classroom of undergraduates and even postgraduates, saying to them, 'The way you learn is through a collective process' … You don't learn on your own! That's why sometimes you don't necessarily put your name to a piece of work, because it's a collective work. I try to get them to really understand that through recounting the collective process of BWG, but they still really struggle with it.

I found I had a copy of a leaflet that we did for one of the Corrie Bill demonstrations. It's a leaflet that we did as the Brixton group putting out a Black woman's perspective on the bill. *[Gail holds up the leaflet to the screen and begins to read from it:]* 'Black Women and Abortion – A woman's right to choose means: the right to abortion on demand, the right to free and *safe* contraception and informed consent.' The leaflet discussed the attack on the Black family, all of that! We were locating it within a wider frame – 'this means fighting against Depo-Provera, fighting against the sterilisation of Black women, fighting tax legislation that specifically discriminates against Black people, fighting the immigration laws.'[16] So again, there was a wider canvas through which we understood any particular issue: abortion legislation, yeah, but it's about these other things too.

---

16 *Editor's note:* This leaflet, 'Black Women and Abortion', is on pp. 102–4 of this collection. The Corrie Bill was introduced in the House of Commons in 1979 by John Corrie (Conservative MP for Bute and Northern Ayrshire) to restrict abortion rights that had been granted under the 1967 Abortion Act. The bill was withdrawn in March 1980, before its Third Reading, following widespread criticism and demonstrations. See 'Abortion Bill: Fight the New Proposals' (*Speak Out*, no. 3), pp. 160–4 in this collection.

Monica: I feel what Gail said about it being a learning process. It was very alive, very provocative, very challenging too, because there were times you would say something, and people would push back.

Takumba: Although I had very little knowledge of Marxism, workers' rights or abortion campaigns, I stuck in there and learnt as much as I could. When [*Black Macho and the*] *Myth of the Superwoman* [by Michele Wallace] was published, I was buzzing. And Claudette and Sylvia grabbed me and said, 'Right, we will review this.' We met at Sylvia's a couple of times to review the book. I had read little bits – they had read it all. I am dyslexic, so reading is hard, but once I had read something I remembered it, as I have a very good memory. I joined in, and Claudette and Sylvia wanted me to be part of the review and valued my contribution. They understood that working-class women who hadn't had much education had as much to say as they did as academics.[17]

Jocelyn: I think that's what, for me, distinguished BWG from other groups that I'd been in, particularly with men. In BWG, we felt safe to get up and challenge each other. If we didn't agree, we could do that because we knew we could have a dialogue. For me, that was a really strong point, that we could do that.

Beverley: I was looking at some *Speak Out* issues and the only article that I could find with a name was the campaign article on Sickle Cell Anaemia, and Elizabeth Anionwu's name is there. I remember we had a discussion about it – she was the only one who had that kind of information at the time, and we wanted people to be able to contact her – her phone number and her address were included in the article, too. We felt that people needed to know who they could get in touch with.[18]

Jade: How did you get the newsletter out to people in the area?

Gail: When we'd go to things, we'd take copies of the newsletter along, I remember that.

Jocelyn: Didn't we go out into Brixton Market?

---

17   *Editor's note*: The review in question – originally published in *Speak Out*, no. 3 – is on pp. 189–93 of this collection.

18   *Editor's note*: For more on Elizabeth Anionwu, see her memoir *Dreams from My Mother* (London: Seven Dials, 2021).

Suzanne: I think we did!

Monica: We went and stood on the streets and stood outside the Tube station.

Beverley: And we sold it in Sabarr! We also sold it or left copies to be sold at places like Pathfinder Press. It was in Waterloo – I think it was a Trotskyist bookstore? But they also had a lot of stuff on Malcolm X.

Monica: I actually remember some people subscribing to *Speak Out* – there were people who would get it regularly.

Suzanne: There is a subscription option on the newsletter.

Gail: That would make sense because of the contact we had with some sisters up in the north. They'd want to be part of the discussions. I'd forgotten that!

Beverley: And at the time, it was the only newsletter of that kind, so it would've gone out to a lot of women.

On anti-imperial feminism

Jade: Throughout this discussion, each of you has mentioned the anti-imperialist core of the group, the anti-hierarchical structure of it and how socialism underpinned your politics. In one of the newsletters, I recall an article about Olive Morris visiting China and some of the links that were being made with other groups nationally and throughout the world. Could you speak about the development of the group's anti-imperialist framework and the different solidarities and relationships that were formed both nationally and internationally?

Beverley: If you're talking about not just having anti-imperialism as a theory but as a *practice*, the support would've been for women in Southern Africa. For example, the women of ANC, SWAPO [South West Africa People's Organisation] and ZANU-PF [Zimbabwe African National Union – Patriotic Front].[19] I think it did expand to include women in China and, certainly, I remember Tamil women coming to us and asking for

---

19 *Editor's note:* For more on SWAPO, see Bience Gawanas's 'Namibia Women's Day' (*Speak Out*, no. 5), pp. 274–8 in this collection.

our support with demonstrations and pickets that they were involved in, because that was the time of the Sri Lankan civil war. So it wasn't just a theory – the idea was that it was important for us to support all those liberation struggles because they were struggles against capitalist dominance in the world. So you supported those movements because they had a direct impact on you as a Black woman in Britain. We always linked what was happening back to the situation in Britain. It was always about the exploitation of Black people and the way in which they moved Black bodies around the world for the benefit of imperialism, so we gave practical support locally and internationally as well.

Sindamani: I was working as an assistant editor on the film *South Africa Belongs to Us*, a film on Winnie Mandela and the women of South Africa.[20] Just down the road from the editing suites, the Lancaster House Talks were taking place between the British government and the Patriotic Front and the Zimbabwe Rhodesian government to end the war of liberation.[21] I became a frequent visitor after work, and one day I invited some of the ZANU-PF women to my sister's flat for dinner with some of the women from the BWG and OWAAD. I do remember Stella [Dadzie] being there. After dinner and discussions, the sisters, who had to be so formal all day at Lancaster House, and who had played a prominent part in the war for independence – both in logistics and in fighting – just wanted to relax and listen to music and dance. It turned into a fun evening. The Zanu-PF women, the next day, were very taken by the women who came to the dinner; it revealed a different way of organising between women beyond the struggle for liberation.

Gail: I do think it does mark a difference between then and now:

20   *Editor's note:* This hour-long documentary, directed by Chris Austin and released in 1980, can be viewed on vimeo.com.

21   *Editor's note:* These talks, which took place between 10 September and 15 December 1979, resulted in the Lancaster House Agreement. Signed on 21 December 1979, this was a significant step leading to the international recognition of an independent Zimbabwe. For more, see D. M. Martin and P. Johnson, *The Struggle for Zimbabwe: The Chirumenga War* (London: Faber & Faber, 1981).

that time … You can hear from the stories, people coming into
BWG were all bringing direct experiences of organising 'back
home', as it were. There were direct links. So, we learnt the
very practicalities of what imperialism and colonial domination
meant. That then made us have an ever-sharpening understanding of why we needed to link issues like the Corrie Bill and
abortion to the question of how the state was operating in
relation to the Black family, generally, and with immigration
legislation and citizenship rights. We might call that 'heter-
onormative' now, but we needed to understand that this was
colonial domination, and we understood that because we
understood how colonialism functioned and we could never
put it in the background. It was the frame through which we
understood society.

I noticed that in *Speak Out*, issue 5, we've got a whole piece
on strip searches in Armagh prison in Northern Ireland.[22] We
understood that as an anti-colonialist struggle. We were learning about those things. It was so core that we would reach out
to make connections with other people because they would also
link to our struggle, and our struggle was linked to theirs. None
of us wanted to dominate any other struggle, but we could only
think about it as our interconnecting field of operations. It was
absolutely central to what we did, how we thought, and how
we helped each other to think and feel. We'd feel it.

Suzanne: I think that we were very much aligned to liberation struggles around the colonised and neo-colonial world.
Many of us used to go to the WPA (Working People's Alliance, Guyana) meetings that were held at Brixton Town Hall.
These movements were very much targeted at the comprador
bourgeoisie – the governing elite, the ruling class. If we talk
about aligning ourselves with those struggles, we're talking
about class struggle within the context of anti-imperialism.

---

22   *Editor's note:* The piece in question, 'Strip Searches in Armagh
Jail' by the London Armagh Co-ordinating Committee (*Speak Out*, no.
5), is on pp. 280–2 of this collection.

On local activism and campaigns

Jade: Beverley, you mentioned that the group's politics were also fundamentally shaped by what was happening on the ground at the time. Could you each speak to some of the activities and campaigns that the group took part in, particularly campaigns that haven't been so well documented?

Monica: I very much remember our concern with what was happening locally and the connections that we forged with local groups. For instance, somebody from the group would attend meetings that were held by different organisations in the community. I remember that I myself went along to a consortium of ethnic minorities, something that the Community for Race Relations in Lambeth had set up, and they were suggesting that if all the groups came together and talked about their needs, then they could position themselves better to get hold of resources. So, we were part of those discussions.

Another one I remember was the Mary Seacole Craft Group, which was founded by one of our members, Olive Gallimore. She worked in an organisation called WellCare and she saw a need for single-parent mothers who were very isolated and not very empowered. She decided that it would be good to get them to come together, ostensibly as a place to meet, have some tea and do some crafts, but in the process of talking to people, also getting them to identify further what sort of things would be helpful. Someone would come from Brixton College to talk to the craft group about what was on offer and helped them through the application process. People from other services would come along and give a talk. It seemed quite low-key, but it was actually quite helpful for a number of people, and I remember distinctly that a couple of them eventually ended up going to Brixton College, studied for their qualifications and went into work.

We were also very much in areas such as Sabarr Bookshop and supplementary education. We were also part of BASH [Black People Against State Harassment], which was founded by Black women in the Black Women's Group.[23] During the

---

23   *Editor's note:* For more on BASH, see Colin Prescod, 'Black People

Brixton Uprising, we did a lot of work locally, such as the Brixton Defence Campaign, which we started off leading. There were others around, such as *Race Today*, but we chaired the meetings, we did a lot of work in the Law Centre defending the people arrested during the uprisings as well as mobilising in the community.

Suzanne: Meetings for the Defence Campaign were at the BWC, weren't they, Monica?

Monica: They were!

Suzanne: Meetings were at the centre every Wednesday evening at seven o'clock.

Monica: We didn't just do Brixton – there were riots taking place in other parts of the country at the time. We went to places like Liverpool and Luton. We gave talks and we told them what we were doing locally in Brixton.

Suzanne: I think it's important to say that although men and women were involved in the Defence Campaign meetings, it was BWG who led that campaign. We were the organisers, the strategists, and we were the ones who made that connection with Brixton Law Centre and the Legal Defence Campaign, and organised the note-taking at the courts.

Amina: I was very involved in the Defence Campaign. Before that, I'd had a left-wing orientation but largely through anti-imperialism, and that was in large part because I am Nigerian. Nigeria has been an independent nation since 1960. I was born in London, but I grew up in Nigeria. Growing up in Nigeria, all my uncles were big nationalists working in education. I understood colonialism and racism, but I learnt about *police* racism because I lived at number 2 Acre Lane.

During the Brixton Uprising, we as the BWG gave people shelter. I saw police assailing people – literally, women with pushchairs being dragged into police vans. They were just mopping up whoever they could. I was appalled! They were picking Black women off the streets! And then they staged the court hearings, and we knew this because we were picketing

against State Harassment (BASH) Campaign – A Report', *Race and Class* 58, no. 1 (2016), 94–100.

outside the courts! That was my exposure to anti-policing
activism.

Monica: I'm really glad that we're having this conversation,
because history is written by those who decide they're going
to write it—

Beverley: —and often just by men!

Monica: Exactly! I remember seeing something that situated *Race
Today* as being central to the Defence Campaign, and that was
not my recollection at all. How did we let this happen?

Suzanne: It wasn't just that we had the Centre. We were able to
take on this role in the community because we were organised.
We had been used to working with other groups and we were
already active in the community. That was the key. I think
other organisations, although they were in Brixton, were quite
inward-looking and self-conscious, whereas I think BWG was
very committed to reaching out. As Black feminists, we were
committed to testing out our feminism in a practical way and
taking our feminism to other groups. So, we were well situated to respond to the uprising because what we were used to
doing was having to coordinate with different people – people
who weren't feminists, who weren't socialists, who weren't
necessarily politically conscious. They were ordinary parents,
brothers and sisters, and so on, who needed a group of people
who were shaped by a particular politics but who could also
reach out to individuals as a part of a community.

Beverley: I just wanted to underscore one other point about the
organisation. Monica touched on it – the flat, non-hierarchical
structure, the network we formed had all of us involved in different organisations. We each had our interests and priorities.
Mine was in education – I was in the WIPAG [the West Indian
Parent's Action Group]. I worked with Gloria Cameron, who
formed that group. Clover and Liz also did work with the
Ahfiwe School. We'd go to these different meetings and then
come and report back on what was happening, and see if there
were things we could support – if there was a supplementary
school or a demonstration, we could get involved. There was a
wide spectrum. Early on in the '70s, there were anti-racist, anti-
fascist groups. I remember one of our members was involved

and she would bring back the reports and tell us about the different demonstrations that were happening. We'd then discuss how many people could go and support. I'm thinking about things like BASH and the Brockwell Three.[24]

It wasn't all about picketing and demonstrations; there were other campaigns that were more about information-sharing, and that's where *Speak Out* came in. Issues like sickle cell, Depo-Provera, and so on. So I just wanted to emphasise that network – that network had to be strong. But it was a lot – *a lot* – of work.

Monica: There were also the events that we put on. I remember there being a Health Day at the centre and wouldn't be surprised if we had other days as well.

Gail: For a while, one of the other things we did at the centre was advice; there was advice around housing, health. We'd have drop-ins for local women to come and get information. I can't remember how long that ran, but that provision was a way of responding to really granular local needs.

Suzanne: We had a case with one woman, Jamilla, who was a mother experiencing a mental health crisis and coming up

---

24   *Editor's note:* On 9 June 1973, following a fireworks display at Brixton's annual Brockwell Park Fair, a white teenager was fatally stabbed during a fight in a crowded fish-and-chip shop. By the time the police arrived, a large crowd had gathered to see what was happening. Claiming to have spotted those responsible for the stabbing, the officers drew their truncheons on nineteen-year-old Horace Parkinson and eighteen-year-old Lloyd James – both Black. At this, the police were met with a volley of bottles and stones thrown by the crowd, in protest at their treatment of Parkinson and James. Police reinforcements arrived, and a larger skirmish developed. Parkinson and James were arrested, along with fourteen-year-old Robin Sterling – also Black. All three reportedly received severe beatings at Brixton Police Station. Although none of them were charged with the stabbing that triggered the incident, they were charged with assaulting police officers and carrying offensive weapons. Following a trial at the Old Bailey in early March 1974, Parkinson, James and Sterling – who came to be known as the 'Brockwell Three' – were each sentenced to three years in prison. A defence campaign soon mobilised, including the founding by students at Tulse Hill Comprehensive, on 27 March 1974, of the Black Students Action Collective (Black SAC). For more, see Waters, *Thinking Black*.

against the care system while fighting for her children. We were trying to get a Black psychiatrist to give an alternative assessment for her. We would make trips to Atkinson Morley Hospital in Wimbledon. I remember Monica and myself would go there with this woman to get an alternative assessment. I remember those sessions being extremely fraught.[25]

Gail: I also remember there was one woman, who was kind of like a semi-member of the group, who returned to us through the advice service during a major crisis in her life. We lost her in the end. There were times when a member became someone who needed advice and support. So all this is an example of the concretisation of BWG's politics. Liz, you used to work in schools and were involved in some of this work?

Liz: It was almost like fulfilling two needs. I remember volunteering at the Saturday school [Ahfiwe] but also learning about Black history at the same time. I remember after I moved to Railton Road and had my first daughter, literally living in the middle of the Brixton riots. I've forgotten how I got involved in all those local activities, but I think I was giving but also receiving so much at the same time.

Gail: I think we all feel that way. I remember it was Suzanne who put me onto *The Hills of Hebron* by Sylvia Wynter [1962]. At the school I went to in London, we didn't know that Jamaicans wrote novels! We all learnt a lot from each other.

Liz: You sort of forget these things; you don't make the links, so I'm just doing a lot of reflection. I remember the Saturday school being really significant for me. I think I combined my experiences with what I got involved in – I was working in education and at the time, I was probably going from bedsit to bedsit, which shaped the path that I took when it came to organising. I remember doing a lot of stuff around the Brixton crèche, for example. Organising was a way to make a lot of the principles we had into reality.

Gail: That's just reminded me of what we were saying about being representatives on other issues. Marlene Bogle was involved

---

25 *Editor's note:* See 'Friends of Jamilla Campaign' (*Speak Out*, no. 4), pp. 235–7 in this collection.

in a committee on child abuse, for example. I didn't live in Brixton the whole time, I was involved in the more London-wide campaigns, like the Depo-Provera campaign that met up in King's Cross. We'd take BWG's thinking and orientation to different things and I know Marlene did, too.

On the Black Women's Centre

Jade: One of the things that has struck me while listening to each of you talk is the centrality of the BWC within local organising and bringing together each of the networks that the BBWG had made links with. Can you talk a bit more about how the Centre came to be?

Gail: The Centre had been squatted by some young white people. We said we wanted it to be a centre for Black women and they left, so that's how we got it. In order to run the centre we needed some money, and, prior to there being a constitution, I remember long, intense, quite heated discussions about whether we should be taking money from the state. Olive Morris was part of that discussion. Some of us were saying, 'No, we shouldn't take money from the state.' Others were saying, 'But this gives us a centre.' I remember it as weeks of intense Sunday meetings.

Suzanne: I think that's really important. In the end, it was Olive Gallimore and the Mary Seacole Crafts Group who put in a joint application. So how did you make the decision to take the money? The money paid for a permanent worker to be employed at the centre.

Gail: That's right, it did. I think in the end, it was the balance of argument about what the money would enable us to do locally in a way that we wouldn't be able to if we held to the idea that we shouldn't take money from the state. There were whole aspects of work that we wouldn't be able to do without it. I have to confess that I always found it very difficult to take the money from the state. We thought we could divide aspects of our work; the work that was linked to the funding – to the worker we employed at the centre and the costs of running the building – and then the [organising] work we've described, which would be linked to the centre but would be separate. So, if we took the money, we could do both kinds of work, but if we didn't get the money, we could only do one kind of work.

Jocelyn: What Gail said, more or less. I think we weighed it up and realised we might be cutting our nose off to spite our face. In the end, I think even the people who weren't comfortable with it did come round and see the argument. For me, having a paid worker at the centre was key, and we could do all the things we wanted to do for the community.

Suzanne: I wasn't there for the application [for the centre], but the challenge for me was that once we got the worker and all of us were on the Centre Management Committee, we then had to manage the centre and the worker in a more formal way than sisters had been used to. I might be wrong, but I think Monica was allocated the mentoring role for our first worker, Zandra [Gairy]. Remember, we all had full-time jobs. Monica had to work with Zandra in a more minute way to manage her. We had wanted a worker for the centre who didn't necessarily reflect us but had strong links to the community and who could bring in other local women, and women's groups. BWG was always separate – we had our identity, and the centre had another identity. We wanted the centre to be a community space for women in the community.

We then had to manage a potential conflict between a Black socialist feminist identity that we brought to the Centre and our desire to open it up to women who were not feminists but also quite suspicious of a Black feminist identity. We were trying to maintain their participation and presence in the Centre alongside us, without us having to concede anything of who we were. I remember that as an ongoing issue. I look back at the minutes and I realise that that was a real conflict.

Gail: I remember, with our first worker, she had a completely different mindset to us and I think she felt compromised. Then we had Caroline, who became our second worker.

Suzanne: There were a lot of activities in the centre. I was amazed when I looked through the minutes! I counted eleven groups who would regularly meet there each week, not counting BWG.

We also had an Easter project for children; we had a summer project. We had BUFP members coming to the centre to organise there. So, the centre was successful; it certainly made its mark in the community.[26]

On BBWG and the Black arts movement

Jade: One of the things that feature heavily throughout *Speak Out* is the role of art within the movement; theatre groups are mentioned, and literature reviews feature throughout the various editions. Can you speak about the relationship between the group and Black arts?

Gail: One thing to remember in terms of the link to Black arts and someone who became very significant within the Black arts movement is that the mural on the wall at the centre was done by Sonia Boyce. I always think of Suzanne and Dorothea as central to BWG's relationship with art.

Beverley: At the centre, we had people like Bernardine Evaristo and other women who were involved in the Black arts movement – she writes about it in *Girl, Woman, Other* [2019]. I remember her being there.

Art has always been integral, from the very beginning. In all Black organisations, art was always part of how you expressed your message. It's part of our culture, it's the way we talk.

Gail: Do you remember when the Jamaican activist theatre group Sistren came to the meetings and we had one whole session or two talking about their work and the connections between their creative practices, working with grassroots working women and the work we were doing as BWG?[27] There were always links, as Beverley just said.

26　*Editor's note:* For more on the funding the group obtained for the centre's work, see footnote 1 in 'News' (*Speak Out*, no. 3) on pp. 148–9; for more on the conflict around the decision to apply for funding, see 'Writing Our Own History: Talking Personal, Talking Political' on pp. 321–37; and for more on the centre's work, see 'Brixton Black Women's Centre: Organising on Child Sexual Abuse' on pp. 315–19.

27　*Editor's note:* For more on the Sistren Theatre Collective, see Honor Ford-Smith, 'Ring Ding in a Tight Corner: Sistren, Collective

When I mention that Suzanne was quite crucial, it was about how what we read as a group could also be in a fictional or poetic form as well, and that this could be just as crucial to learning and understanding our situation as reading Walter Rodney. That was important.

Suzanne: And it was a crucial time, I think. You had publishers like Bogle-L'Ouverture that were publishing.[28] We were getting these books for the first time; it was really exciting to read African American writers for the first time, and Caribbean writers for the first time. I think Sinda was the one who commissioned a lot of people; I remember her asking me to write pieces for the newsletter.

I think you're right, Gail and Beverley – culture and self-expression are so important in every liberation struggle and every organisation. Women started to use the centre to rehearse. Jackie Kay has talked about coming down to the centre to rehearse her play there and, of course, Bernardine has written about coming down to the centre.

I just heard Bernardine talk about it in an interview recently. She said she'd just left Rose Bruford College and had come to Brixton with two other women. We gave them room, and that was really the beginning of her experience as a writer and as a theatre practitioner. As with Sonia Boyce, they all went on to do great things.

Liz: I was really into my music. For me, a lot of the messages I was hearing as a young Black person was that we didn't have

Democracy, and the Organization of Cultural Production', in *Feminist Genealogies, Colonial Legacies, Democratic Futures*, ed. M. Jacqui Alexander and Chandra Talpade Mohanty (New York: Routledge, 1996), 213–58.

28   *Editor's note*: For more, see Philippa Ireland, 'Laying the Foundations: New Beacon Books, Bogle-L'Ouverture Press and the Politics of Black British Publishing', *E-rea: Revue électronique d'études sur le monde anglophone* 11, no. 1 (2013); Karen Sands-O'Connor, 'Britain, Black Empowerment and Bogle-L'Ouverture: Independent Black Publishing of the 1960s–1980s', in *Children's Publishing and Black Britain, 1965–2015* (New York: Palgrave Macmillan, 2017); and Laurence Byrne, 'Bogle-L'Ouverture Publishing House', British Library *Untold Lives* blog, 19 September 2019, blogs.bl.uk/untoldlives.

Black history taught in school. People like Bob Marley had hit the scene; all of these experiences came together for me.

I was really involved with my music, and I used to play with a sound system. One of my memories is sitting in the BWC with Sylvia and a few other people, and that's where Sister Culture, which was the female sound group, was born. I remember us playing out to women-only audiences. It's always been a very positive experience.

Sindamani: Art is a vital component of our lives, and especially so when we are struggling to change society – and especially so for women who are often invisible in the artistic expression of destruction and/or optimism.

I think there were two phases in the impact of creative women in the BWG/BWC. The first wave of women who were around in the late '70s and early '80s floundered a bit in the all-white world of the arts. There was one sister at Chelsea College of Arts and she had a very difficult time, as did many of us who were entering the big institutions of the arts and communications. Gerlin helped many sisters through those turbulent times – artists, it seems to me, have to tug at their souls, and it can be quite shattering if you are not strong enough – and some were not. It was the same with some of the intellectuals in the BWG, for example Sylvia Erike, who had a formidable intellect. There was a high cost to pay.

I remember the poet and writer, the late Jean 'Binta' Breeze, living in Brixton, and perhaps she too came to the centre. I bumped into Iyamide Hazeley at the British Library last year. She organised writing workshops at the centre, and some of the poems and short stories were published. My poem about my mother, 'She Lives between Back Home and Home', came out of one of those workshops.[29]

---

29 *Editor's note:* Published in Rhonda Cobham and Merle Collins, eds, *Watchers and Seekers: Creative Writing by Black Women in Britain* (London: Women's Press, 1987).

On the evolution of the BBWG

Jade: This conversation has been really important in showing how integral the BBWG has been, the spaces that the group provided and the group's role in shaping Black culture in this country.

Stella: I've been captivated! I'm so impressed by people's memories! What's striking me is how much of BWG's politics influenced the formation and the development of OWAAD. I'm listening to this and I'm thinking, 'Yes, we did that,' and, 'I remember that person.' We were all connected in some way. There was a really powerful network. When we talk about anti-imperialism, when we talk about studying Marx, all of that stuff – I came to it through a different route, but I was doing the same thing in different organisations. Somehow, we kind of coalesced. I really want to acknowledge how much Gerlin and Olive, who were there in those early OWAAD days, did. They really, really did influence our thinking.

Another thing that occurred to me as you were speaking was how much of this kind of activity was going on in different parts of London and the country. I remember other Black women's groups who were not doing all that BWG was doing but doing facets of it, and when you look at it as a whole you see a really important and quite often unacknowledged subtext to most of the UK civil rights struggles. Women were there, beavering away, giving up their time and doing all these things in a way that has yet to be acknowledged. That's why I'm excited about this book, because it begins to put all this stuff on the map. As somebody said earlier, if we don't tell our history, who's gonna tell it?

Jade: You've each mentioned that this was a lot of work to take on alongside all your other responsibilities. Could you each speak to how your relationship with the group evolved over time?

Suzanne: I think we left at a similar time.

Beverley: Yes, I think I left just before *Heart of the Race* came out, when we were in the middle of writing it. For me, I think the Group changed over time; the group that started in '73 was very different from the group we had by '83. The basic political ideas didn't change so much, certainly up until *Speak*

Out no. 4 came out – which is the one I remember being most heavily involved in, especially the editorial on Black feminism. We felt we had to write it and we sat down on a Sunday until we got what we thought was a clear idea that we wanted to put out and share. By the time I left, I felt I wasn't getting that much out of the group itself. I was really just very tired and, by that time, I had children. We kind of skirt around these things, but to have children and to have a full-time job, doing a postgraduate degree, writing a book, and to be in an organisation where you felt like you were giving more than you were receiving was quite a lot! I just couldn't give any more, after more than ten years in that organisation. For me, it was just too much.

Jocelyn: I don't think I made a positive decision to leave, as such. I started drifting away after my baby daughter Acacia died, and there was so much going on with the riots and everything else. And then I went to Trinidad. When I came back and the centre was functioning, I was kind of around for a bit, had a couple of kids, then left to work in the Cayman Islands in '87. Technically, that's when I left the group.

I think individual people seemed to leave because of their own journey and where they were going to go next. I don't necessarily recall anyone that I know of who left because they weren't happy with the group. It wasn't as simple as that. They were just going off to do something else or going in a different direction. I'm trying to remember – you said it's amazing how much people remember, Stella, but I'm amazed by just how much I've forgotten!

Suzanne: I think we've all forgotten things we did! I was looking through [BBWG documents] and I saw my name on things I couldn't remember doing! When you see your name on all these meetings and agendas and minutes you think to yourself, 'When did we find the time?'

Beverley: Can I just add something? Going back to what Gail said about taking money from the state, I think it played a part [in the end of the group] in a funny sort of way, because before that, you might think, 'I can't leave the group because there won't be anyone to do this or that.' Once we had that funding and there was somebody working in the centre and keeping the doors open, you thought, 'Oh, maybe I can take a backseat now.' I think that ties into the way in which people don't connect in the same way within an organisation once there's government funding involved.

Suzanne: I can't quite remember why I stopped going but I think I left around the same time that you did, Bev and Monica. I think a lot of things hit me quite hard: Gerlin left to go to Zimbabwe and Monica left to go to Tanzania, and I think you were writing your application to go back to Jamaica, Bev, and then Jocelyn had left temporarily. Somehow, I felt that the centre of the group was falling apart.

The other factor was the effect of all the hard work we did around the uprisings and the Defence Campaign – that was an immense amount of work and a huge commitment. It really didn't leave us time to think about our original commitment to a Black socialist feminist group. It was also a challenge to work again in a mixed group with men; it required a lot of skills to keep it all going. Speaking personally, I felt that we were doing all the work; I remember being the one taking the minutes, and all of us – in particular Monica and Neelim [Sultan] – did all the liaison work with the courts, such as finding solicitors, keeping files on defendants, keeping a rota of people to go to courts, and so on, as well as having full-time jobs. And so it happens with history: none of the women who were central to the concrete, material, everyday survival of the victims of state harassment have been asked to come and talk about their roles in the aftermath of the uprising.

So, it was a combination of things. Finally, I think that all groups change, and I think it was time for another set of women who had a different perspective and clearer view of what they wanted from BWG, a clearer view of the centre, to make their mark. Marlene [Bogle] did work very differently in the centre in a very transformative way – she was a very keen member of the new formation of the group. That's why the group survived another five or six years, because there was fresh thinking and a new perspective.

Beverley: That's the point I wanted to make! All groups change and there's no problem with that evolution. The fact that it could continue ... it was a celebration of new things happening.

Jade: How do you reflect on your time in the BBWG?

Beverley: Maybe in the moment it didn't always seem positive, but I certainly reflect back on it as a very positive experience. If I compare it to being in the Panthers – even though I was working hard in the Panthers and was seen as somebody serious enough who might one day go on to 'higher leadership' – I found my voice in BWG. That was a time when you felt like you were in a space where you were safe enough to give voice to your understandings, your critiques and to ask questions. You could ask really difficult questions or maybe even really basic questions – you could ask all those questions! I appreciated the way in which it was structured, and it's fed into my life. In fact, that experience in BWG has been part of my professional life ever since; it was part of what brought me back to Jamaica.

Suzanne: I agree completely. The ideas around collectivism and the importance of a class analysis are so important in the contemporary period, and with what we're witnessing with the new formations of social and political structures and individual identities.

Beverley: You could ask, 'What is dialectical materialism?'

Suzanne: It was such a safe space! I think those ways of working and thinking on the everyday level have informed my practice as a worker and my view of the world.

Takumba: For me, BWG was a place of action, of learning and sharing and going out and speaking to women, supporting them and sharing with them what I had been learning. There were campaigns everywhere to make changes in working-class women's lives, both big and small, and I was in there adding my energy. I left because I moved to Manchester. As soon as I got there, I joined Abasindi Black Women's Group in Moss Side from '82 to '95.[30] My sisters from BWG and Abasindi are still a big part of my life.

---

30 *Editor's note:* See D. Watt and A. D. Jones, *Catching Hell and Doing Well: Black Women in the UK – The Abasindi Cooperative* (London: Institute of Education Press, 2015).

Stella: An important sense of sisterhood came out of the experience of organising. That was a real lasting legacy, and you can see that from the way all of us are still connected in some way forty years on—

Suzanne: Even among the sisters who weren't able to come today!

Stella: It's shocking, really, how that grapevine has survived and survived, in some really important ways – not just on the political arena but in terms of our personal lives and what we share. We're all pretty much entering grandmotherhood now. The reality is that these are the women who have shared my journey. I should say it now: I'm absolutely honoured to have shared it with such powerful women. It's really humbling to think about what an impact they've had on my life, and I hope that it's been mutual. I adore Gerlin; she was my mentor. As for these two sisters [Beverley and Suzanne], whether we like it or not, our names are connected forever.

Beverley: I like it!

Stella: But I just think we should put that on record, too: We didn't all get on. There were some people you liked more than others. That's the reality of any human interaction, but that strong sense of sisterhood, of shared experience, of shared politics, of surviving some of the things that we've lived through – what a generation! What we lived through is just phenomenal! It would have been a much lonelier place if it wasn't for these phenomenal women.

Index